DISCOVER AMERICA ONLINE

America Online Toolbar

America Online

File Edit Go To Mail Members Window Help

Icon	Function	Description
	Read New Mail	Mailbox flag goes up when "You've Got Mail!"
	Compose Mail	Write E-mail and send files.
	Channels	AOL's content by category.
	What's Hot	New and exciting areas to explore.
	People Connection	Chat live with other members!
	File Search	Select from thousands of files to download.
	Stocks & Portfolios	Up-to-date Wall Street information.
	Today's News	Your 24-hour news service.
	World Wide Web	Direct access to the Internet!
	Marketplace	Shop online for great deals!
	My AOL	Customize AOL to suit your needs.
	Online Clock	Find out how long you've been online.
	Print	Print the current file.
	Personal Filing Cabinet	View your saved E-mail and downloads.
	Favorite Places	View your favorite places. Drag heart icon here.
	Member Services	Online help and account information.
	Find	Members, files, places, and more!
	Keyword	Go directly to any America Online area.

Online Terms: Learn the Lingo

Chat room	An area where AOL users can interact directly by typing at each other. Some chat rooms have specific purposes for people who share an interest, other chat rooms are for general interaction.
Download time	A guesstimate made by AOL about the length of time it will take to download a file from AOL to your local drive.
Emoticon	A shortcut word that means an emotion icon, which you can create from your keyboard to indicate your mood.
FAQ	Frequently Asked Questions. Many FAQ files are available on AOL that describe specific AOL features.
Flame	An angry message left on a message board or in a newsgroup. Flaming is usually attacking someone instead of discussing an issue.
Flash Session	An automated way to retrieve your e-mail and any files you've selected for downloading.
Forum	An area on AOL that is dedicated to a particular subject.
Freeware	Software that is available for downloading that you can use without paying any fees.
Gateway	A connection between two computers. When you are connected to AOL it provides a gateway from its computers to the computers on the Internet.
Guide	An AOL staff person who is available to help you when untoward interaction between users occurs, usually in a chat room.
Instant Message	A device that enables an AOL user to send a note to somebody who is currently signed on. The note appears in the recipient's AOL window.
Keyword	A one-word entry that moves you to a specific area of AOL.
Local Access Number	A telephone number in your area code that you dial to reach a local AOL computer. That computer, in turn, connects you to the main AOL computers.
Master Account	The first screen name you create when you sign up on AOL becomes the master account and it controls any additional accounts (screen names) you create.
Newbies	A term used by veteran AOL users to describe new AOL users.
Post	A message added to a message board or a newsgroup. You can use the words message and post interchangeably.
Screen name	The name that is assigned to you while you are on AOL. It also is your e-mail address (along with @aol.com) when other people send you e-mail.
Thread	The specific topic being discussed on a message board or in a newsgroup.

DISCOVERY CENTRAL

DISCOVER AMERICA ONLINE®

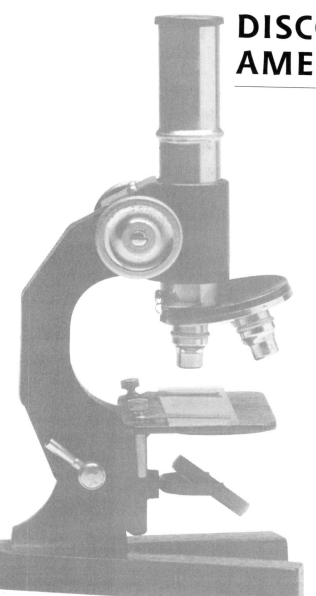

DISCOVER AMERICA ONLINE®

BY KATHY IVENS AND
THOMAS E. BARICH

IDG BOOKS WORLDWIDE, INC.

AN INTERNATIONAL
DATA GROUP COMPANY

FOSTER CITY, CA • CHICAGO, IL •
INDIANAPOLIS, IN • SOUTHLAKE, TX

Discover America Online®

Published by
IDG Books Worldwide, Inc.
An International Data Group Company
919 E. Hillsdale Blvd., Suite 400
Foster City, CA 94404

http://www.idgbooks.com (IDG Books Worldwide Web site)

Library of Congress Catalog Card No.: 96-79755

ISBN:0-7645-3057-7

Printed in the United States of America

10 9 8 7 6 5 4 3 2

1B/ST/QW/ZX/FC-IN

Distributed in the United States by IDG Books Worldwide, Inc.

Distributed by Macmillan Canada for Canada; by Transworld Publishers Limited in the United Kingdom; by IDG Norge Books for Norway; by IDG Sweden Books for Sweden; by Woodslane Pty. Ltd. for Australia; by Woodslane Enterprises Ltd. for New Zealand; by Longman Singapore Publishers Ltd. for Singapore, Malaysia, Thailand, and Indonesia; by Simron Pty. Ltd. for South Africa; by Toppan Company Ltd. for Japan; by Distribuidora Cuspide for Argentina; by Livraria Cultura for Brazil; by Ediciencia S.A. for Ecuador; by Addison-Wesley Publishing Company for Korea; by Ediciones ZETA S.C.R. Ltda. for Peru; by WS Computer Publishing Corporation, Inc., for the Philippines; by Unalis Corporation for Taiwan; by Contemporanea de Ediciones for Venezuela; by Computer Book & Magazine Store for Puerto Rico; by Express Computer Distributors for the Caribbean and West Indies. Authorized Sales Agent: Anthony Rudkin Associates for the Middle East and North Africa.

For general information on IDG Books Worldwide's books in the U.S., please call our Consumer Customer Service department at 800-762-2974. For reseller information, including discounts and premium sales, please call our Reseller Customer Service department at 800-434-3422.

For information on where to purchase IDG Books Worldwide's books outside the U.S., please contact our International Sales department at 415-655-3200 or fax 415-655-3295.

For information on foreign language translations, please contact our Foreign & Subsidiary Rights department at 415-655-3021 or fax 415-655-3281.

For sales inquiries and special prices for bulk quantities, please contact our Sales department at 415-655-3200 or write to the address above.

For information on using IDG Books Worldwide's books in the classroom or for ordering examination copies, please contact our Educational Sales department at 800-434-2086 or fax 817-251-8174.

For press review copies, author interviews, or other publicity information, please contact our Public Relations department at 415-655-3000 or fax 415-655-3299.

For authorization to photocopy items for corporate, personal, or educational use, please contact Copyright Clearance Center, 222 Rosewood Drive, Danvers, MA 01923, or fax 508-750-4470.

 is a trademark under exclusive license to IDG Books Worldwide, Inc., from International Data Group, Inc.

ABOUT IDG BOOKS WORLDWIDE

Welcome to the world of IDG Books Worldwide.

IDG Books Worldwide, Inc., is a subsidiary of International Data Group, the world's largest publisher of computer-related information and the leading global provider of information services on information technology. IDG was founded more than 25 years ago and now employs more than 8,500 people worldwide. IDG publishes more than 275 computer publications in over 75 countries (see listing below). More than 60 million people read one or more IDG publications each month.

Launched in 1990, IDG Books Worldwide is today the #1 publisher of best-selling computer books in the United States. We are proud to have received eight awards from the Computer Press Association in recognition of editorial excellence and three from *Computer Currents'* First Annual Readers' Choice Awards. Our best-selling *...For Dummies®* series has more than 30 million copies in print with translations in 30 languages. IDG Books Worldwide, through a joint venture with IDG's Hi-Tech Beijing, became the first U.S. publisher to publish a computer book in the People's Republic of China. In record time, IDG Books Worldwide has become the first choice for millions of readers around the world who want to learn how to better manage their businesses.

Our mission is simple: Every one of our books is designed to bring extra value and skill-building instructions to the reader. Our books are written by experts who understand and care about our readers. The knowledge base of our editorial staff comes from years of experience in publishing, education, and journalism — experience we use to produce books for the '90s. In short, we care about books, so we attract the best people. We devote special attention to details such as audience, interior design, use of icons, and illustrations. And because we use an efficient process of authoring, editing, and desktop publishing our books electronically, we can spend more time ensuring superior content and spend less time on the technicalities of making books.

You can count on our commitment to deliver high-quality books at competitive prices on topics you want to read about. At IDG Books Worldwide, we continue in the IDG tradition of delivering quality for more than 25 years. You'll find no better book on a subject than one from IDG Books Worldwide.

John Kilcullen
CEO
IDG Books Worldwide, Inc.

Steven Berkowitz
President and Publisher
IDG Books Worldwide, Inc.

Eighth Annual Computer Press Awards ➤1992

Ninth Annual Computer Press Awards ➤1993

Tenth Annual Computer Press Awards ➤1994

Eleventh Annual Computer Press Awards ➤1995

IDG Books Worldwide, Inc., is a subsidiary of International Data Group, the world's largest publisher of computer-related information and the leading global provider of information services on information technology. International Data Group publishes over 275 computer publications in over 75 countries. Sixty million people read one or more International Data Group publications each month. International Data Group's publications include: ARGENTINA: Buyer's Guide, Computerworld Argentina, PC World Argentina; AUSTRALIA: Australian Macworld, Australian PC World, Australian Reseller News, Computerworld, IT Casebook, Network World, Publish, Webmaster; AUSTRIA: Computerwelt Osterreich, Networks Austria, PC Tip Austria; BANGLADESH: PC World Bangladesh; BELARUS: PC World Belarus; BELGIUM: Data News; BRAZIL: Annuário de Informática, Computerworld, Connections, Macworld, PC Player, PC World, Publish, Reseller News, Supergamepower; BULGARIA: Computerworld Bulgaria, Network World Bulgaria, PC & MacWorld Bulgaria; CANADA: CIO Canada, Client/Server World, ComputerWorld Canada, InfoWorld Canada, NetworkWorld Canada, WebWorld; CHILE: Computerworld Chile, PC World Chile; COLOMBIA: Computerworld Colombia, PC World Colombia; COSTA RICA: PC World Centro America; THE CZECH AND SLOVAK REPUBLICS: Computerworld Czechoslovakia, Macworld Czech Republic, PC World Czechoslovakia; DENMARK: Communications World Danmark, Computerworld Danmark, Macworld Danmark, PC World Danmark, Techworld Denmark; DOMINICAN REPUBLIC: PC World Republica Dominicana; ECUADOR: PC World Ecuador; EGYPT: Computerworld Middle East, PC World Middle East; EL SALVADOR: PC World Centro America; FINLAND: MikroPC, Tietoverkko, Tietoviikko; FRANCE: Distributique, Hebdo, Info PC, Le Monde Informatique, Macworld, Reseaux & Telecoms, WebMaster France; GERMANY: Computer Partner, Computerwoche, Computerwoche Extra, Computerwoche FOCUS, Global Online, Macwelt, PC Welt; GREECE: Amiga Computing, GamePro Greece, Multimedia World; GUATEMALA: PC World Centro America; HONDURAS: PC World Centro America; HONG KONG: Computerworld Hong Kong, PC World Hong Kong, Publish in Asia; HUNGARY: ABCD CD-ROM, Computerworld Szamitastechnika, Internetto online Magazine, PC World Hungary, PC-X Magazin Hungary; ICELAND: Tolvuheimur PC World Island; INDIA: Information Communications World, Information Systems Computerworld, PC World India, Publish in Asia; INDONESIA: InfoKomputer PC World, Komputek Computerworld, Publish in Asia; IRELAND: ComputerScope, PC Live!; ISRAEL: Macworld Israel, People & Computers/Computerworld; ITALY: Computerworld Italia, Macworld Italia, Networking Italia, PC World Italia; JAPAN: DTP World, Macworld Japan, Nikkei Personal Computing, OS/2 World Japan, SunWorld Japan, Windows NT World, Windows World Japan; KENYA: PC World East African; KOREA: Hi-Tech Information, Macworld Korea, PC World Korea; MACEDONIA: PC World Macedonia; MALAYSIA: Computerworld Malaysia, PC World Malaysia, Publish in Asia; MALTA: PC World Malta; MEXICO: Computerworld Mexico, PC World Mexico; MYANMAR: PC World Myanmar; NETHERLANDS: Computer! Totaal, LAN Internetworking Magazine, LAN World Buyers Guide, Macworld Netherlands, Net, WebWereld; NEW ZEALAND: Absolute Beginners Guide and Plain & Simple Series, Computer Buyer, Computer Industry Directory, Computerworld New Zealand, MTB, Network World, PC World New Zealand; NICARAGUA: PC World Centro America; NORWAY: Computerworld Norge, CW Rapport, Datamagasinet, Financial Rapport, Kursguide Norge, Macworld Norge, Multimediaworld Norge, PC World Ekspress Norge, PC World Nettverk, PC World Norge, PC World ProduktGuide Norge; PAKISTAN: Computerworld Pakistan; PANAMA: PC World Panama; PEOPLE'S REPUBLIC OF CHINA: China Computer Users, China Computerworld, China InfoWorld, China Telecom World Weekly, Computer & Communication, Electronic Design China, Electronics Today, Electronics Weekly, Game Software, PC World China, Popular Computer Week, Software Weekly, Software World, Telecom World; PERU: Computerworld Peru, PC World Profesional Peru, PC World SoHo Peru; PHILIPPINES: Click!, Computerworld Philippines, PC World Philippines, Publish in Asia; POLAND: Computerworld Poland, Computerworld Special Report Poland, Cyber, Macworld Poland, Networld Poland, PC World Komputer; PORTUGAL: Cerebro/PC World, Computerworld/Correio Informático, Dealer World Portugal, Mac*In/PC*In Portugal, Multimedia World; PUERTO RICO: PC World Puerto Rico; ROMANIA: Computerworld Romania, PC World Romania, Telecom Romania; RUSSIA: Computerworld Russia, Mir PK, Publish, Seti; SINGAPORE: Computerworld Singapore, PC World Singapore, Publish in Asia; SLOVENIA: Monitor; SOUTH AFRICA: Computing SA, Network World SA, Software World SA; SPAIN: Communicaciones World España, Computerworld España, Dealer World España, Macworld España, PC World España; SRI LANKA: Infolink PC World; SWEDEN: CAP&Design, Computer Sweden, Corporate Computing Sweden, Internetworld Sweden, it.branschen, Macworld Sweden, MaxiData Sweden, MikroDatorn, Nätverk & Kommunikation, PC World Sweden, PCaktiv, Windows World Sweden; SWITZERLAND: Computerworld Schweiz, Macworld Schweiz, PCtip; TAIWAN: Computerworld Taiwan, Macworld Taiwan, NEW ViSiON/Publish, PC World Taiwan, Windows World Taiwan; THAILAND: Publish in Asia, Thai Computerworld; TURKEY: Computerworld Turkiye, Macworld Turkiye, Network World Turkiye, PC World Turkiye; UKRAINE: Computerworld Kiev, Multimedia World Ukraine, PC World Ukraine; UNITED KINGDOM: Acorn User UK, Amiga Action UK, Amiga Computing UK, Apple Talk UK, Computing, Macworld, Parents and Computers UK, PC Advisor, PC Home, PSX Pro, The WEB; UNITED STATES: Cable in the Classroom, CIO Magazine, Computerworld, DOS World, Federal Computer Week, GamePro Magazine, InfoWorld, I-Way, Macworld, Network World, PC Games, PC World, Publish, Video Event, THE WEB Magazine, and WebMaster; online webzines: JavaWorld, NetscapeWorld, and SunWorld Online; URUGUAY: InfoWorld Uruguay; VENEZUELA: Computerworld Venezuela, PC World Venezuela; and VIETNAM: PC World Vietnam.   3/24/97

Welcome to the Discover Series

Do you want to discover the best and most efficient ways to use your computer and learn about technology? Books in the Discover series teach you the essentials of technology with a friendly, confident approach. You'll find a Discover book on almost any subject — from the Internet to intranets, from Web design and programming to the business programs that make your life easier.

We've provided valuable, real-world examples that help you relate to topics faster. Discover books begin by introducing you to the main features of programs, so you start by doing something *immediately*. The focus is to teach you how to perform tasks that are useful and meaningful in your day-to-day work. You might create a document or graphic, explore your computer, surf the Web, or write a program. Whatever the task, you learn the most commonly used features, and focus on the best tips and techniques for doing your work. You'll get results quickly, and discover the best ways to use software and technology in your everyday life.

You may find the following elements and features in this book:

Discovery Central: This tearout card is a handy quick reference to important tasks or ideas covered in the book.

Quick Tour: The Quick Tour gets you started working with the book right away.

Real-Life Vignettes: Throughout the book you'll see one-page scenarios illustrating a real-life application of a topic covered.

Goals: Each chapter opens with a list of goals you can achieve by reading the chapter.

Side Trips: These asides include additional information about alternative or advanced ways to approach the topic covered.

Bonuses: Timesaving tips and more advanced techniques are covered in each chapter.

Discovery Center: This guide illustrates key procedures covered throughout the book.

Visual Index: You'll find real-world documents in the Visual Index, with page numbers pointing you to where you should turn to achieve the effects shown.

Throughout the book, you'll also notice some special icons and formatting:

 A Feature Focus icon highlights new features in the software's latest release, and points out significant differences between it and the previous version.

 Web Paths refer you to Web sites that provide additional information about the topic.

 Tips offer timesaving shortcuts, expert advice, quick techniques, or brief reminders.

 The X-Ref icon refers you to other chapters or sections for more information.

Pull Quotes emphasize important ideas that are covered in the chapter.

 Notes provide additional information or highlight special points of interest about a topic.

 The Caution icon alerts you to potential problems you should watch out for.

The Discover series delivers interesting, insightful, and inspiring information about technology to help you learn faster and retain more. So the next time you want to find answers to your technology questions, reach for a Discover book. We hope the entertaining, easy-to-read style puts you at ease and makes learning fun.

Credits

ACQUISITIONS EDITOR
Ellen Camm

DEVELOPMENT EDITOR
Barbra Guerra

TECHNICAL EDITOR
Cary Torkelson

COPY EDITORS
Kelly Oliver
Michelle Shaw

PROJECT COORDINATOR
Susan Parini

QUALITY CONTROL SPECIALIST
Mick Arellano

GRAPHICS AND PRODUCTION SPECIALISTS
Renée Dunn
Ed Penslien
Christopher Pimentel
Jude Levinson
Elsie Yim

PROOFREADERS
Christine Sabooni

INDEXER
Anne Leach

BOOK DESIGN
Seventeenth Street Studios
Phyllis Beaty
Kurt Krames

About the Authors

Kathy Ivens has written more than two dozen books about computers as a result of her compulsion to prove that old people can learn about computers, too. She's had a number of other careers — none of which involved the use of computers, but they provided lots of education and interesting times.

Thomas E. Barich is relatively new to the authoring game. A former computer book editor turned author, he's now learning what it's like to be on the other side of the fence. He's been involved with computers since he got his first XT back in the days when 256K was "more than enough" memory to handle most jobs. In addition to writing computer books, he also runs a CD production company designing and building computer software CDs.

PREFACE

Discover America Online is written to help you learn about the vast cyberspace community available once you log on to this service. Reading this book will help you configure the AOL software and your AOL personal information, and it will also give you an idea of what's waiting for you on AOL and the Internet.

How This Book Is Organized

There are a number of components in this book, and you can skip around and find the information you need as your need occurs.

Quick Tour

The opening section Discover America Online is a Quick Tour, which is a brief overview of some of the important issues and instructions we discuss throughout the book. It's a way to get started quickly and to satisfy your curiosity before reading about a subject in depth.

Real Life Vignettes

What "real life" applications might AOL have for you? Check out the vignettes that appear with each part opener. These are stories about experiences of other AOL subscribers — how they've optimized AOL services for their best use, how they came to choose AOL in the first place, and some humorous episodes along the way.

Part One: Getting Started

Here's where you learn about the details you have to attend to in order to log on, become a member, and get yourself a screen name and password. There's a lot of information about the basic features of AOL, the ones you'll use the most.

Part Two: Communicating

In Part II we give you all the tips and tricks you need to know when you want to communicate with other cyber-residents. From e-mail to AOL chat rooms, you'll learn how to use the features, how to get the best out of them, and how to avoid making mistakes.

Part Three: Visiting AOL Sites

There is so much to see and do on AOL that you'd grow old before you had a chance to view it all. In this section you a tour some of the types of activities, information, and fun available. This way you can decide which features grab your interest and head for them without wasting days — or weeks or months — trying to learn what's out there.

Part Four: Using the Internet

Even though AOL isn't the Internet, you can use AOL as a gateway to all features of the Internet. We explain the parts of the Internet and how to get the most out of them.

Discovery Center

Check out the Discovery Center in the back part of the book. It's a graphical map to all the highlights of the book. It's also useful for reviewing what you learned in the chapters or to get a quick lesson in case you want to travel around AOL before you read all the chapters in this book.

The CD-ROM

The CD-ROM in the back pocket of this book contains the software you need to join and use America Online, whether you are using Windows 95, Windows 3.x, or a Macintosh. You will find specific installation information in Appendix B and C. Since you will want to tear into the CD-ROM packet right about now (if you haven't already!), take a minute to check the License Agreement. If you have any questions for the America Online folks, their customer service number is 1-800-827-6364.

Acknowledgments

The authors extend their gratitude to all the members of the talented team at IDG Books Worldwide. Ellen Camm was supportive and involved throughout the process, defining the job of Acquisitions Editor as it should be. Barb Guerra invested time, energy, and a great deal of talent to make sure this book was everything we hoped it would be (and wouldn't have been without her). Technical Editor Cary Torkelson checked the technical accuracy so we wouldn't make fools of ourselves, and Copy Editors Kelly Oliver and Michelle Shaw straightened out our grammar and spelling errors so our high school teachers wouldn't be embarrassed.

CONTENTS AT A GLANCE

CONTENTS

INTRODUCTION

This book is designed to get you up and operating in America Online as quickly as possible. We've included all sorts of easy-to-follow instructions for the basic steps you have to take to sign on, sign off, and configure AOL so it's convenient and fun to use.

Besides all the technical stuff that shows you how to operate the software and navigate through all of AOL's areas, we picked some of the popular places and examined them for you. This gives you some information about the services available on AOL and gives you a head start on knowing what to expect. There are tips about the neat AOL areas and how to get the best out of them, and some information on where to browse to find more nifty things.

Each chapter concentrates on a particular set of tasks or a particular AOL area of interest. For those chapters that are concerned with technical tasks that get you around AOL, we've been as thorough and careful as possible to make sure you don't run into problems or delays. The chapters that deal with interests are designed to give you a whirlwind tour and whet your appetite to discover even more when you get there.

You'll find tips that we think will make your time on AOL more productive (or more fun) and cautions to give you warnings about things that might cause problems. We've even included the jargon you'll need when you interact with other AOL users (so nobody knows you're a *newbie* — the AOL term for a new user).

We think you're going to love the virtual world waiting for you on AOL. Whether you stay within the AOL areas or venture onto the Internet and all the excitement and information available there, this book will hold your hand throughout the trip.

AMERICA ONLINE QUICK TOUR

PRACTICE USING THESE SKILLS

No matter what your favorite AOL area is, it's a safe bet that you spend time visiting your mailbox. E-mail is the one feature that everybody loves, and, in fact, it doesn't take long before you're dependent on it. It's fast, it saves money over long distance calls, and it's easy.

Sending Mail

To send mail, click the Compose Mail icon — the pencil and paper — on the Toolbar, which opens the Compose Mail window (see Figure 1).

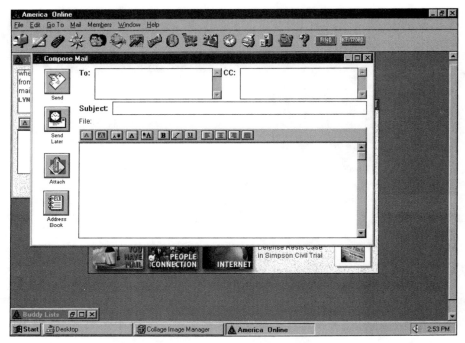

Figure 1   Send letters to family or friends without licking stamps or walking to the mailbox.

The simple way to send a message is to fill out the fields:

✳ Put the recipient's e-mail address in the field named To (for AOL users, just enter the screen name).

✳ To send copies to others, enter their e-mail addresses in the CC field.

✳ Use the large text window to enter your message.

✳ Click Send to deposit the message in the recipient's electronic mailbox.

You can also try your hand at formatting your message so it's fancy, using the buttons on the message Toolbar to change the look, color, or justification of the text.

Looking in Your Mailbox

When people send you mail, it's placed in your AOL mailbox. When you sign on, the voice that welcomes you adds a message that you have mail. If you don't have a sound card, you'll have to remember to peek at the mailbox on the Toolbar. When there's mail in it, the flag goes up and the corner of an envelope can be seen. Click it to see the contents of your mailbox (see Figure 2).

Figure 2 Letters, we get letters...

* Click a message and choose Read to see what's inside. It stays in your mailbox for a few days before disappearing into the dead mail area (never-never land, which means AOL deletes it).

* Choose Ignore to let AOL send the message to the dead mail area as if it were read, without having to read it (good for junk mail).

* Choose Keep As New after you've read it to have it treated as a new message (you'll be told you have mail).

* Choose Delete to get rid of the message right away, whether you've read it or not.

Reading Your Mail

When you choose Read, the message opens in its own window (see Figure 3).

There are several things you can do with a message to save its contents:

* Print the message by clicking the Print button on the Toolbar while the message is displayed.

* Save the message by choosing File → Save from the Menu Bar, and then naming the file.

After you've read a message, a red check mark appears on the mail icon when you next look in your mailbox.

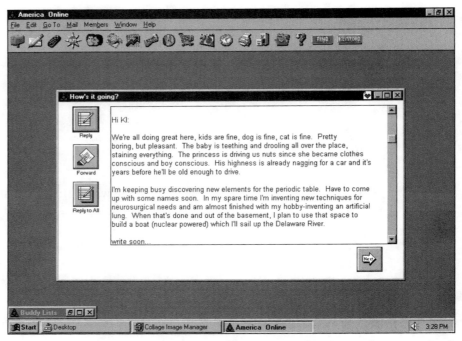

Figure 3 Use the scroll bar to read the entire message if it's longer than a couple of paragraphs.

Replying to Mail

Click the Reply icon to open a new message window with the recipient's name and the subject already filled in. If the message was sent to other recipients besides you and you want everyone to receive your reply, choose Reply to All.

Forwarding Mail

If you think someone else would be interested in the information you received in the message, click the Forward icon. A message window opens so you can fill in the name of the recipient (see Figure 4).

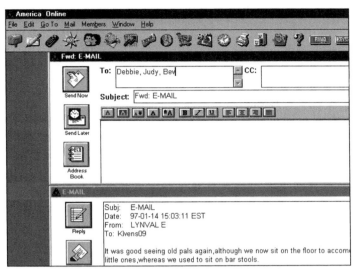

Figure 4   The other people who came to the party might like to see this note from one of the group.

All the contents of the message (including the name of the original sender) are sent when you click the Send Now icon.

PART ONE

GETTING STARTED

THIS PART CONTAINS THE FOLLOWING CHAPTERS

CHAPTER **1** SIGNING UP AND SIGNING ON

CHAPTER **2** LEARNING THE BASICS

CHAPTER **3** CONFIGURING AOL

In Part 1 you'll learn how to get started with AOL. Signing up is easy! You just have to agree to pay for your service and then you have to decide on a name and a password. Then you'll learn how to use the basic services AOL provides, and you'll configure your AOL software to match the way you want to use it.

Behind the icons, Menu Bars, channels, and chat rooms, real live people are waiting to take your call. Not all of them are actual AOL employees. Some, like Kim Tedrow, are community leaders — AOL volunteers who help bridge the gap between the megalithic online service and the regular people at their keyboards, especially the "new" regular people.

Kim runs the live Q&A of AOL's Reference channel, the place where you ask questions you can't find the answers to elsewhere on AOL, ranging from the banal to the esoteric. Besides helping disoriented new members find their niche in cyberspace, Kim trains other volunteers like herself to field questions from their homes or other real-world computers. She also responds to suggestions and helps set up new databases for the reference section.

Volunteers like Kim often need to help members get comfortable with using computers in general, in order to help them take advantage of the service. "A lot of new people don't know the keyword system right away, so I'll tell them how to find the keyword box via the Menu Bar or the hot key combination. I've had members ask me what the Menu Bar is. Fortunately, AOL itself has been responding to that need with some more basic areas, such as Reach Out and Family Computing," she said.

As to misconceptions users might have about AOL, Kim said, "I remember one member asking me how to order a pizza on AOL. I still wonder if he was serious."

The biggest hurdle beginners confront when acclimating to AOL, Kim claimed, is in remembering how to get "back" to areas they've visited and enjoyed. She prescribes two remedies for this: keywords and Favorite Places. "If members can familiarize themselves with how to use the keyword search, they'll have little difficulty in finding what they need online," she explained. "With version 3.0 of the AOL software, members can now put their 'ear marks' (little red hearts) into a member-refined feature called Favorite Places.

Kim's original favorite place was the Writer's Club: "Someone mentioned to me that there was a poetry workshop in that conference room once a week, so I dropped in on it. This is a real-time workshop held in a chat room, with a host, and with poems by one of the members sent out in advance. The other members of the workshop would take turns commenting on the work. It was as fine and insightful a workshop as I've attended in a university setting. I eventually hosted the workshop myself for a year, which, in combination with my other skills, led me to qualify as a community leader for the Reference Channel."

CHAPTER ONE

SIGNING UP AND SIGNING ON

1

IN THIS CHAPTER YOU LEARN THESE KEY SKILLS

N ow that you've installed AOL, it's time to open the software for the first time and use it to get signed on with the AOL service. This is not a complicated procedure, but there are a few steps involved. You have to make sure your modem and AOL get introduced to each other. And, the folks at AOL want money from you, so you'll have to tell them about your credit card and give them permission to bill you through that credit card (or make arrangement with your bank and AOL to establish an automatic withdrawl for your AOL bill). You must have a sign-on name and a password. And, of course, you have to find out what telephone number you can dial to reach AOL in your city or town.

This chapter walks you through all the steps you need to take to complete the signing-up process. We'll cover all the specific tasks as you give AOL the required information, and then we'll help you sign on to AOL for the first time.

Setting Up

A merica Online (AOL) software is dependent upon two pieces of hardware in order to work: a modem and a telephone line. Although technically you might not think of a telephone line as hardware, it is a physical entity that is necessary to dial out using your computer, so I'm going to call it hardware.

Before you start the setup process, you have to understand the hardware you have and you also have to know exactly what's required to make it work properly with AOL. In the next sections, you'll learn what you have to know and why. You'll use the information during the actual setup process. Don't worry; we'll get there.

Also, make sure you know the registration number and password that came with your AOL disk.

Understanding telephone lines

You may be wondering "What's the big deal with understanding telephone lines?" It's not the *line* you have to understand — it's the way the line works. The type of telephone installation and the features installed on the line have to be considered when you set up AOL.

If you're using AOL on an office computer, there's a good chance that your telephone line is also a computer device — a computer installed in the office to run the phone system. This could mean your company has an automated PBX-type system (instead of the old non-automated PBX systems that required operators who plugged jacks into phone lines in order to connect employees with people on the outside).

Another good bet is that you can punch some numbers on the phone (less than seven numbers) to reach somebody else inside your company — an inter-office call. If that's true, how do you tell your telephone "Attention please, I'm dialing somebody who doesn't work here"? The usual answer is that you have to dial a 9. If this describes your office, you'll have to set up AOL to dial 9 before dialing into AOL. Otherwise, some other employee is going to be extremely annoyed about answering the phone and hearing your modem screech.

Whether you're calling from the office or from home, you also have to know whether the telephone line is equipped for touch-tone service or pulse service (*pulse* means rotary dialing).

TIP **Just because you're able to punch numbers on your telephone doesn't mean you have touch-tone service. There are phone instruments that translate those buttons that you touch into pulses in order to communicate with the pulse telephone line. The way to test a touch-tone phone to see if it's connected to a touch-tone line is to press and hold down one of the buttons. If you hear a beep that continues to beep the whole time you're pressing the button, you have touch-tone service. If the beep just sort of squawks at you and then is silent while you continue to hold down the button, you have a pulse telephone line.**

The last thing you need to know is whether or not the line is equipped for call waiting (generally not a problem from an office). If it is, there's a way to tell AOL to turn off call waiting while you're using it. Don't worry, though; as soon as you hang up from AOL, call waiting returns. AOL doesn't require that you turn off call waiting just because it doesn't want to share you or your phone line. This isn't a fit of jealousy; it's a technical problem with the way data is transmitted.

If you could hear the sounds in your telephone line while you're connected with another computer via modem (which is what's happening when you dial in to AOL), you'd hear squawks, screeches, and other rude noises. Each one of those noises is meaningful, and you can think of every little sound as representing a character on your keyboard. In fact, there are some characters you can't easily type from your keyboard, and they're being sent between computers too. The noise that call waiting makes on your telephone line gets interpreted as an official computer squawk or squeal or screech and is inserted in the characters streaming between you and AOL. Neither your computer nor AOL's computer can interpret them correctly, and this causes problems.

Understanding modems

You need a modem because your computer and the telephone lines speak totally different languages, and the modem can translate in both directions. Although that is really an oversimplification of all the techy stuff that goes into modem communications, it's a pretty good way to envision what's happening.

Your computer — actually the data that's output by your computer — is *digital*. The standard telephone line is *analog*. (We're not going to bother going into long, complicated explanations of those words here. Take my word for it that digital and analog are two different things.)

The data from your computer (remember, that's digital data) is handed over to the modem, which translates it into analog form (remember, that's what the telephone line needs). The technical term for this activity is *modulating*. (I don't know why that term was coined, but that's the word for it.)

At the other end of the telephone connection, there's a modem receiving the analog data from the telephone line and translating it into digital form so that it can be passed to the receiving computer. The technical term for this activity is *demodulating*.

Now, if you've followed this, you can picture one modem modulating and the other demodulating as data is exchanged. Somebody (or maybe some company — it all happened before I was interested in computers, so I wasn't paying attention) took those two terms and put them together in shortened form. Mod-demod is really what's happening, but people would feel silly going into a store and asking for a mod-demod, so it was shortened to *modem*.

Having said all that, I have to point out that there are digital forms of telephone lines (called ISDN lines). However, they are not yet universally available, and they require special equipment in your computer. They generally are complicated enough that if you're using an ISDN line, you're probably not buying books on using AOL (you're probably running an Internet node on your computer). Therefore, that's all I plan to say on that subject.

If you have a fairly new computer, you probably have a modem built in. If your computer did not come with a built-in modem, you have to buy a modem and either install it inside your computer (an internal modem) or attach it to a serial port on your computer (an external modem). I'm not going into long, detailed explanations about how to install the modem (physically install it, I mean); you'll have to read the instructions that came with the modem if you're facing this chore. It's actually quite easy.

TIP **If you have a new computer and you're not sure whether or not it came with a modem already installed, peek at the back of the computer. (I'd suggest you read the manual, but nobody ever seems to do that.) You'll see a number of thingys that look metallic and technical. Some have pins sticking out; others have holes. If you see a hole that looks like a telephone jack, you have an internal modem. Stick a phone cord into it and put the other end of the cord into the wall jack.**

You should know the speed of your modem because in many locations there are certain AOL telephone numbers dedicated to certain modem speeds.

Speed for a modem is a measurement of the number of bits of data it will modulate/demodulate in a second. The jargon for this is *bps* (bits per second), and all modems have a bps rating. The higher the number, the faster the modem. Today's standard modems are 28,800 bps or 33,600 bps. If you have an older modem (perhaps 14,400 bps or 9,600 bps) you could get along with it, but you should start dropping coins into a jar to save up for a faster one. If you have a modem that's slower than 9,600 bps, you're going to face a lot of frustration and wasted time.

You must also know the serial port to which your modem is attached. If it is an internal modem, it's probably using COM3. The physical serial ports on your computer are using COM1 and COM2 — they can be seen from the back of your computer, and they have pins. One of them probably has a mouse attached. External modems generally use either COM1 or COM2, depending upon where you attached the cable.

If the modem connectors aren't labeled as COM1 and COM2 and you're not sure, the installation process your operating system goes through in order to recognize the modem will produce the correct port number for you. Follow the instructions in the operating system help files to install and configure the modem.

Understanding the costs

AOL isn't free. You need to have your credit card number handy to set up your AOL software. The Internet is free, but unless your computer is directly connected to a computer that's part of the Internet, you have to pay somebody to provide the doorway to the Internet. (Most of the direct Internet connections are in universities and government offices.) AOL provides Internet access in addition to all the features that are built into AOL's own sites. In fact, you can get your money's worth out of AOL without ever stepping foot into Internet territory.

Today, you can choose a fee plan for AOL, either paying for each minute of time you're online or paying a flat fee every month without any limit to the time you spend using the service. If you use AOL only for occasional e-mail or you spend only a couple of hours a month on AOL for some specific use, you might want to go with the hourly fee. Otherwise, the flat rate arrangement works best.

Making a list and checking it twice

Are you ready? Have you gathered all the information you need? Here's a reminder of what you need to know:

* The unique registration number and password that is in your AOL disk package. (Check the installation appendix if you're using the CD–ROM from this book.)

* The credit card number and expiration date you'll use to pay for AOL service.

* Your modem's speed.

* The type of telephone service you have (touch-tone or pulse).

* The access number to get an outside line (if you're calling AOL from an office).

The first time you use AOL, you're automatically taken through the setting-up and signing-up processes, which are covered in the next sections.

Signing Up

If you start the software immediately at the end of the installation process (which is an option), you can skip this section on starting the software for now. However, make sure you read it at some point because the next time you use AOL, you'll have to launch it yourself.

To start the AOL software:

* If you use Windows 95, double-click the desktop icon that was installed during installation (if there isn't one, read the paragraphs after this list).

* If you use Windows 3.x, open the America Online program group and then double-click the America Online icon.

* If you use a Macintosh, double-click the America Online folder and then double-click the America Online icon.

Having any problems completing this first step? Let's talk about some common problems that are usually found in Windows 95 or on a Mac.

Let's do the Mac first, because there's really only one common problem with starting AOL for the first time — not being able to find the folder. AOL installs itself in your System folder; however, during the installation process, you can choose a different location. Many people who choose a different folder don't remember where they put it when they attempt to use the software for the first time. If you didn't write it down and you've forgotten where you installed the software, use the Find command on your File menu.

For Windows 95 users, the common problem is that there's no AOL icon on the desktop after the installation is completed (even though the AOL installation program announces there will be one waiting for you). If this happens, you'll probably find that the installation process also failed to place AOL on the Programs list of your Start menu. Relax; you didn't do anything wrong, and you didn't skip any steps. AOL just didn't keep its promise. This happens frequently.

Here's the cure:

1. Open Explorer (if there isn't an Explorer icon on your desktop, it's on the Programs menu — usually the last item).

2. Find the AOL30 folder and click it to display its contents in the right pane.

3. In the right pane, double-click the file named Aol.exe (see Figure 1-1).

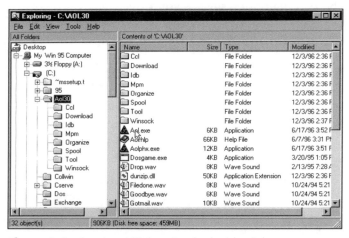

Figure 1-1 Starting AOL is a simple double-click maneuver.

I sure don't want to open Explorer, find the folder, find the file, and then double-click it every time I want to use AOL. I find that to be a real pain in the neck.

If you agree, follow these simple steps to put an AOL shortcut on your Windows 95 desktop:

1. Follow the previous steps 1 and 2 to get to the file named Aol.exe.

2. Drag the file onto any blank space on your desktop.

When you release the mouse, a shortcut to AOL is on the desktop. It's permanent; just double-click it whenever you want to use it.

**Don't try this trick for making Windows 95 shortcuts with any files
except program files. If you drag a document file from the Explorer
window to the desktop, you've *moved* it. You'll probably never find it
again when you want to use it with the software that created it.
However, if the file is one that launches a program (those files have an
extension of .exe or .com), Windows 95 doesn't move the file to the
desktop; it automatically creates a shortcut to the file.**

Beginning the setup

Starting the software for the first time brings up AOL's welcoming message (see
Figure 1-2), which includes some information about what AOL is planning to do
next to complete the setup procedures.

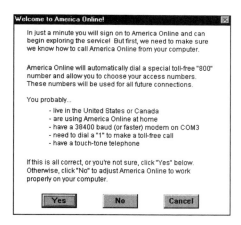

Welcome to America Online!

In just a minute you will sign on to America Online and can
begin exploring the service! But first, we need to make sure
we know how to call America Online from your computer.

America Online will automatically dial a special toll-free "800"
number and allow you to choose your access numbers.
These numbers will be used for all future connections.

You probably...

- live in the United States or Canada
- are using America Online at home
- have a 38400 baud (or faster) modem on COM3
- need to dial a "1" to make a toll-free call
- have a touch-tone telephone

If this is all correct, or you're not sure, click "Yes" below.
Otherwise, click "No" to adjust America Online to work
properly on your computer.

[Yes]   [No]   [Cancel]

Figure 1-2 If you're not using Windows
95, the window looks a
bit different but says the
same thing.

As shown in Figure 1-2, AOL makes some assumptions about your setup
information. The following list tells you what these assumptions mean. Answer
No if any of them are incorrect, and then follow the simple instructions to
change the information.

✱ If you live in the U.S. or Canada, you can select an access telephone
number from a database. If you live outside the U.S. or Canada, AOL
tells you how to get an access telephone number.

✱ If you are using AOL at home, you probably don't have to dial a
number to get an outside line before dialing the AOL access number. If
you're using the software at your office, AOL asks which digit gets you
an outside line (usually 9).

✱ You may very well not have a modem at the speed that AOL assumes,
and it may be connected to a different port. You read the beginning of
this chapter and you've done your homework, so you know the correct
answers.

* The assumption that you must dial a 1 before making a toll-free (800) call is probably correct.

* If you have call waiting, you must know the characters to dial to turn it off (it's usually #70, but check the front of the phone book or call the telephone company). AOL will dial those characters for you every time you sign on.

* Today, it's probably safe to assume you have touch-tone telephone service.

If you need to correct AOL's assumptions, click No/Other Options/Change Options (depending on your operating system). The windows that display are simple to use; they walk you through the changes in a straightforward manner.

TIP If you have to dial a number to get an outside line, when you tell AOL about it, you must enter a comma after the number to indicate a one-second pause (or multiple commas if it usually takes more than a second to get a line).

By the way, every time you log on to AOL you have an opportunity to make changes to the setup. Even if you make changes to your system later, you don't have to reinstall AOL to change the configuration.

Eventually, AOL displays a window reminding you that you need the registration number and password from your software and that you need a credit card number. Click OK to move to the next step.

Getting an access telephone number

Unless you live in the same town as America Online, which is located in Virginia, it could be quite expensive to dial directly into the AOL computer. To save you all those long-distance charges, AOL has set up computers with modems all over the place. You dial into the closest computer, and then that computer connects you to the main AOL computers. (AOL picks up the long-distance tab — although the money you pay every month offsets this expense.)

All the available telephone numbers are in a database; AOL uses your modem to dial into that database by using an 800 number. When the connection to the database is complete, the process of choosing a local access number begins. Enter your area code and then press Enter or click Continue (see Figure 1-3).

If you live in a large city, you're going to find multiple numbers to choose from (see Figure 1-4). Some area codes have fewer numbers, and some local access numbers may involve toll charges even though they carry the same area code.

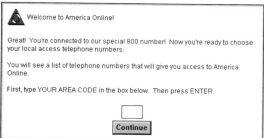

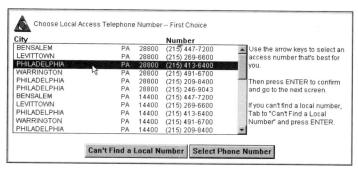

Figure 1-3 To get to the right part of the database, AOL needs some information.

Figure 1-4 Don't forget to look at the baud rate for a phone number and match it to your modem.

TIP If your modem speed isn't listed (for example, you may have a 9,600 baud modem), go for the next highest speed. It won't make your modem faster, but you won't have to slow down to the next slowest rate (2,400 bps). When two modems communicate, they do so at the speed of the slower of the two.

To set up your local access numbers, follow these steps:

1. Scroll through the list. When you find an appropriate number, choose Select Phone Number. If there is no local number, choose Can't Find a Local Number. You'll see the window illustrated in Figure 1-3 again — this time enter another area code (the one closest to yours).

2. AOL presents the same numbers again, this time asking you to select a secondary number that will be dialed if the first number is busy or doesn't answer. Select a number and then click Select Phone Number, or click Same as First Choice to tell AOL to redial the original number for the second try.

3. AOL confirms your access number selections. Choose Continue to move to the next phase of the signup process.

AOL continually adds access numbers to its database, and you can change the ones you're dialing at any time. See the Bonus section at the end of this chapter to learn how to accomplish this.

Registering with AOL

Now AOL knows which number to dial in order to establish a connection between your computer and its access computer. Without hesitation, it uses that information. The connection to the toll free number with the database is broken (that means AOL hangs up), and the local number is dialed. You don't have to do anything to make this happen. It's all automatic.

TIP **If the first number is busy or doesn't answer, AOL will try the second number. If that number is busy too, you'll get a message that a connection couldn't be made. Just wait a few moments and try again. Try to avoid the busy hours (about 6:00 p.m. to 11:00 p.m.).**

When the modem on the local AOL computer answers your call, the registration process begins (see Figure 1-5).

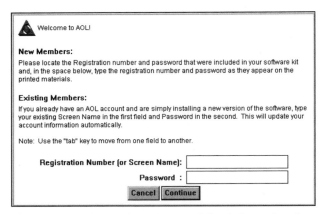

Welcome to AOL!

New Members:
Please locate the Registration number and password that were included in your software kit and, in the space below, type the registration number and password as they appear on the printed materials.

Existing Members:
If you already have an AOL account and are simply installing a new version of the software, type your existing Screen Name in the first field and Password in the second. This will update your account information automatically.

Note: Use the "tab" key to move from one field to another.

Registration Number (or Screen Name):
Password :
Cancel Continue

Figure 1-5 This is where you need that information that came with your AOL disk.

To register yourself with AOL, follow these steps:

1. Enter the Registration number, and then press Tab to move to the Password box. Fill in the two-word password that came with your software. It will be a weird combination of words, such as STUPID UNCLE or BANANA FISH. Click Continue when you have filled in the information. AOL displays a screen explaining the next few screens that will appear.

2. An information screen asking you for your name, address, and telephone number appears. Use Tab to move from field to field and fill in

the information. This information is for AOL billing purposes and won't appear to any other AOL users.

3. The next screen asks you to select a payment method. It lists all the popular credit cards (Visa, MasterCard, and American Express). If you plan to pay for AOL with one of these, click the card's name and then press Enter.

4. If you want to use a Discover Card or have your AOL bill paid directly from your checking account, choose More. Then select one of those options.

5. In the next window, you fill in the specific information about the payment method you chose. Your credit card number and expiration date (or your bank account number) are required. Choose Continue when you have entered all the data.

The business part of registration is complete at this point, and it's time to move on to the personal stuff, such as picking a name.

Naming yourself on AOL

AOL presents a screen so you can invent your AOL identity. The first thing you need is a screen name. This is the name you'll use when you send and receive e-mail, and it's the name that appears when you enter a chat room.

You can use a variation of your own name, invent a totally fictitious and whimsical name, or name yourself after your favorite movie or book character. You can do almost anything you want with your screen name.

There are, however, a couple of rules about your screen name:

✳ It must be between three and ten characters long.

✳ The first character must be a letter. After that, letters, numbers, and spaces are fine.

✳ Caps, lowercase, or a combination of both is fine.

✳ The name cannot be obscene, offensive, or insulting.

✳ It must be unique so that only you can receive your e-mail. (There are millions of users on AOL, and this is frequently the hardest rule to follow.)

Now that you have the rules, here are some additional things to think about:

✳ The uniqueness of the name is going to be a problem unless you want a variation of your real name, which happens to be Zkkjyk Brllppn. Anything less unusual than that will probably be rejected because it's not unique — it's amazing how often that happens.

✳ If the name you select isn't unique, AOL will offer to accept it with a number after it (to differentiate you from all the other people with the same screen name). For example, I figured there wouldn't be anybody else out there with the name Kivens, but I ended up being Kivens09.

* Actually, AOL frequently offers you the screen name USER*XXXXXX*, where each *X* stands for a number. Don't accept it! It's an announcement that you are a rank amateur at this, and people in chat rooms will make fun of you.

* Some names are so popular (such as anything from Star Trek or Star Wars, or a host of other movies and TV shows that are popular with teenagers) that if you want to use them, you will definitely have many numbers tagged on to your name.

* You may want to consider using some form of your real name, just in case you have to send e-mail in which you want to be taken seriously. Remember, this is your e-mail name and it's not a good idea to send serious e-mail to a business associate from ImAPunk2.

AOL permits up to five screen names for an account, so you can indulge your fantasies with the additional names and keep this original screen name for dignified use.

 See Chapter 3 for information on how to create additional screen names.

Now that you understand the concept, enter your screen name and click Continue. The AOL computer churns away, checking the name and looking for duplicates. If your name follows the rules and isn't duplicated anywhere, you're finished. If there's a problem, you'll be asked to re-enter a screen name. (AOL will insert a suggestion, but you don't have to follow it.) This continues until you have selected a unique screen name that passes all the rules.

You're not finished, though. You have to select a password to go with this name. And, of course, there are rules for the password:

* Your password must be between four to eight characters long.
* It can be letters, numbers, or a combination of both.
* It does not have to be unique — it's attached only to your screen name and not to any other AOL user.

And, of course, I have some suggestions:

* Don't pick something connected to you if you're worried about security (especially if you are using an office computer that others can access). For instance, don't use your spouse's name — it's one of the first words that people will try.
* Pick something you're going to remember. There's no easy recovery from a lost password.

* If you are afraid you'll forget it and want to write it down, put the paper in your wallet. Don't write the password on a Post-it note and stick it on your monitor.

* Make it easy to type because you will not see the letters you're typing when you enter it (this is a security measure so that nobody can look over your shoulder and get your password). If you always make mistakes when you type numbers, don't use numbers in your password.

Now that you understand passwords, enter the password in the AOL Password screen. Notice that you don't see the letters you're typing; you see only asterisks.

After you type the password the first time, press Tab to move to the second password box and enter the exact same password again. You have to enter it twice so that AOL knows you can enter your password without making a typo. This also ensures that you didn't enter a typo the first time you typed the password.

If you enter the second password differently, AOL will make you start all over again. After you've successfully entered the password twice, click Select Password.

Understanding the rules

The last step in the sign-up process is to read the Terms of Service. These are the rules of behavior that AOL has developed to make sure everybody's time on the service is as pleasant as possible. After you've read them, press Enter to indicate that you have done so and that you accept the rules and will follow them.

TIP **In AOL chat rooms, when somebody is acting improperly or being excessively annoying or insulting, you'll frequently see other members warn that person by using the term TOS. This means Terms of Service, and anyone who fails to follow the rules can be prevented from using AOL (see Chapter 5 for details).**

You're finished. You've signed up. You're a bona fide AOL user. And, you're disconnected. AOL disconnects you after the sign-up process is finished so that you can sign on using your new screen name and password. You don't have to do that right away, though. Whenever you have time to play on AOL, just start the software and sign on. The next section walks you through a normal sign-on.

Signing On

Everything's set. You're a regular AOL user now, and you can sign on anytime you want to and use all the features and facilities. So, let's see what it's like when you do a normal sign-on.

Just follow these easy steps:

1. Launch the software by double-clicking its icon. The AOL window opens. The Welcome screen is nestled in the middle of the window (see Figure 1-6).

Figure 1-6 The Welcome screen starts you off whenever you want to use AOL.

2. The Select Screen Name box has your screen name filled in already (if you have multiple screen names, it will display the last name you used to sign on). Click in the Enter Password box to put your cursor there, and then enter your password. Type carefully; remember that you can't see the letters you're typing.

3. Click SIGN ON.

That's it — pretty simple. AOL performs a whole bunch of steps at this point, and it sends you messages that announce each step so you know what's happening. The steps include initializing the modem, dialing the local access number, confirming the modem connection, contacting the main AOL network, giving the network your name and password, and waiting for verification of your password. Whew — lots of work. You don't have to do anything, though; AOL does all the work.

If the first number is busy, AOL tells you that it's going to try the other number (see Figure 1-7). The other number may be the same number as the first one, depending upon the way you configured your local access numbers, but that's okay because there's a chance it may not be busy anymore when it's redialed.

Figure 1-7 It's certainly nice of AOL to tell me what's going on.

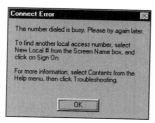

If the second number is also busy (this is likely to happen during the evening or on weekends), AOL gives up (see Figure 1-8). Click OK and start the process again by entering your password and clicking Sign On.

Figure 1-8 I can't sign on at the moment, so I'll try again in a few minutes.

TIP If this occurs frequently, when you do finally sign on to AOL, check to see if there are additional access numbers available for your area code. See the Bonus section at the end of this chapter for instructions.

Getting the new user treatment

I told a lie earlier when I said that signing on to AOL after you finish setup would be normal and just like everybody else's sign-on procedure. The first time you sign on, you get some special treatment. So, after *that*, sign-on will be a routine event. Let's talk about the special treatment.

"WELCOME — YOU'VE GOT MAIL"

As soon as the sign-on process is completed, you'll hear a deep voice say "Welcome." Almost immediately, that voice will announce "You've got mail." It doesn't help to talk back, but I couldn't resist retorting "Your grammar needs work." Grammatically stated or not, you've got mail. If you don't have a sound card, you won't hear the welcoming voice; however, you can tell if you have mail by looking at the mailbox icon on the AOL Toolbar. If the flag is up, there's mail for you.

To read your mail, click the mailbox. As a first-time user, you'll find a letter from the head of AOL, welcoming you to the service. He doesn't expect a reply, and, in fact, he doesn't particularly want one, so read it and delete it (or print it if you want a memento of your first sign-on).

X-REF For the scoop on e-mail, read Chapter 4.

TAKE THE NEW USER TOUR

The other special treatment offered to you as a newbie is a Quick Start tutorial to introduce you to all the features of AOL (see Figure 1-9).

Figure 1-9 It might not be a bad idea to take a few moments to tour AOL.

You can take the tour now by clicking Yes. You'll be given some choices about the kind of tour you want to take, and then you'll see the highlights of AOL services, along with some hints about using them. All the information presented during the tour is covered throughout this book.

If you choose No, you're merely postponing your new user tour. Every time you sign on, you'll see the Quick Start window with the same offer. After you take the tour, click Been There, Done That the next time you see the Quick Start window, and AOL will stop offering it.

TIP   **Don't tell them I told you, but you can lie. If you don't want to take the tour now, later, or ever, click Been There, Done That as soon as you see the Quick Start window. The tour won't be offered again.**

After you've finished the tour (or postponed it, or told AOL you've already finished it), mosey around AOL. The chapters in this book give you plenty of information about what there is to do and see, how to get there, and what to do when you get there.

Leaving AOL

Eventually, you probably have to leave the fun and go back to regular computer software and get some real work done. Or, you have to leave the computer and finish those household chores that have piled up since you discovered the way time flies when you're signed on to AOL.

You have two choices for leaving AOL:

* Exit the software, which signs you off, disconnects your modem, and also closes down the AOL software.

* Sign off without closing down the software, which disconnects your modem, but leaves the AOL software open on your screen (which makes it easy to sign on again).

To close down the software and disconnect from AOL, choose File→Exit from the Menu Bar. The software closes and you're ready to do other work on your computer.

To sign off, but keep the AOL software open on your screen, choose either one of these steps:

* Choose <u>G</u>o To→Sign Off from the Menu Bar
* Choose <u>S</u>ign Off→<u>S</u>ign Off from the Menu Bar

Either choice brings up the Goodbye window (see Figure 1-10).

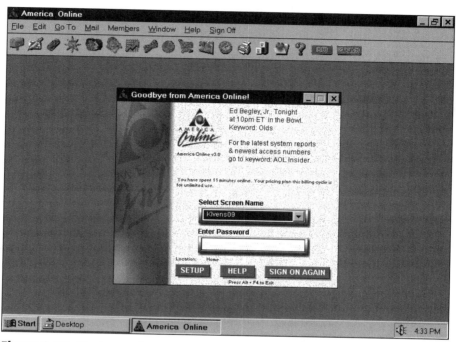

Figure 1-10 You are no longer connected to AOL but the software is still running so you can change the configuration or sign on again.

The Goodbye window has three choices available:

* Choose SETUP to change the configuration of your sign on routine.
* Choose HELP to look up topics on signing on.
* Choose SIGN ON AGAIN to go back to AOL.

If you find you're not going to use any of the buttons on this window, you can close the software by using the normal software exit routine for your operating system.

BONUS

Because signing on is really a matter of dialing into a local AOL computer and letting AOL take it from there, it's worthwhile discussing two important features for local access numbers: finding new ones and creating a setup for local access when your locale changes temporarily.

Adding Access Telephone Numbers

AOL is constantly adding local access numbers to its system. If you find that it's difficult to dial in (those busy signals are frustrating), you should see if there are other numbers available for your area code. I figure that many AOL users either don't know they can do this (they didn't buy this book) or don't bother. That means any new access number you find might not have quite so many people trying to dial it.

To find the latest and greatest list of access numbers, you have to be signed on to AOL. Then just use the keyword **Access** to bring up the Accessing America Online window (see Figure 1-11).

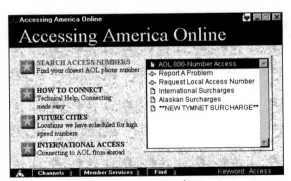

Figure 1-11 All the information about accessing AOL is found in one place, which is rather handy.

Click Search Access Numbers and a search box opens. Enter your area code, the name of your city, or the standard abbreviation for your state, and then click List Articles. Because this is a search box, it behaves like one, returning the matching entries. For example, if you listed the area code, the article is named *Access numbers for area code XXX* (where *XXX* is the area code you entered). Double-click the entry to bring up the file (see Figure 1-12).

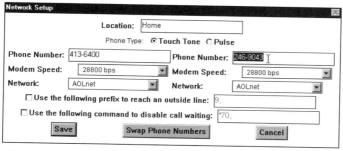

Figure 1-12   Pick a number, but don't forget to pay attention to the baud rates next to the numbers.

Write down the information for the number you want to use (or click the Print icon on the Toolbar and print out the entire list).

Then follow these steps:

1. Sign off, and when the next window displays, choose SETUP.

2. Choose Edit Location from the Network & Modem Setup window.

TIP   **If you have created additional locations (perhaps you travel and require local access numbers for other cities), you have to select the location for which you want to make the access number change. Then choose Edit Location.**

3. When the Network Setup window displays (see Figure 1-13), select the old number and type in the new one. Remember that the number on the left side of the window is the one AOL tries first, and you can replace either the first or second number (or both) with the new access number(s).

Network Setup

Location: Home

Phone Type: ⊙ Touch Tone ○ Pulse

Phone Number: 413-6400   Phone Number: 246-9043

Modem Speed: 28800 bps   Modem Speed: 28800 bps

Network: AOLnet   Network: AOLnet

☐ Use the following prefix to reach an outside line: 9,

☐ Use the following command to disable call waiting: *70,

[Save]   [Swap Phone Numbers]   [Cancel]

Figure 1-13   Changing an access number is quick and easy.

4. Choose Save to save the information on this window, and then choose OK when the original setup window reappears.

Now when you sign on, the system will use the new access number(s).

Adding Locations

If you travel, you certainly don't want to lose contact with AOL. And, you don't want to dial back to your home access number and pay those long-distance charges. The solution is to set up additional locations for all the places you might be when you want to dial in to AOL.

To set up an additional location, follow these steps:

1. At the opening AOL window, choose Setup.

2. In the Network & Modem Setup window, choose Create Location.

3. When the Network Setup window displays (see Figure 1-14), enter a name for this location (make it appropriate, such as West Coast Office or Grandma's House).

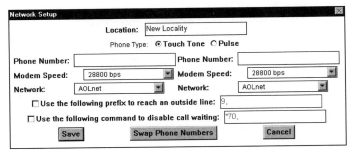

Figure 1-14 Tell AOL about the new location and the way the phones work in the new location.

4. Enter the local access phone numbers for this location (which you had to get when you were signed on, of course).

5. If necessary, add or change the information about prefixes to reach outside lines and disable call waiting.

6. Choose Save to create the location and return to the previous window, and then choose OK to finish this task.

You can add as many new locations as you want. If you have a number of locations and there are any you no longer use, you can delete them. Just select an out-of-date location to highlight it, and then choose Delete.

Summary

There's nothing terribly difficult in the process of signing on and signing off, but it's important to set up your system properly. This chapter covered the basic issues you need to reach AOL, so dive in to the other chapters to learn about all the fun and education available now that you're an AOL user.

CHAPTER TWO

GETTING THE BIG PICTURE

2

IN THIS CHAPTER YOU LEARN THESE KEY SKILLS

N ow that you've signed on, you are probably anxious to get going and find out what America Online is all about. You could jump right in and just start clicking helter-skelter, but chances are you'd end up getting annoyed and frustrated. It would be like going into the local library and wandering through the aisles hoping to find something of interest. Not that it couldn't happen, but your chances are a lot better if you know what's available and how to find it. Your best bet is to take a few minutes and learn a little about what the service has to offer and how best to use it to your advantage.

In this chapter, you learn to use the basic navigational tools that enable you to get where you want to go with the least amount of effort. In addition, this chapter offers a brief overview of the basic features and services that AOL has to offer, some of which are initially presented to you by way of the Welcome screen, and others that you will encounter along the way.

Getting Around in AOL

I f you do any traveling at all, you know that no matter where you go and no matter how great the place, you can't really enjoy yourself unless you know how to get around. Spending all your time either lost or taking the long way to get somewhere because you don't know better can turn a pleasure trip into a nightmare. AOL is no different. There's a lot to see and do, but if you can't get to it, you may miss out on some great experiences. Therefore, one of the first skills to master is the ability to navigate through the vast number of areas and services available and hone in on those that truly interest you. Fortunately, AOL offers several ways to accomplish this.

Ordering from the Menu Bar

Over the years, a certain amount of standardization has occurred in the world of computers. One item that is now common to most software programs is the Menu Bar. It is that thin, narrow bar that contains words only, each with one underlined letter, at the top of the screen just below the title bar (see Figure 2-1).

Figure 2-1 The Menu Bar offers complete access to AOL's extensive features.

The concept behind the Menu Bar is simple and straightforward. The menu heading indicates the general category of features to be found within the menu itself. The menu contains options to perform an action or take you to a screen where you can perform a related action (see Figure 2-2).

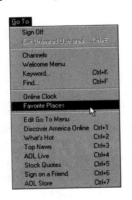

Figure 2-2 The drop-down lists of the Menu Bar offer many options.

To open a menu, follow these steps:

1. Move your mouse pointer to the heading of your choice.

2. Click the menu heading.

3. Move your mouse pointer down the menu to the option of your choice.

4. Click the option to perform the action or go to the related screen.

No matter where you go in AOL, the Menu Bar is always available. You never have to worry about finding yourself somewhere without access to an important feature or function.

TIP The <u>G</u>o To menu reveals several AOL sites as standard options to jump to. However, if you find that you have other spots you frequent more often, you can change the <u>G</u>o To menu to eliminate the sites that you don't visit and add the ones that you do. To customize these options, open the <u>G</u>o To menu by clicking <u>G</u>o To→Edit Go To Menu or by using the hot key Alt+G and clicking Edit Go To Menu. At the Favorite Places screen, make the necessary modifications and click Save Changes. The next time you open the <u>G</u>o To menu, the available options reflect your changes.

Tackling the Toolbar

While the Toolbar does not display as many features as the Menu Bar, it does provide quicker and easier access to the most popular AOL features (see Figure 2-3). Clicking any of the icons on the Toolbar takes you to the related area immediately. One click and you're there. It couldn't get much simpler. Although there's a lot of truth to the old adage that a picture is worth a thousand words, it's not always the case when it comes to computer icons. Understanding icons often requires the use of at least a few words. AOL is aware of this and provides little pop-up notes called ToolTips that give a brief description of the feature represented by the icon. To display ToolTips, simply move your mouse pointer over the icon and hold it there momentarily. Within a second or two, the ToolTip appears.

Figure 2-3   To get to the Marketplace quickly, you can't beat the Toolbar.

TIP Unless you have e-mail in your New Mail box, the Mailbox icon at the left end of the Toolbar appears to be completely nonfunctional — you don't even see a ToolTip when you place your pointer on it. As a matter of fact, the only time it does anything is when you receive mail. At that point, the little red flag pops up, the door opens, and a letter appears in the mailbox, alerting you that someone has sent you e-mail.

Putting keywords to work

Keywords offer another means of getting around AOL. You can use keywords to locate specific AOL areas or pages on the World Wide Web, or you can use them to search for AOL areas that contain information related to a keyword or keywords (see Figure 2-4).

To jump to an AOL area, follow these steps:

1. Click the Keyword button at the right end of the Toolbar to open the Keyword window.

2. Enter the name of the AOL area you want to visit in the text box to the right of Enter Words(s):

3. Click Go.

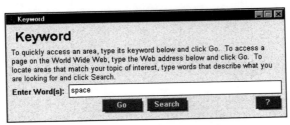

Figure 2-4   AOL's Keyword feature takes you to AOL areas as well as sites on the World Wide Web.

If the keyword you entered is the correct name of an AOL area, you are immediately transported to that area. If no such site exists, you are presented with existing keywords that are related. Either choose one of those keywords or try another keyword.

In the event that you are interested in a topic but can't figure out which area it is in, you can use the Keyword Search function to locate all areas that contain related information.

To perform a Keyword Search, follow these steps:

1. To open the Keyword window, click the Keyword button on the Toolbar.

2. In the text box, enter the word or words to search for.

3. Click Search.

TIP   **To make keyword searching easier and faster, remember that there is no need to worry about using capital letters or articles such as "a," "an," or "the." AOL's Find feature totally ignores both capitalization and small articles when conducting a search.**

Finding your way around

AOL's Find feature is a simple yet surprisingly sophisticated tool for uncovering information of the "needle in a haystack" variety. This unassuming little feature can be found on the Toolbar next to the Keyword button. At first glance, it appears to be just another window with a couple of options. However, closer examination reveals that it is actually a power tool in disguise. Aptly titled Find It On AOL!, the AOL Find feature packs a lot of search power into a relatively small package (see Figure 2-5). This is one example.

Figure 2-5 If you can't locate it with Find, it probably doesn't exist.

Click the Find button in the Toolbar to open the AOL Find window and discover a wealth of search options:

* **Search.** Type a keyword or keywords and click Search.

* **Places & Things.** Click this tab to display of list of AOL search areas for — you guessed it — places and things.

* **People.** This tab contains areas such as the Member directory and Buddy Lists as well as other tools for locating people.

* **Events.** For contests, live chat events, and auditorium events, this is the tab for you.

* **The Essentials.** Click this icon to jump to The Essentials window (see Figure 2-6), which contains links to the AOL Directory, the Member Directory, AOL Software Libraries, and the Internet & World Wide Web. For a quick tour of basic AOL features, click the Start button in the Get the Facts box.

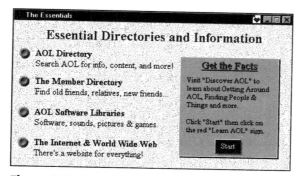

Figure 2-6 Sometimes all it takes is getting back to "the essentials."

* **Browse Channels.** This is one of my favorites. Use this icon to jump to the Channel Find feature (see Figure 2-7), which allows you to select a channel and search its subcategories alphabetically or by topic.

Figure 2-7 Channel Find is your guide to "what's on" AOL.

* **Find Help.** Still confused about how to find what you're looking for? Just click Find Help to get some suggestions, including other directories, other Help areas, and some good search tips (see Figure 2-8).

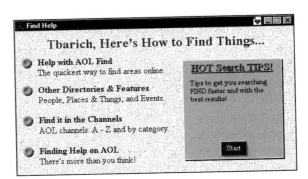

Figure 2-8 Find Help offers tips and suggestions for improving your success rate at locating information.

Saving Favorite Places

A tremendous number of resources are available on AOL, and you will undoubtedly spend a good deal of time exploring new and interesting areas. However, your primary interests and passions will probably keep you returning time and time again to certain sites. To eliminate the need to burrow through several layers of menus and windows each time you want to visit one of your chosen sites, AOL provides a Favorite Places feature.

To save an area as a Favorite Place, follow these steps:

1. Jump to the area using your preferred method.

2. Click the little red heart next to the Minimize button in the title bar (see Figure 2-9) to bring up the Add dialog box.

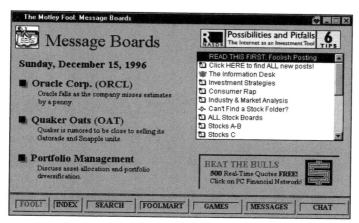

Figure 2-9 All it takes to add a Favorite Place is a couple of mouse clicks.

3. To add the site, select Yes.

After you've added a site to Favorite Places, getting back to it is a snap.

To return to a Favorite site, follow these steps:

1. On the Toolbar, click the Favorite Places icon (the folder with a heart) to open the Favorite Places window (see Figure 2-10).

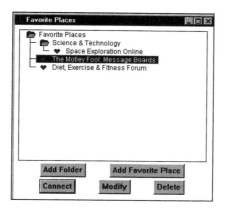

Figure 2-10 Favorite Places are stored in folders for easy retrieval.

2. Highlight the Favorite Place you want to return to.

3. Click Connect to jump to the site.

TIP To keep your Favorite Places orderly and ready to use, you should create additional folders in the Favorite Places window for each general area you visit frequently. You might have a folder for news, fitness, personal finance, and so on. After you've created the new folders, you can drag your Favorite Places and drop them into the appropriate folder. By double-clicking the folders, you can collapse and expand them to see or hide the contents.

Exploring the Welcome Screen

After you sign on to AOL, you are greeted — verbally (if you have a sound card and speakers that are turned on) and visually. The visual greeting is in the form of the Welcome screen. This is a jumping-off place to begin your AOL adventure. It includes links to the most commonly used features as well as items of special interest (see Figure 2-11). The seven main features — Channels, What's Hot, Mail Center, People Connection, Internet, Top News Story, and Learn AOL — remain constant. Three additional features change depending upon when and where you sign on. They provide local information, special offers, and AOL news.

Figure 2-11 The Welcome screen is your road map to AOL's basic features.

Viewing Channels

One of the main reasons most people are tuning in to AOL is to access the large volume of content available on a variety of topics. It is often argued that online services such as AOL cannot compete with the Internet for the sheer amount of information provided at the same or lower cost. Such an argument fails to address one thing, however. To borrow a phrase from the political arena, "It's *organization*, stupid!" Organization is an invaluable commodity that is in short supply on the Internet but generously available on AOL.

If you're looking for information on a certain topic or subject, head for the channels. Channels are your gateway to areas dedicated to information, news, opinion, discussion, and just about anything else you can think of. The Channels screen contains over twenty different categories to choose from, including health, education, finance, fashion, music, art, and literature — just to name a few (see Figure 2-12).

Figure 2-12   Channels: If you can't find it here, it's probably against the law.

Learning what's hot

Just hang on a minute! Before you start loosening your clothes and getting any ideas, this is not that kind of place. It is, however, the place to find out what everyone's talking about and the areas that are currently most popular (see Figure 2-13). Stop here to see which sites the members have selected as the best online areas. Find out what is available on AOL that can't be found anywhere else. It's also a good idea to check here occasionally to see what new features have been added to AOL. If you can't resist a sale, perhaps you should skip What's Hot, rather than be tempted by the Real Deals feature. This is also the place to find out about all the contests that are going on.

Using the Mail Center

At the AOL Mail Center, you can read and write messages, send files, sign up for mailing lists, and more (see Figure 2-14).

Electronic mail, better known as e-mail, has become the most efficient and effective means of exchanging information around the corner or around the world. Its cost is minimal (nonexistent if you consider it a fringe benefit of your online service), and neither time nor distance significantly affect its operation.

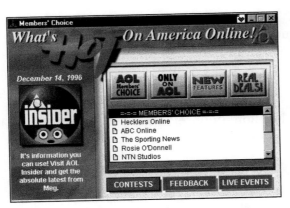

Figure 2-13 Stop here first to find out what's happening on AOL.

As long as your correspondent has an online e-mail account (AOL or another service provider), you can exchange e-mail. The nice thing about e-mail is the fact that it is practically instantaneous, but both the sender and the receiver have the flexibility to deal with it at their own convenience. You don't have to wait for a "decent" hour to send it, and you can choose to ignore incoming messages until you have time for them.

Figure 2-14 Tired of licking stamps? Stop at the Mail Center.

Connecting with people

When you go out to dinner, do you often find your waiter hanging around your table eyeing the check with anticipation while stifling a series of yawns and turning up all the chairs on the surrounding empty tables? Are you always the last one to leave a party? Is your phone bill slightly smaller than the national debt? Then you might be a good candidate for AOL's People Connection (see Figure 2-15). This network of AOL chat rooms offers you a chance to chat "live" with members from all over with a wide variety of interests. The chat rooms are divided into three groups: Public, Member, and Private. The Public and Member rooms are further divided into categories of interest. Private rooms are by invitation only, or you can create your own and invite others to join you.

For more information on chat rooms see Chapter 5.

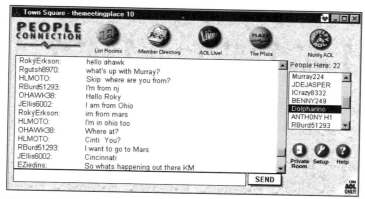

Figure 2-15 There's rarely a lull in the conversation at the People Connection.

Accessing the Internet

 Of course, the online experience would not be complete without access to the Internet. Like a large, bustling city, the Internet has a lot to offer, but it is easy to get lost, and there are a number of pitfalls. If the quantity of diverse information doesn't entice you, the promise of adventure in an electronic world where almost anything goes might. Fortunately AOL offers easy access to the main features of the Internet, including the World Wide Web (WWW), Usenet newsgroups, Gopher, and FTP (see Figure 2-16).

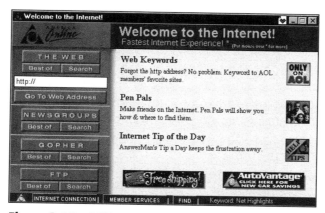

Figure 2-16 AOL's on-ramp to the Information Superhighway.

Touring AOL

If you hate wandering around and learning by trial and error, this is your ticket to a crash course in using AOL. Here you find detailed instructions on how to navigate through AOL, how to send and receive e-mail, how to join a chat room, and more. The AOL Tour, as it is also known, provides brief lessons as well as quick tips on ten of the service's most popular features and facilities (see Figure 2-17). The step-by-step lessons for each topic are broken down into a series of mini tutorials that cover specific features and functions. As a result, you are free to take the entire lesson, from beginning to end, or jump around and find only the particular help you need.

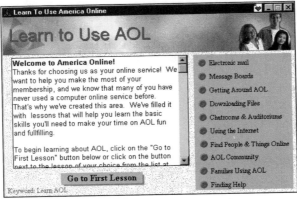

Figure 2-17 Sharpen your AOL skills with step-by-step lessons.

TIP If you are new to computers as well as AOL, it might be good to check out the AOL Quick Start, which includes a tutorial for "absolute beginners." To reach Quick Start, click the Keyword button on the Toolbar, enter Quick Start, and then click Go.

Keeping up with the news

There's no doubt about it, we live in the information age. The wealth of information available to us is phenomenal and for the most part invaluable. Unfortunately, the sheer volume can sometimes become more of a hindrance than a help. This is especially true when it comes to news. Satellites and computers have made the entire world a global community, with instant communication from even the most remote areas a reality. Consequently, it is difficult to keep informed without being overwhelmed. AOL's Top News Story feature, which can always be found at the lower-right corner of the Welcome screen, enables you to take a quick look at the Reuters Hourly News Summary and determine which news, sports, business, or entertainment information you want to explore (see Figure 2-18).

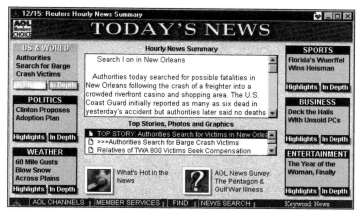

Figure 2-18   Get the news you want, when you want it, with AOL's Top News Story feature.

Using AOL Core Features

Certain features are either found in or can be accessed from a multitude of different areas. These features form the backbone of the AOL structure and can provide a great deal of assistance and enjoyment after you become familiar with them. I'm referring specifically to Message Boards, Chat Rooms, Buddy Lists, Member Services, and File Downloading. After you learn your way around AOL and master these core features, you can put AOL's wealth of information to work for you.

Getting your message across

One of the nice things about AOL is that it has been around for quite a while and it has a large membership. This means that if you have a question about a topic of interest, there's a good chance that someone else has an answer — or at least an opinion. The place to find both is on the area's Message Boards. The Message Boards provide a forum for people to ask questions, make comments, and trade insights and experiences on specific subjects. The format for the information exchange is similar to e-mail except that the messages are not sent to anyone in particular, but instead are posted for all to read. Any one channel may have a number of Message Boards specific to subtopics of the main category. By selecting different subcategories, you can often find an appropriate Message Board.

Suppose you're looking for some advice on how to get in shape. It seems that everything the experts, articles, and marketing departments (for fitness equipment) have to offer is either too good to be true or impossible for a mere mortal to achieve. How about real people? How do they do it? A great place to find out is on the Personal Fitness Message Boards.

The first step is to get there:

1. On the Toolbar, click the Keyword button to open the Keyword search window.

2. Enter the Keyword **fitness**.

3. Click Go to open the Fitness Main window (see Figure 2-19).

Figure 2-19 The Fitness Main window offers a number of options, including Message Boards.

4. Click the small square to the left of Message Boards to enter the primary Message Board window (see Figure 2-20).

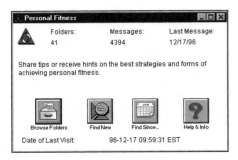

Figure 2-20 The primary Message Board window gives statistics and options for scanning the messages.

5. Click the Browse Folders icon to view the various topics being discussed by the group. The Folders window appears with a list of the subjects covered, the number of messages contained in each folder, and relevant dates (see Figure 2-21).

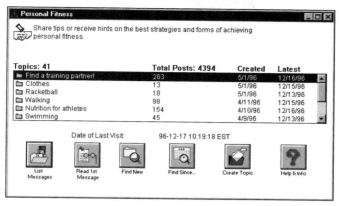

Figure 2-21   The Message Board folders offer a wide variety of subjects and options.

In addition to having a number of topics to choose from, the Message Boards also offer a selection of options for using the boards effectively:

* **List Messages.** Displays a scrollable list of all the messages in the highlighted folder.

* **Read 1st Message.** Takes you to the first (by date) message in the highlighted folder.

* **Find New.** If you've been here before, AOL remembers your last visit and displays only those messages posted to the highlighted file since you were last here.

* **Find Since...** This option allows you to specify the messages you want to see by how recent they are.

* **Create Topic.** If you don't find a folder that addresses your concern, start one of your own.

* **Help & Info.** Provides help on using the Message Boards.

TIP   The Message Boards have a limited capacity for folders and at times become full. When this happens, the Create Topic icon returns a message indicating that no more folders can be added. If you feel there is a real need for your topic, you might contact the forum leader and request that an additional folder be added.

6. Highlight a topic of interest and select List Messages to display a list of all the messages contained in the folder (see Figure 2-22).

7. To read a message, double-click it. Or, highlight it and click the Read Message icon.

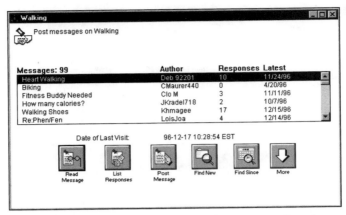

Figure 2-22 The folder messages and responses reflect the questions, opinions, and advice of other AOL members

8. To read the responses to a message after you have opened the message, select Read 1st Response. From there, you can cycle through all the responses by using the arrow icons.

You can also add your own message by choosing Add Message, or you can post a response to a message by selecting Post Response. The bottom line is that you can either find the answer to your question or pose it to the entire community. Of all the AOL members out there, someone is bound to have the answer, a similar experience, or at the very least an opinion on the matter.

Chatting online

One of AOL's most popular features is its chat rooms. This is where the AOL community gathers around the old pot-belly stove to discuss news, sports, politics, sex, gossip, and just about anything else you can think of. Like any public forum, you are bound to encounter chat rooms you love and chat rooms you hate. The best strategy is to avoid topics that don't interest you and find ones peopled by members with similar interests and temperaments.

TIP Be advised that there is a great deal of frank discussion of a sexual nature being carried on in many of the chat rooms. Even those that are clearly of a non-sexual nature occasionally are visited by those who want to shock or liven things up. Therefore, it is an especially good idea to use the parental controls to ensure that young children are not exposed to these areas.

The quickest way to get started is with a single mouse click. To enter the People Connection (see Figure 2-23), simply click the Chat icon on the Toolbar (hint: it's the one with the two faces).

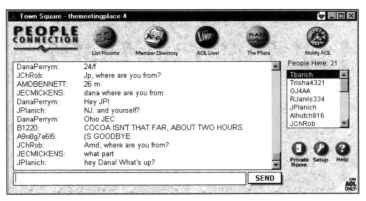

Figure 2-23 The People Connection is the entryway to AOL's chat rooms.

Upon entering the People Connection, you are immediately whisked into the first Town Square Lobby with an open seat. You can either hang around and see if there's anything interesting being discussed or move on to a room of your choice. To get around, you should familiarize yourself with the People Connection options:

* **List Rooms.** Click this icon to open the Public Rooms window, which displays a list of topics on the left and a list of related chat rooms on the right.

* **Member Directory.** This option allows you to search for member profiles or open and modify your own.

TIP If you find someone in the chat room who seems interesting, you can quickly find out the basics about the person by double-clicking the member's screen name in the list and then clicking Get Info. If the user has filled out a member profile, it appears with what information the member has provided. Since cyberspace offers a cloak of anonymity, many members choose to create fanciful online indentities for themselves. As a result, the member profiles are not always one-hundred percent accurate.

* **AOL Live.** Something akin to the community bulletin board. This is where you can find out what live events are taking place or coming up.

* **The Plaza.** Links to interactive games, channel chat rooms, romance, and more.

Cruising the Information Superhighway

It's almost a sure bet that even someone who has never seen or used a computer has heard of the Internet. It's the hottest topic around. Now that you're on AOL, you have the opportunity to find out what everyone is talking about. As is usually the case, the difference between media hype and reality can be substantial. You may even be somewhat disappointed at first glance. However, with a little patience and some understanding of how to best use the Internet, you will find it to be an invaluable tool for many tasks.

Before you travel too far down this electronic expressway, you should familiarize yourself with a few terms and concepts that you are about to encounter:

* **The Internet.** A worldwide network of computers linked together to provide nearly instant access to information of all varieties.

* **World Wide Web (WWW).** That part of the Internet that uses easy-to-navigate HyperText Markup Language (HTML) pages to provide information.

* **Web browser.** A software program that enables you, through the use of a modem, to connect to and interact with all the computers that make up the World Wide Web.

* **URL (Uniform Resource Locator).** This is the address of a particular page on the World Wide Web. It is the equivalent of your street address, city, state, and Zip code used for mail delivery.

* **Search engine.** A service or program that locates specific WWW sites and pages using keyword searches.

Another stop you might make prior to diving headfirst into the Internet is at AOL's Step-by-Step Lessons for Using the Internet.

To access the lessons, follow these steps:

1. Select Learn AOL from the Welcome screen to open the Member Orientation window.

2. Click the "Click here to Learn AOL!" sign to enter the Learn to Use AOL area (see Figure 2-24).

3. Select the Using the Internet lesson by clicking the red dot to the left of it.

4. This brings you to the lesson introduction. To take the tutorial, click the Step-by-Step Lessons button.

After you've got the basics down, you're ready to travel. To start your journey, click the World Wide Web (WWW) icon (the mini globe) on the Toolbar. You are immediately transported to AOL's Welcome to the Web page (see Figure 2-25). You are already on the Internet! By clicking the WWW icon, you have actually launched AOL's Web browser and been transported to a World Wide Web page — in this example, AOL's home page.

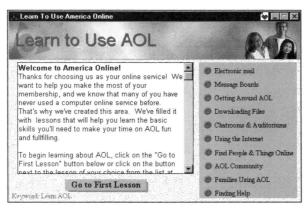

Figure 2-24   Learn to Use AOL offers tutorials on most AOL basic features.

Figure 2-25   Nothing to it! One mouse click and you're on the road to cyberspace.

Downloading files

It's frustrating to go to the library to do research and find the perfect book — only to have the librarian give a stern look of disapproval and say, "You know that you can't take reference books out. I'm afraid you'll just have to stay here and do your research." Well, thanks to file downloading, it won't happen to you online, except on rare occasion. Downloading is simply saving text, graphics (pictures), computer programs, and even WWW pages to the hard disk on your computer. You can then view or use them at a later time, at your convenience. The most frequently downloaded files are computer programs and utilities. Fortunately, AOL offers a tremendous selection of software files to download.

To begin, follow these steps:

1. Click the Keyword button on the Toolbar.

2. Enter "file search" when the text box opens.

3. Click Go to open the Software Search window, which is shown in Figure 2-26.

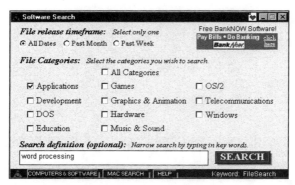

Figure 2-26 Search an entire category or narrow it down with a keyword search.

4. Select a release time frame.

5. Choose a file category.

6. If you have a more specific idea of what you're looking for, you can enter a keyword in the Search Definitions text box to narrow your search.

7. Click Search to open the File Search Results window (see Figure 2-27).

8. To get detailed information about a file, highlight the title and click the Read Description icon.

9. If you want to download a file immediately, highlight the title and click Download Now.

10. In the Download Manager dialog box, either accept the default file name and destination folder on your hard drive or change them to reflect the name and place you prefer.

11. Click Save to begin the download process.

TIP If you plan to download more than one file, use the **Download Later** option. It allows you to add files to your download list. When you have chosen all the files you want to download, select File→Download Manager from the Menu Bar and modify your download list or begin the download process.

Figure 2-27 All files that meet the search criteria are listed in the File Search Results window.

Although file downloads appear to provide a source of free software, it is important to understand that not all downloaded software is without cost. Different types of software files are available on AOL (and the Internet) with which you should be familiar:

* **Public Domain.** Software that is not copyrighted and may be used and copied freely.

* **Freeware.** Software that is copyrighted but is available for free personal use. Depending on its End User License Agreement (EULA), it may or may not be available for commercial use and redistribution.

* **Shareware.** Software that is copyrighted and distributed for evaluation for a limited period of time. After the evaluation period has ended, the user is required to either pay a registration fee or delete the program from all computers on which it resides.

* **Demoware.** Marketing versions or crippled versions of software that give the user a demonstration of some of the features but doesn't enable the functionality of the full, working program.

Making good use of Member Services

When you have questions or concerns about your community services, where do you go? City Hall, of course. Well, the AOL community has its city hall too. It's called Member Services. If you want account and billing information, come to Member Services. Want to find out if any AOL services are temporarily down for maintenance and upgrading? Stop at Member Services. Need to get in touch with an AOL representative? Yep, you guessed it — Member Services. To get to the main Member Services window, click the Help icon (question mark) in the Toolbar (see Figure 2-28).

Figure 2-28 If you have a question or a concern about the AOL service, you'll find the answer here.

To use Member Services effectively, you have to first understand what services are available. Here are just some of the things you can find in Member Services:

* **Quick Answers.** A database of help information on most of AOL's extensive features. The main categories include E-mail, Downloading, Internet/WWW, Connecting to AOL, Error Messages, Exploring AOL, Accounts & Billing, and Graphics & Multimedia (see Figure 2-29).

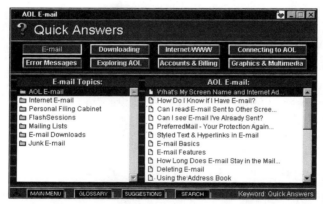

Figure 2-29 Get answers to the most frequently asked questions about AOL features.

* **Download 101.** A quick tutorial on downloading files.
* **Contact Us.** Information on how to contact AOL representatives online, by phone, fax, bbs, or e-mail.
* **Sign on a Friend.** If you get a friend or family member to join AOL for at least three months, AOL pays you a "finder's fee" of $20. Like all promotions, this one is subject to change at any time, so check before enlisting all your friends and neighbors to sign up.

✳ **Accounts & Billing.** Everything and anything you want to know about the subject of accounts, pricing plans, and billing terms (see Figure 2-30).

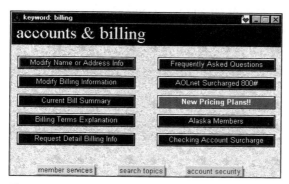

Figure 2-30 Review your account, modify your billing information, or check out the current pricing plans at accounts & billing.

✳ **Members Helping Members.** A community bulletin board where members exchange information about AOL services.

✳ **Connection Help.** Information on modems and connections problems. However, since you have to be connected to access any Member Services, this won't be of much help to you if your problem is that you can't get connected.

✳ **Helpful AOL Books.** Books that cover AOL and that can be purchased online.

✳ **AOL Insider.** An AOL area with news, tips, and updates about the AOL service.

✳ **Scheduled Maintenance.** Notices of downtimes for services and features due to maintenance and upgrades.

Getting help before it's too late

Occasionally, we all need a little help. AOL is aware of this and has kindly provided some assistance for those times when you find yourself lost or just dazed and confused. There are a number of ways to access Help. If you are new to AOL and need help with AOL's basic features, the best place to begin is in the Quick Answers found in Member Services and covered earlier in this chapter. Your next line of attack is the Help menu on the Menu Bar. From the Menu Bar, you can access the standard Windows-style Help that includes tips and tricks, security, modem, connection, troubleshooting help, and more (see Figure 2-31).

Figure 2-31 Technical help is available with the America Online Help Topics.

To access this Help window, select Help→America Online Help Topics. You can then select a Help topic or use the Index feature to perform a keyword search. Another great Help tool is the online support found in Member Services, especially the Member Help Interactive. Interactive Help places you in a chat room with an AOL rep who will answer any questions you may have (regarding AOL).

To access Member Help Interactive, follow these steps:

1. Click the Help icon (question mark) in the Toolbar to open the Member Services window.

2. Select Contact Us.

3. From the list on the right side of the window, double-click Member Help Interactive. This brings you to the Member Help Interactive window with three options as shown in Figure 2-32.

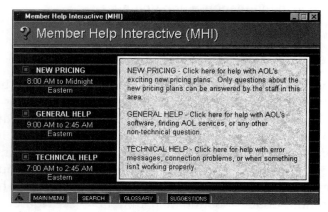

Figure 2-32 The Member Help Interactive (MHI) area of AOL shows you when, where, and how to get help.

You can choose from Pricing, General, and Technical Help. If you select the wrong one, you may waste your time waiting in line only to find you have to go into a different area. If a large number of members are attempting to get interactive Help, there may be a wait. In the event there is, a screen appears telling you how long the wait is and offering you an opportunity to search the AOL database for an answer while you're waiting. You can search without fear of losing your place in the queue. Just remember to check back and see if your number is up.

TIP There are a couple of things you can do to make your interactive Help session quick and smooth. First, be sure you're in the right area. Next, don't pose a question until you are greeted by the AOL support technician. There can be as many as six members in a support room at one time. The technicians take questions in the order you entered the room. Have your question well thought out and make it as concise as possible. Finally, don't dawdle. When you're through, say thanks and exit. Remember that there are people in line behind you.

4. Select the appropriate Help area.

5. Follow the on-screen instructions.

Other Help options include Online Support and the Quick Reference Guide, both of which can be accessed from the Help menu on the main Menu Bar.

BONUS

The amount of information and the number of different areas available on AOL is almost limitless. There is no way to see or do everything. But there are a number of avenues to help you become more familiar with America Online and assist you in getting around comfortably.

The AOL Highlights Tour

To get a quick taste of what AOL has to offer, take the America Online Highlights tour by using the keyword **tour**. This short excursion through twelve commercial and non-commercial sites covers a wide range of topics. It isn't meant to do anything more than whet your appetite, and that it does.

The Channels Screen Disappearance < poof >

After you become familiar with the AOL environment and feel comfortable getting around using the Toolbar, the keyword search, and Favorite Places, you may find that the Channels screen is no longer necessary. It may even become an annoying nuisance. If you find that you no longer need or want the screen to appear each time you sign on, you can get rid of it with a few mouse clicks.

Follow these steps:

1. From the Menu Bar, select Members→Preferences to open the Preferences window (see Figure 2-33).

Figure 2-33 Customizing AOL is easy with the Preference options.

2. Click the General icon to open the General Preferences window (see Figure 2-34).

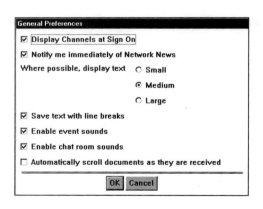

Figure 2-34 General Preferences allow you to control the way AOL operates.

3. Click Display Channels at Sign On to deselect (remove the check mark) for this option.

4. Select OK to return to the Preferences window.

5. When you are finished with the customizing options, close the window to return to AOL.

Howdy, Y'all!

One of the nice things about computers is the fact that they can do all kinds of neat things. AOL has taken advantage of this and created a little surprise for those who are curious, adventurous, or just fortunate enough to stumble on the Howdy window, hidden behind the Welcome Screen. The Howdy window, which can be opened by clicking the AOL logo on the Welcome Screen, contains a daily cartoon to start your day on the right note (see Figure 2-35). In addition, you can find links to the Vault, Rate O Rama, Interact!, And Behind the Curtain, all of which lean toward the lighter side of life.

Figure 2-35 The Howdy window is always good for a laugh.

A Hot Key Combo to Go, Please

Although the mouse is easy and intuitive to use, it is not always the best tool to accomplish a given task. There are times when the keyboard can be quicker and easier, especially if you use hot keys. Hot keys are combinations of keys that, when pressed simultaneously, cause an action to be performed. Table 2.1 lists the basic hot keys available in AOL 3.0.

TABLE 2-1 Basic Hot Keys in AOL

Action	Hot Key
KEYWORD SEARCH	Ctrl+K
FIND	Ctrl+F
COMPOSE MAIL	Ctrl+M
READ NEW MAIL	Ctrl+R
PRINT	Ctrl+P
CREATE A NEW FILE	Ctrl+N
OPEN AN EXISTING FILE	Ctrl+O
SAVE A FILE	Ctrl+S
UNDO LAST COMMAND	Ctrl+Z
CUT	Ctrl+X
COPY	Ctrl+C
PASTE	Ctrl+V
SELECT ALL	Ctrl+A

Summary

Did you ever see a dog owner being dragged down the street by a large canine? It makes you stop and wonder who's really in charge. Your relationship with AOL has the same potential. If you learn how to get the most from it, you will find it an invaluable resource and a source of great enjoyment. If, however, you let it drag you down the street, you may find that you are simply wasting a lot of time that could be spent better elsewhere.

CHAPTER THREE

CONFIGURING AOL

IN THIS CHAPTER YOU LEARN THESE KEY SKILLS

ESTABLISHING YOUR ONLINE IDENTITY   PAGE 59

SETTING PERSONAL PREFERENCES   PAGE 68

3

AOL boasts of a membership of nearly seven million users, and you can bet that each and every one of them wants AOL to function just a little differently. Fortunately, AOL provides the tools necessary to "have it your way." The devices that permit you to customize the service are the *configuration options*. They range from choosing your screen name to eliminating junk e-mail — and a whole lot in between.

In addition to setting up many of AOL's features as you encounter them, you may find that some of the choices you made during the initial AOL setup need to be modified. In either case, it is AOL's extensive configuration options that allow you to mold the service into a comfortable and efficient online environment that suits your needs.

Establishing Your Online Identity

When you first set up AOL, you began defining who you are when you're online. As you become familiar with the service, it is often necessary to change some of the initial information you provided because of changes in the data. If you move, get married, or have children, you can reflect those changes in your online persona. Perhaps you're tired of your screen name or *handle*. As friends come and go, you create new Buddy Lists and modify old ones. All these things are accomplished by changing your AOL configuration settings, also known as preferences.

Adding screen names

Because AOL is very much a family place, it affords different members of the household an opportunity to sign on and customize the service independently. There's no doubt that the kids' favorite places are going to be different from yours. In the event they coincide, you may decide it's better that they don't. The use of different screen names allows each family member to sign on with preferences set to accommodate individual needs and tastes. In addition, the primary account holder can limit the access of the other four accounts, thereby enabling you to apply the oft-needed parental discretion.

To set up or change screen names, follow these steps:

1. From the Toolbar, click the Keyword button.

2. Enter **screen names** and then click Go to open the Create or Delete Screen Names window.

3. Double-click Create a Screen Name to open the Create a Screen Name window (see Figure 3-1).

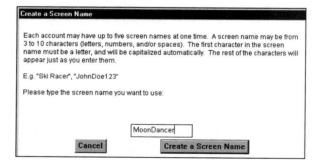

Figure 3-1 Don't be shy; get creative with your screen name.

4. Enter the screen name of your choice and then click Create a Screen Name. If the name is not available, you will receive a message indicating that "The name you requested is already in use. Please try another name."

5. Click OK to return to the Create a Screen Name window and try again.

6. After you have entered an available screen name, the Set Password window opens and requests that you enter a password twice (the second time for confirmation).

7. Select Set Password to access the Parental Control window (see Figure 3-2).

8. Choose the appropriate age group, and then click OK.

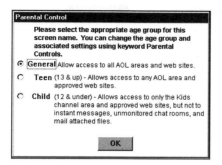

Figure 3-2 Select the age group for the new screen name.

To use a newly created name, you must sign off and then sign on again using the new name. If you want to continue without signing off, simply click OK and ignore the message telling you to sign on again.

Changing your password

Please remember that your password is the key to your AOL account. To ensure the security of your online account, *never* give your password to anyone — including the AOL support staff. As you make your way through the various areas of AOL, you encounter reminders everywhere informing you that AOL staff will never request your password for any reason. Therefore, anyone who might request it is not only unauthorized but also probably has less than honorable intentions.

It is a good idea to change your password regularly just to be on the safe side.

To do this, you:

1. Click the Keyword button on the Toolbar.

2. Enter **password** in the text box, and then select Go.

3. From the opening window, select Change Password.

4. In the Change Your Password window (see Figure 3-3), enter your old password, and then enter the new password twice. When you're through, click Change Password to finalize the change.

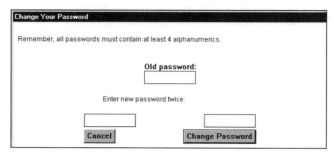

Change Your Password

Remember, all passwords must contain at least 4 alphanumerics.

Old password:

Enter new password twice:

Cancel   Change Password

Figure 3-3 Change your password regularly to safeguard your account.

TIP   It's tempting to use a familiar name, word, or date for your password to ensure that you don't forget it. However, anyone trying to break into your account will first try things such as birth dates, the names of children or pets, and so on. If you spend any amount of time in chat rooms, you can very easily divulge much of that type of information to the entire electronic community. So be sure to create a password that cannot be easily guessed by someone with whom you have casually exchanged personal information.

Modifying your member profile

Your Member Profile is your personal "bio" that is made available to the entire AOL community through the membership directory. It consists of as little or as much basic information as you want to provide. If you are searching for online friends with similar interests, this is the place to look.

To change your Member Profile, follow these steps:

1. Click the Keyword button on the Toolbar.

2. In the Keyword text box, enter **Member Profile** to open the Edit Your Online Profile window (see Figure 3-4).

3. Enter as much information as you want.

4. When you are finished adding or changing your profile, click the Update button to save the changes.

TIP   The online community is no different from the real world when it comes to the variety of people who populate it. They come in all sizes, shapes, and temperaments. This means that there are bound to be a handful of unscrupulous scoundrels lurking around the electronic back alleys. To avoid putting you or your family at risk, it is a good idea to not include your street address or telephone number in any of your

Member Profiles. As a matter of fact, you might want to go so far as to leave out the city in which you live to prevent anyone from finding you in the phone book. You should check your children's profiles periodically to make sure they are not supplying any information with the potential for misuse by others.

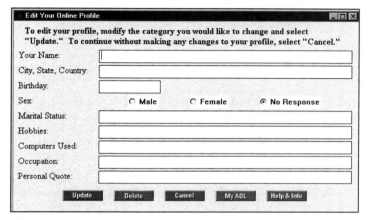

Figure 3-4 Create your online identity with the Member Profile form.

Creating Buddy Lists

Do you spend a lot of time online hangin' out with the guys? Do you get together with the girls online for regular bull sessions? Do you have a group of online friends that you enjoy debating politics with? If the answer to any (or all) of those questions is yes, then you should have some Buddy Lists set up. Like any large metropolis, AOL can be a lonely place even when you're surrounded by multitudes of people. By creating Buddy Lists, AOL instantly alerts you when any of your online friends signs on.

Creating Buddy Lists is simple:

1. From the main Menu Bar, select Members → Buddy Lists to open the Buddy Lists window (see Figure 3-5).

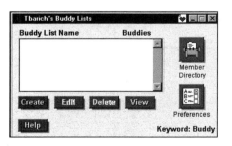

Figure 3-5 Keeping in touch with your AOL friends is easy with the Buddy List.

2. Click Create to open the Create a Buddy List window (see Figure 3-6).

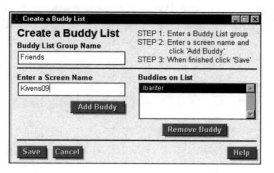

Figure 3-6 Create separate Buddy Lists for family, friends, and business contacts.

3. Enter the name of the list (Family, Friends, and so on) in the Buddy List Group Name text box.

4. Press Tab to move to the Enter a Screen Name text box.

5. Enter the person's screen name.

6. Click Add Buddy to include the individual on the current Buddy List.

7. Repeat the process until you have added all the names for this list or until you have reached the limit, which is sixteen per group.

8. When you are satisfied with the list, click Save to save the list.

SETTING BUDDY LIST PREFERENCES

Like most of AOL's features, you can set the options for Buddy Lists to suit your needs.

To customize your Buddy Lists, follow these steps:

1. From the Menu Bar, select Mem**b**ers → Buddy Lists to open the main Buddy List window.

2. Click the Preferences icon to open the Buddy List Preferences window (see Figure 3-7).

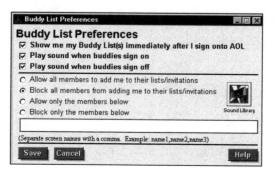

Figure 3-7 Control Buddy Lists' sight and sound with Buddy List preferences.

3. Set the options by selecting (indicated by a check mark) or deselecting each one.

Buddy List Preferences provide the following options:

✴ **Show me my Buddy List(s) immediately after I sign onto AOL.** Select this option to have your Buddy List(s) automatically pop up as soon as you sign on.

✴ **Play sound when buddies sign on.** If you want to be alerted with a sound when someone on your Buddy List signs on, select this option. Remember, you must have a sound card and speakers for this to work.

✴ **Play sound when buddies sign off.** Similar to the previous option, this one, when selected, will play a sound to alert you when one of your buddies leaves the AOL service.

 TIP To play the sounds, you must first download the AOL sound installer, a handy utility that installs the BuddyIn and BuddyOut sound events onto you computer. Click the Sounds Library icon, double-click Door Bell/Slam Sound Installer, and then select Download Now.

The next four option buttons offer you the opportunity to selectively decide whether or not to allow others to include you on their Buddy Lists. However, you can choose only one of the four.

✴ **Allow all members to add me to their lists/invitations.** Select this if you want everyone to be able to add you to their Buddy Lists.

✴ **Block all members from adding me to their lists/invitations.** This is a must for all misanthropes (people haters). It allows no one to add you to a Buddy List.

✴ **Allow only the members below.** If you wish only a select group of people to be able to add you to a Buddy List, select this option and fill out the text box below it with their screen names.

✴ **Block only the members below.** Select this option to prevent specific individuals from adding you to their Buddy Lists. Fill out the text box below with the screen names of those whose lists you want to avoid.

4. After you have set all the options, click Save to save your Buddy List Preferences.

USING THE BUDDY LIST

The BuddyView is your Buddy List organizer and is available whenever and wherever you want. If you select the Show me my Buddy List(s) immediately after I sign onto AOL preference, the Buddy List automatically appears each time you sign on to the service. If you deselect that option, you can still access the Buddy List by using the keyword **buddyview**. The Buddy List's features allow you to easily manage your lists and contact your buddies with little or no effort (see Figure 3-8).

Figure 3-8 Use the BuddyView to find and communicate with your online buddies.

* Display window. The BuddyView window displays your Buddy Lists and which members of each list are currently online.

* Locate. To see if a particular buddy is in a chat room, click the Locate icon. If the selected buddy is in a chat room, you are told which one and offered the option (click Go) of joining the room. If the buddy is not in a chat room, you are informed of that fact and offered the opportunity to send an Instant Message (IM).

* IM. If you could care less where your buddy is but want to send a quick note, highlight the buddy name and click the IM (Instant Message) icon. This activates the Send Instant Message window (see Figure 3-9), in which you can type a short note that will immediately pop up on your buddy's screen when you click Send.

Figure 3-9 Instant Message provide a direct communications link with buddies no matter where you are on AOL.

* Invite. If you want to get together with some of the members on your Buddy List for a private chat, you can send a group invitation (see Figure 3-10) by clicking the Invite icon.

Figure 3-10 Get everyone together for a chat session with the Invite option.

Used properly, the Buddy Lists can provide you with a direct link to those online friends with whom you spend most of your time. Keeping in touch is important whether you're on land, sea, or in cyberspace.

Changing a billing method

As of this writing, AOL only offers two billing methods: credit card or checking account debit card. The credit card method is preferable simply because it does not carry the monthly surcharge of three dollars as does the bank debit card.

If you want to modify your billing information, follow these steps:

1. Click the Keyword button on the Toolbar.

2. Enter **billing** in the text box, and then choose Go to activate the accounts & billing window (see Figure 3-11).

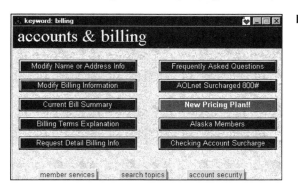

Figure 3-11 The accounts & billing window provides easy access to all your account information.

3. Select Modify Billing Information, enter your password, and then click Continue.

4. To use the checking account billing method, click Checking Account. Then from the next screen, select Use Checking Account to open the checking account billing form (see Figure 3-12).

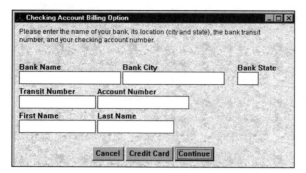

Figure 3-12 To select the checking account billing options, fill out this form.

5. To use the credit card payment option, select Credit Card to open the credit card billing form (see Figure 3-13).

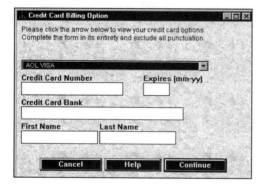

Figure 3-13 Use this form to select the credit card billing option.

TIP Remember that billing options can only be modified from the master account. If you have more than one screen name, be sure to sign on using your original screen name whenever you want to change your account information.

Setting Your Preferences

There is one thing that most people have in common, and that is the fact that they are all different. Many of those differences surface in small personal preferences. Fortunately, AOL has provided a means for users to tailor many of the service's features to suit their needs. Most of the major features have a group of options, called Preferences, that can be set in order to make the particular feature as user friendly as possible.

Chat Preferences

If you are spending any amount of time in chat rooms, you should be sure to check out the Chat Preferences. Here's your opportunity to create a chat environment to your liking. If you're the inquisitive type, you'll want to know when people are coming and going and who's in the room. If you like sounds, you'll want to enable them; on the other hand, if they drive you crazy, you'll want to eliminate them.

To perform these actions:

1. From the Menu Bar select ⬛ **Members** → ⬛ **Preferences** to open the Preferences window (see Figure 3-14).

Figure 3-14 What's your preference?

2. Click the Chat icon to open the Chat Preferences window (see Figure 3-15).

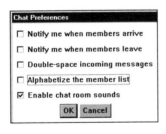

Figure 3-15 Make the chat rooms your kind of place by setting Chat Preferences.

3. To turn an option on, click it to add a check mark to the box that's to the left of the option. To turn an option off, click it to remove the check mark.

   The following options are available for chat sessions:

   ✳ **Notify me when members arrive.** Select this option to be informed each time a member enters the chat room you're in.

   ✳ **Notify me when members leave.** To be informed as members leave the chat room, select this option.

   ✳ **Double-space incoming messages.** Sometimes having single-spaced lines can make reading the chat sessions a little difficult. If you find that to be a problem, turn on the double-space option.

* **Alphabetize the member list.** Use this option to organize the list of members currently in the room. It makes it easier to find someone you might be expecting.

* **Enable chat room sounds.** Either you love 'em or you hate 'em. There doesn't seem to be much middle ground. Either way, the choice is yours. Turn chat room sounds on or off with the click of a mouse button.

4. When you are satisfied with your chat room option choices, click OK to save the settings.

Graphic Preferences

It's hard to miss the fact that AOL is a visually oriented service with lots of graphics. To make life a little easier for you, AOL provides a few options to make dealing with graphics somewhat simpler. Of all the different types of files that are transmitted to your computer from AOL's when you're online, graphics files are some of the biggest. This means that every time you enter an area containing graphics (which is just about every area on the service) you have to wait for the graphics, or art, as AOL refers to them, to download to your computer. This is time consuming and — if you have sufficient disk space — unnecessary. By setting the Graphics Preferences, you can control how your system handles AOL art. Graphics Preferences include:

* **Maximum disk space to use for online art.** Every AOL area that you enter contains a certain amount of art, or graphics, that must be downloaded to your computer — unless they already reside on your computer (from a previous download). AOL, by default, sets aside twenty megabytes of your hard disk space to store artwork. By changing this option, you can allocate more or less of your hard disk space for the storage of online graphics. The more you are able to store, the less you have to download and the quicker your access to different AOL areas (after the first visit).

* **Display image files on download.** When you are downloading image files from AOL or from software libraries, you can choose to display the image at the time you download or wait until you have downloaded and display them at your own leisure. By waiting, you accelerate the download process and spend less time online. However, if you wait to view them later, you must have a separate graphics viewer installed on your computer. Because there are many available from the shareware libraries on AOL, this is not a major stumbling block; however, it should be taken into consideration when deselecting this option.

* **JPEG compression quality.** This option is best left selected. It changes the image quality of JPEG graphics. Unless you are well-acquainted with graphics, you can do more harm than good by changing this.

* **Set Color Mode.** To ensure the best quality viewing of colors on AOL, the program automatically attempts to determine how many colors your computer is set to use. Occasionally, this information is not properly communicated from your computer to the AOL software. In that case, you may have to change the color settings.

TIP If, while in AOL, you find that you are getting strange colors or that the graphics on your screen are starting to do weird things, the problem may be with your color settings. The first thing to do is check your Windows color settings by bringing up your Windows task bar and then selecting Start → Settings → Control Panel. Double-click the Display icon, select the Settings tab, and then look at the Color palette settings. The color palette settings tell you how many colors your computer is set to use. Then return to the AOL Graphics Preferences window, select Set Color Mode, and click the appropriate option that matches your Windows color palette settings (Windows 95's High Color setting is equal to AOL's More than 256 colors setting).

To access the Graphics Viewing Preferences window, follow these steps:

1. Select Members → Preferences from the Menu Bar to open the Preferences window.

2. Click the Graphics icon to open the Graphic Viewing Preferences window (see Figure 3-16).

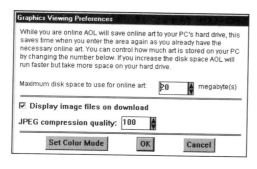

Figure 3-16 Managing the way your computer handles graphics can improve AOL performance.

3. When you have set all your graphics options, select OK to save the settings.

General Preferences

As you become more familiar with AOL, you may decide that some of the standard settings are not quite right for you. Do you always want to see the Channels window when you sign on? Is the e-mail text big enough for you to comfortably read? Or perhaps it's too big? Either way, the choice is yours, along with some others. In the General Preferences window, you find:

* **Display Channels at Sign On.** When you begin your AOL experience, you probably find the Channels screen to be helpful. It directs you to the main AOL areas with a simple mouse click. As you become more familiar with AOL and begin saving Favorite Places and using keywords, you may decide that the Channels screen is no longer necessary. Deselecting this option eliminates the screen from automatically appearing each time you sign on.

* **Notify me immediately of Network News.** This is probably a good one to have checked because it automatically alerts you to important announcements made by AOL's network center. There are relatively few announcements, so it is not much of a hassle.

* **Where possible, display text.** Your choices are small, medium, and large. This affects only the text displayed in e-mail and certain other areas, not AOL in general.

* **Save text with line breaks.** Selecting this option saves text with the AOL formatting. If it looks good to you on AOL and you want it to look similar when you save it to a text file, select this option.

* **Enable event sounds.** Those are the verbal welcome and good-bye greetings you get when you sign on and off and the notification that you have mail in your mail box. Of course, if you don't have a sound card and speakers installed, then you won't be hearing those sounds, and this option will be meaningless to you. If, on the other hand, you have a sound card and speakers, you turn those sound on or off with this option.

* **Enable chat room sounds.** As with event sounds, this option allows you to turn chat room sounds on or off (see the "Chat Preferences" section for more details).

* **Automatically scroll documents as they are received.** Unless you are connecting at 2400 baud, there is probably no reason to select this option. Selected, it does just what it says — it automatically scrolls documents as they are received on your computer.

To access the General Preferences window, follow these steps:

1. From the Menu Bar, select Members → Preferences to open the Preferences window.

2. Click the General icon to open the General Preferences window (see Figure 3-17).

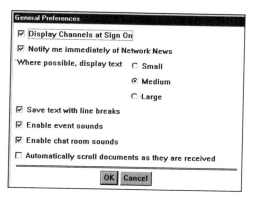

Figure 3-17 General Preferences control some service-wide features.

3. Set the options you desire, and then click OK to save your settings.

Download Preferences

The vast amount of software available for downloading on AOL ensures that this is a feature that gets a lot of use. There are tons of games, applications, and utilities to try out in addition to any file attachments that may accompany your incoming e-mail. If you find yourself doing a lot of downloading, you may discover that AOL's download options come in quite handy.

Here's how to set download preferences:

1. Open the Preferences window by selecting `Members` → `Preferences` from the Menu Bar.

2. Click the Download icon to open the Download Preferences window (see Figure 3-18).

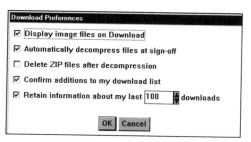

Figure 3-18 Don't download without setting your options first.

Available download options include

✳ **Display image files on Download.** Images are displayed on your AOL screen when you download them. To save time, turn this option off and view the images at a later time.

* **Automatically decompress files at sign-off.** To cut down on transmission time when downloading, many files are compressed. They are basically compacted before being sent and must be decompressed before they can be used. With this option selected (the default is "on"), AOL will automatically decompress the files. If you have a compression utility such as WinZip or PKZip, you can deselect this option and decompress the files yourself.

* **Delete Zip files after decompression.** Most compressed files are of the Zip variety. After the original file(s) are extracted from a Zip file, you can delete the Zip (compressed) file or keep it as a backup. The Zip files still retain copies of the original compressed file(s). Selecting this option causes AOL to automatically delete the Zip file after it has been decompressed. This is useful if you are short on hard disk space.

* **Confirm additions to my download list.** If you decide not to download files immediately, you can add them to a download list and transfer them at a later time. Selecting this option causes AOL to prompt you for a confirmation each time you add something to the download list.

* **Retain information about my last [###] downloads.** AOL keeps a list of the items you download. The list can be found in the Download Manager or in your Personal Filing Cabinet. If you prefer not to keep track of downloaded files, deselect this option. If you want to keep a list, but more or less titles than the default of one hundred, select the option and change the number to suit your needs.

3. Click OK to save your settings and exit.

Mail Preferences

E-mail is one of AOL's most frequently used features. It provides near instantaneous communication with anyone around the world who has AOL or Internet access. For the quick, long distance exchange of information and data, it has no equal. To get the most out of such a handy tool, you should take advantage of the options provided by AOL in Mail Preferences.

Here's how:

1. From the Menu Bar, select Members → Preferences to open the Preferences window.

2. Click the Mail icon to access the Mail Preferences window (see Figure 3-19).

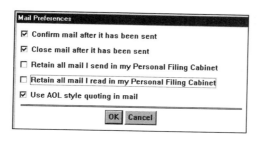

Figure 3-19 E-mail provides a great "electronic" trail if you set your options to save messages received and sent.

Mail Preferences offer the following options:

* **Confirm mail after it has been sent.** Select this option to be notified after an e-mail message is sent.

* **Close mail after it has been sent.** If you do not select this option, e-mail messages you create remain open, even after you send them, until you close them yourself. By turning this feature on, AOL automatically closes the message as soon as you send it.

* **Retain all mail I send in my Personal Filing Cabinet.** If you send e-mail that is of any value to you, this feature is a must. By selecting this option, a copy of all e-mail messages that you send will be kept in your Personal Filing Cabinet. If you later have a question about the content or even the fact that you sent a message, you can easily find out by checking your Personal Filing Cabinet.

* **Retain all mail I read in my Personal Filing Cabinet.** Like the previous feature, this option (when turned on) causes e-mail messages to be stored in your Personal Filing Cabinet. In this case, it is the incoming messages that are stored.

* **Use AOL style quoting in mail.** It's always a good idea to include the portion of an e-mail message to which you are responding in your reply. Frequently, the sender will not recall the exact information or question posed in the original note — especially in a long message. This option allows you to paste any part of the original message into your reply by simply highlighting the text to copy and paste and selecting Reply (or Forward). The text is immediately placed in the new message. In addition, it is enclosed in double brackets to indicate that it is "quoted."

3. Click OK to save your settings and return to the previous window.

Web Preferences

Whether it is sooner or later, there is no doubt that the Internet will eventually lure you onto the Information Superhighway. When you begin accessing the Internet through AOL, you can customize many of the features by changing the

AOL Internet Properties. These options include everything from selecting screen colors to controlling the content accessed through your computer.

 For more details on these options see Chapter 15.

Filing Cabinet Preferences

Your Personal Filing Cabinet (PFC) is an extremely useful tool for keeping track of much of the information and data that you accumulate as you travel through cyberspace. Unfortunately, the virtual world, just like the real world, has lots of "stuff." Even though it may be virtual stuff, you still need some place to store it. Are you familiar with the old adage (somebody's law?) that work expands to fill the time available? Well, stuff is the same way. It has a habit of expanding to fill the storage space available. AOL, being aware of these laws of nature, has created the Personal Filing Cabinet to help you keep all your virtual stuff under control. The Personal Filing Cabinet Preferences help you to use the Personal Filing Cabinet as effectively as possible.

To access the Personal Filing Cabinet Preferences, follow these steps:

1. Select ⬛Mem**b**ers → ⬛**Preferences** to open the Preferences window.

2. Select the Personal Filing Cabinet icon to open the Personal Filing Cabinet Preferences window (see Figure 3-20).

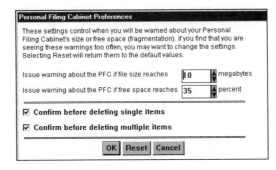

Figure 3-20 Personal Filing Cabinet Preferences are your key to an efficient electronic storage system.

You find the following options in Personal Filing Cabinet Preferences:

✳ **Issue warning about the PFC if file size reaches [xxxx] megabytes.** Because the Personal Filing Cabinet is really just a portion of your hard disk set aside for storing your old e-mail, files, and other information, it is important to keep its size under control. By setting this option, you can have AOL warn you when the amount of space occupied by the Personal Filing Cabinet reaches a certain size. Set this number depending on the size of your hard disk and the amount of space available.

* **Issue warning about the PFC if free space reaches [xx] percent.** As you delete files from your Personal Filing Cabinet they are marked as deleted, but they are not actually removed. As a result, your PFC often contains a lot of unused space that is "reserved" for deleted files. You can reclaim this free space by compacting the PFC. The free space warning alerts you when the specified percentage of unclaimed space is reached. Since there's no reason to waste disk space on deleted files it's a good idea to keep an eye on this warning.

* **Confirm before deleting single items.** It's easy to make a mistake. We all do it. Unfortunately, deleting the wrong e-mail or file is one of those mistakes that cannot be rectified. Unlike many applications that have an Undelete feature, the AOL Personal Filing Cabinet does not. By turning this option on, AOL prompts you to confirm that you have made the right choice before deleting an item from the PFC.

* **Confirm before deleting multiple items.** A nice feature when doing a little housekeeping in your Personal Filing Cabinet is the ability to mark several items and delete them all at once. Because this is an irreversible action, however, it is a good idea to set this option to ask for confirmation before deleting multiple items... just in case.

3. When you have finished selecting options, click OK to save the settings and return to the previous screen.

Marketing Preferences

We all know that marketing makes the world go round. It's the only reason that we have the extensive radio and television programming that is available today. It generally keeps the cost of newspapers and magazines at a reasonably affordable level. However, there comes a time when enough is enough. AOL does a fair amount of its own marketing, but it gives the user the option to put some limitations on the scope of it.

To access the Marketing Preferences:

1. Click the My AOL icon in the Toolbar to open the My AOL window (see Figure 3-21).

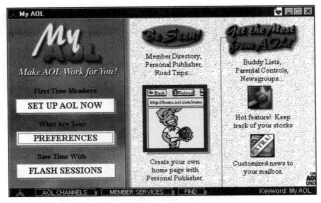

Figure 3-21 The My AOL window offers an array of options.

2. To open the Preferences window, select Preferences (see Figure 3-22).

Figure 3-22 The Preferences window provides access to the main AOL preferences available.

3. Choose Marketing Preferences and then Set Up Now to open the Marketing Preferences list of choices (see Figure 3-23).

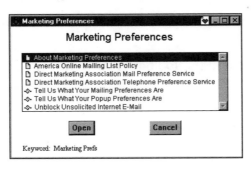

Figure 3-23 Marketing Preferences allow you to limit the amount of unsolicited advertising you are exposed to.

In addition to preference options that can be set, Marketing Preferences include information on how to reduce the amount of unsolicited mail and telephone offers you receive. The options you can set are:

* **Tell Us What Your Mailing Preferences Are.** If you are interested in receiving direct marketing material from specific groups of advertisers, make your selections on this form. If you do not want to receive any unsolicited offers, select the last box by placing an X in it.

* **Tell Us What Your Popup Preferences Are.** AOL does a certain amount of online advertising through the use of popup offers. If you want to receive them, indicate the categories in which you are interested by placing an X in the box. If you do not want to receive popup offers, select the last option. This brings up a Popup Preferences window (see Figure 3-24) with only one option. To eliminate popup offers, click the option so that a check mark appears in the box.

Figure 3-24 Just say no to popup advertising.

* **Unblock Unsolicited Internet E-Mail.** This option filters out unsolicited junk e-mail. This option is on by default. If you want to receive unsolicited e-mail, select I want junk e-mail.

4. Select the settings of your choice. Make the necessary changes and then click OK to save the changes.

Multimedia Preferences

For most users, the Multimedia Preferences default settings are probably adequate. However, those with slower modems or connections might want to make some changes.

To modify the Multimedia Preferences, follow these steps:

1. Select the My AOL icon from the Toolbar to open the My AOL window.

2. Choose Preferences to open the Preferences window.

3. Select Multimedia Preferences and then Set Up Now to open the Multimedia Preferences window (see Figure 3-25).

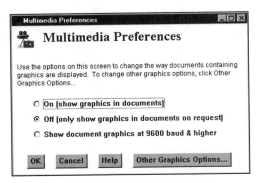

Figure 3-25 Cutting back on graphics can speed things up dramatically.

The following Multimedia options are available:

✴ **On (show graphics in documents).** Turning on graphics in documents is the default setting. This setting causes graphics to be automatically downloaded into all documents. Although this is certainly more pleasing to the eye, it can be a serious drawback when using a slow modem or connection.

✴ **Off (Only show graphics in documents on request).** To download graphics by request only, check this option.

✴ **Show document graphics at 9600 baud & higher**. If you have a fast modem but frequently are unable to connect at speeds above 9600 baud, you might want to check this option. When this option is selected, graphics are not downloaded unless you are connected at 9600 or faster.

4. Select OK to exit and save your changes.

BONUS

Not only does AOL offer a lot in the way of configuration options, it also offers some value-added features. If you have a hankering to become a part of the World Wide Web, you can create your own home page that will be available to the entire Internet community. Another nice feature is the FlashSessions, which allow you to work offline and connect to upload or download at designated times. This feature is great for picking up e-mail and downloading files at times when the traffic might be diminished — therefore resulting in a quicker session.

Creating Your Own Home Page

As we all know, the world is made up of watchers and doers. In cyberspace the watchers surf and browse other peoples' sites. The doers, not content just to watch, create their own pages and become part of the action. AOL provides every member the opportunity to stake a claim to a little piece of the Internet by providing the space and the tools necessary to build your own Web page. Each account is allocated a total of ten megabytes of space for Web pages. For each screen name, you can use up to two megabytes — every member of the family can have his or her own page.

To begin, you should first download Personal Publisher, AOL's software tool for designing and creating Web pages.

To access Personal Publisher, follow these steps:

1. Click the Keyword button on the Toolbar.

2. Enter **personal publisher** in the text box, and then select Go.

3. Choose Download Now.

After you have the software and are ready to begin your career as a Web publisher, the first place to head for is the Web Diner. This is an AOL area dedicated to Web site design. It includes tutorials, notes, actual classes, chat rooms, message boards, and more. Everything you find in this area is directly related to the creation of Web pages. No matter how much or how little you know, this is one place you can be sure to pick up the information and help you need. If you've never even heard of the World Wide Web, you will come out of the Web Diner with the tools you need to build your own home page.

To enter the Web Diner:

1. Click the Keyword button on the Toolbar.

2. Enter **web diner** in the text box and select Go to open the Web Diner Main Menu (see Figure 3-26).

The main menu contains a large selection of choices. If this is your first time here, you should probably start with New? Click Here! This is the place to find the notes and tutorials that enable anyone and everyone to create a Web page in no time. In addition, you find graphics and shareware, as well as tips and tricks to assist you in every aspect of Web development.

Figure 3-26 All the Web publishing information you can digest.

FlashSessions

If you have decided against switching over to AOL's new, unlimited use plan, you should consider using FlashSessions. They can dramatically reduce the amount of time (and, thereby, the cost) you spend online doing such mundane chores as sending and receiving e-mail and downloading. If you compose e-mail and read e-mail while you're online, you are accomplishing nothing that you couldn't do off line. FlashSessions allow you to:

* Compose e-mail messages offline and upload them at a designated time.
* Automatically retrieve all unread e-mail and any attached files.
* Automatically retrieve unread newsgroup messages.
* Compose newsgroup messages offline and upload them automatically.

To set up a FlashSession, follow these steps:

1. Click the Keyword button on the Toolbar.

2. Enter **flashsession** in the text box, and then choose Go to open the FlashSessions window (see Figure 3-27).

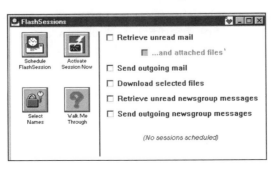

Figure 3-27 Use FlashSessions to spend more time working and less time online.

3. To walk through setting up a FlashSession with step-by-step instructions, select the Walk Me Through; otherwise, design your FlashSession using the options on the right side of the window.

4. If you choose to set up the FlashSession using the on-screen options, you must also choose the screen names to include in each session. To do this, click the Select Names icon to open the Select Screen Names window (see Figure 3-28).

Figure 3-28 Each FlashSession can include one or all of the screen names on your account.

5. For each screen name you want to include, place a check mark to the left by clicking the Screen Name, and enter the appropriate password in the text box.

6. When you've entered all the information, click OK to save your settings and return to the FlashSessions window.

7. To automate FlashSessions, select the Schedule FlashSession icon and open the Schedule FlashSessions window (see Figure 3-29).

Figure 3-29 Let FlashSessions do all the work — when *you* want it done.

8. To use the scheduler, first enable it by clicking on Enable Scheduler to place a check mark in the box to the left.

9. Select a starting time for the first FlashSession to occur.

10. Choose the days you want FlashSessions to take place.

11. From the How often: drop down list, select how frequently they should occur.

12. Click OK to return to the previous window.

13. If you want to begin a session immediately, select the Activate Session Now icon.

Even if you're on the unlimited plan, you may find that automating some of AOL's mechanical tasks with FlashSessions provides you with more time to spend on the fun stuff.

Summary

From your first introduction to AOL, it was probably clear that the service has a lot to offer. Now you can see that in addition to being feature-rich, AOL also has a wealth of options to assist you in customizing all those features. The ability to mold the software into your kind of environment makes AOL a comfortable and homey place to spend time in cyberspace.

COMMUNICATING

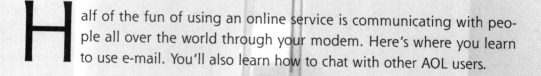

Half of the fun of using an online service is communicating with people all over the world through your modem. Here's where you learn to use e-mail. You'll also learn how to chat with other AOL users.

What does a dedicated traveler do when unable to travel? Travel online, of course. America Online makes it easy to sample the offerings of countries around the globe without leaving our ergonomic office chair. It also makes it easy to make arrangements to visit those places in real life, compare airfares, chat with other members about places to stay, and learn about the customs of those countries.

But first we need to get properly outfitted, even for pretend. In the Travel Store (keyword: **Travel Store**), I can get the only umbrella that will fit into my briefcase (handy for tropical monsoons), a Swiss army knife with at least 12 gizmos, a travel alarm clock, and a universal adapter. I can order by credit card online, and AOL has it set up so that we can add items one at a time into our virtual shopping cart, and "check out" when we are finished shopping.

Fully outfitted, we can proceed to any corner of the universe via the International Channel, which features a world map — one click per continent. When you click a continent, you get a list of resources organized by country.

Let's get exotic: Africa! Click the African hotspot in the world map, and up comes a list of resources, alphabetized by the names of the countries of Africa. I choose Ghana, because I have a friend there. I click Traveler's Corner - Ghana. There's a resource like this for every country. It lists a city-by-city tour, an introduction, DOs & DON'Ts, and a potpourri.

You could find these resources directly on the Web without AOL, but AOL does us the favor of collecting all these links and making them available from a central location like this. This is especially handy for Web novices.

The introduction contains a brief but intriguing historical overview, a description of the country's lush scenery, and an advisory for travelers, emphatic enough to make me forgo any notion of doing business on the black market. Potpourri offers tiny slice-of-life descriptions of the customs of the place, especially from the point of view of western travelers.

For a personal note, we can check the Message Boards, common to all special-interest sections on AOL, where we can get whatever we need to know virtually first hand — that is, from native Ghanaians or other travelers. The most diverse and unpredictable is the Culture & Society section, which contains topics ranging from Ghanaian art and music to tribal tummy markings to propositions for international business ventures.

To get more into the thick of things, we can enter the political arena by clicking Politics, where we find postings speculating on the upcoming elections and pronouncements about what Ghana "really" needs.

On our way out we can stop for a rollicking rendition of Ghana's national anthem, available as both MIDI and WAV files.

USING E-MAIL

IN THIS CHAPTER YOU LEARN THESE KEY SKILLS

4

Do you ever get tired of telling the kids that they can only talk to cousin Janie, who lives on the other side of the country, for a few minutes in order to keep the cost down? Or that they have to wait until tonight to call mom on her business trip? It's especially trying when they give you that look that says if you knew anything, you'd realize that they have too much to tell cousin Janie in a "few minutes," and what they have to tell mom can't possibly wait until tonight. Thanks to e-mail, you can let them take all the time they need and send a message out whenever they want without worrying about cost (assuming you've switched to AOL's flat monthly rate or you use FlashSessions) or timing.

After you've used e-mail, you wonder how you ever got along without it. It places the power of inexpensive, instant, global communication in the hands of anyone who has access to a computer. It enables you to communicate without concern for time zones or time limits. Documents and data files can be exchanged in the blink of an eye. Thankfully, one of the many benefits AOL membership provides is access to e-mail. Each screen name of your account has its own address and mailbox. This means that if you have five members with five different screen names, each has his or her own private e-mail system.

Getting Started with E-Mail

When you initially sign on to AOL, you automatically receive your first piece of e-mail. It is from AOL, welcoming you aboard. Chances are that you know someone who has access to e-mail, so you're probably anxious to send a message and let him or her know you're online. If you have given your e-mail address to friends and family who are either on AOL or another service with e-mail access, you may find yourself with a full mailbox in no time. To take advantage of e-mail, you first need to know some of the basics.

Your e-mail address

Your e-mail address is just like your physical mailing address. It identifies the specific location of your electronic mailbox to which all your electronic mail is delivered. Without an e-mail address, you are among the ranks of the electronically "homeless." Fortunately, as soon as you create a screen name, you simultaneously create an e-mail address for that screen name. As a matter of fact, for exchanging e-mail with other AOL users, your screen name *is* your e-mail address. For communicating with non-AOL members, simply add **@aol.com** to the end of your screen name.

Accessing e-mail

As is the case with most of its features, AOL offers several options for accessing e-mail. Which method you use depends upon the task you want to accomplish.

THE TOOLBAR

If you have a sound card and speakers and your sound feature is turned on, AOL audibly notifies you any time you have e-mail in your mailbox. It also gives you a visual cue by changing the mailbox icon (on the left end of the Toolbar) to a lighter color, with an open door, and the flag up. When the Mailbox icon indicates you have mail, simply click the icon to open the New Mail window (see Figure 4-1), and then double-click the message you want to read.

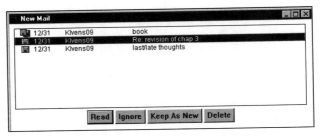

Figure 4-1 You never have to brave the elements to pick up your e-mail.

The easiest way to send e-mail is by clicking the Compose E-mail icon or the Toolbar. It is the pencil and paper icon to the right of the Mailbox icon.

THE WELCOME SCREEN

Each time you sign on to AOL, you are greeted by the Welcome screen, which includes a link to the Mail Center (see Figure 4-2). At the Mail Center, you can perform some (but not all) e-mail functions and find quite a bit of e-mail help.

Figure 4-2 Not getting enough e-mail? No problem; stop at the Mail Center and sign up for all 80+ mailing lists.

Although some e-mail features cannot be accessed through the Mail Center, there is still quite a bit you can do here:

* **Read New Mail**. If you have new (unread) mail, click here to open the New Mail window. However, be aware that you cannot reread old mail here.

* **Compose Mail**. Create and send a new e-mail message.

* **More E-mail Functions**. This button provides access to Mail Controls and the E-mail Message Exchange.

* **Basic E-mail Help**. Here you can find answers to common e-mail questions.

* **Beyond the Basics**. Answers to more advanced e-mail questions.

* **Message Exchange**. Member Message Boards dealing strictly with e-mail issues.

* **Ask the Mail Team**. In theory, this area should provide direct communication with the AOL e-mail support team. However, at the time of this writing, it merely offered access to the e-mail message boards and e-mail help.

* **Newsletters**. Over eighty free online newsletters covering a multitude of topics.

* **Other things you can do with e-mail**. Information on e-mail extras such as mailing lists and pen pals.

TIP If you've been tooling around on AOL for any length of time and have a jumble of windows open, you may not be able to locate your Welcome screen. For quick access to the Mail Center, you can also use the keyword search by clicking the Keyword button on the Toolbar, entering **mail**, and selecting Go. (Psst! If you go there a lot, add it to your Favorite Places.)

THE MENU BAR

For complete access to all e-mail features, your best bet is the Menu Bar. From the Menu Bar, you can read old mail, new mail, and mail that you've already sent. You can also create new mail, edit your Address Book, reach the Mail Center, and set up and use FlashSessions. To open the Mail menu (see Figure 4-3) select Mail from the Menu Bar, then choose the option to use.

Figure 4-3 For the full range of e-mail features, use the Mail menu.

The following Mail menu options are available:

* **Mail Center**. Takes you to the Mail Center.
* **Compose Mail**. Opens the Compose Mail window.
* **Read New Mail**. Takes you to the New Mail window.
* **Check Mail You've Read**. Use this option to reread old mail that has been saved.
* **Check Mail You've Sent**. Click here to read mail that you composed and sent at an earlier time.

TIP In order to keep an "electronic" trail of your dealings with others, it is a good idea to save much of the e-mail you send and receive. The best way to do this is by setting the Mail Preferences to retain e-mail (sent and received) in your Personal Filing Cabinet. For more details, see Chapter 3.

* **Edit Address Book....** Use this option to add, change, or delete entries in your e-mail Address Book.

* **Set Up FlashSession**. To configure and schedule FlashSessions, click here.
* **Activate FlashSession Now**. After you have set up a FlashSession, you can override the automatic scheduling and have all preprogrammed functions performed immediately by using this option.
* **Read Incoming FlashMail**. Click to open the Incoming FlashMail window.
* **Read Outgoing FlashMail**. Click to open the Outgoing FlashMail window.

Receiving E-Mail

I can hear the grumbling. Enough talk already, let's get to the fun stuff and actually use e-mail. Sending and receiving e-mail is somewhat akin to the old chicken and egg question. Which comes first? Because your earliest experience with AOL e-mail is as a receiver, I suppose it's as good a place as any to start. There's no trick to receiving e-mail. As long as the sender has your correct address and you have not set your e-mail options to block e-mail, you don't have to do a thing.

However, after you get it, you have a number of options for dealing with it. First you've got to read it. Well, that's not entirely true — in cases where it is clearly junk e-mail or is from a sender with whom you have decided to eliminate all communication, you may choose to scrap it without bothering to read it first. Whether you want to read it or delete it, you must first access the New Mail window (see Figure 4-4). The simplest way to do that is by clicking the Mailbox icon when it indicates new mail is present.

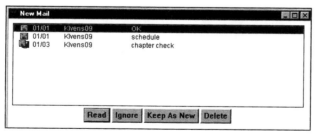

Figure 4-4 The New Mail window displays all unread e-mail in your mailbox.

Reading messages

To read mail, select the message you want to read and double-click it. This opens the e-mail and offers you several options for dealing with the message and its contents (see Figure 4-5).

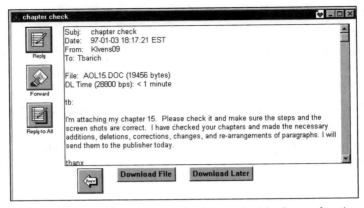

Figure 4-5 E-mail is a communications tool with plenty of options.

If you would prefer to delete the message without reading it, select it and then click Delete.

Replying to messages

Assuming that you have decided to read at least some of your e-mail, you may find that you want to respond to the sender. One of the nice things about replying to an existing e-mail rather than sending a new message to the sender is that you don't have to fill out a new e-mail form. Simply click the Reply button to the top left of the message itself. This opens a Compose Mail window with the mail to address and the subject already filled in (see Figure 4-6).

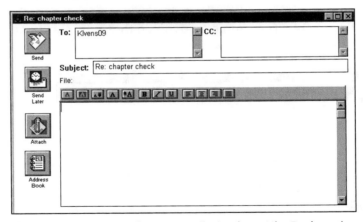

Figure 4-6 To respond to an e-mail, simply use the Reply option.

TIP It is often helpful when responding to an e-mail to include part of the original message in your reply. This is especially true of long messages that cover more than one topic. An easy way to accomplish this is by highlighting the desired text in the original message before selecting

Reply. When you click Reply, the highlighted text is automatically copied to the new message and enclosed in double brackets.

In the event that you receive an e-mail that has been sent to several people, including yourself, you can reply to all the folks who received the original message by clicking the Reply to All icon. This automatically includes all their e-mail addresses in your reply.

After you've typed your response, click the Send icon to mail your reply to the original sender.

Forwarding messages

In some cases, e-mail you receive may not require a response to the sender but does contain information that should be supplied to a third party. When this happens, you can send the message on to that other person by clicking the Forward icon on the E-mail window (it's to the left of the message contents). This opens a Compose Mail window with the subject already filled in (see Figure 4-7). From your Address Book, select the person to whom you want to forward the e-mail, type a message of your own to preface the forwarded mail, and then click Send Now.

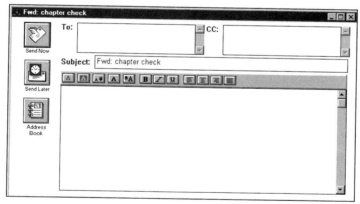

Figure 4-7 Forwarding offers a quick and easy way to pass information on to the right person.

Downloading attached files

One of e-mail's handiest features is the ability to attach files to your messages. You can include word processing, spreadsheet, database, and all other computer files with your e-mail messages. If you happen to be on the receiving end of an e-mail with a file attachment, you can immediately tell by the small file icon that appears behind the Message icon in the New Mail window (see the message titled Chapter Check back in Figure 4-4). Another indication is the presence of two download buttons beneath the message content after you open the message to read it (see Figure 4-8).

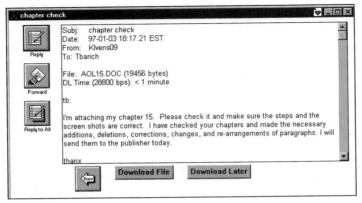

Figure 4-8   AOL offers you the option of downloading the attached file now or later.

If you want to download the file now, click the Download File button. To add the file to your Download Manager list, select Download Later.

TIP   **When to download depends on a number of factors. If you have many files that you will be downloading, either from various e-mail messages or from the software libraries, it makes sense to download them all at one time. Therefore, adding them to the Download Manager makes sense. Another factor to consider is the size of the file. The larger the file, the longer it takes to download. To help you make that decision, AOL provides the file size and estimated download time (DL Time) as part of the message header.**

If you choose to download now, AOL presents you with the Download Manager dialog box, from which you must select a destination on your hard drive for the file and then confirm the name to save it under.

Saving e-mail

Did you ever write down an important number or address on a slip of paper and then have it disappear just when you need it? Well, if you communicate via e-mail and save your messages, you will always be able to find that important information. Another dilemma that often arises from human communication is the fact that no two people seem to remember the details of a conversation exactly the same way. If you are exchanging important information or making or receiving commitments, whether personal or business, it is a godsend to be able to look over your saved e-mail and verify anything that may be in doubt.

AOL automatically retains all e-mail for three to five days and then may delete it. To keep both incoming and outgoing messages until you decide to delete them, you must reset your Mail Preferences.

Here's how:

1. From the Menu Bar, select **Members** → **Preferences** to open the Preferences window.

2. To open the Mail Preferences window (see Figure 4-9), click the Mail icon.

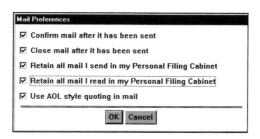

Figure 4-9 Mail Preferences offer several options for using AOL e-mail.

3. Click the Retain all mail I send in my Personal Filing Cabinet option (a check mark appears next to it when you click it) to save a copy of each of your outgoing messages.

4. Click the Retain all mail I read in my Personal Filing Cabinet option to save all your incoming mail.

5. Click OK to save your changes.

Printing e-mail

Do you remember all the hype about the "paperless office" of the future? The advent of the personal computer was going to eliminate the need for paper. Everything would be done electronically. I can tell you from my own experience that the paper manufacturers are laughing all the way to the bank. Until I owned a computer, I never used half the paper I do now. Electronic data is wonderful, but it is ephemeral and can disappear at the wave of a magnetic wand. Paper copies of data (a.k.a. *hard copies*) are generally more durable, if somewhat more difficult to store. So, for at least the short term, most of us choose to keep hard copy back-ups of our important information. E-mail often contains some of that important information that you may want to commit to hard copy.

Of course, to save data on hard copies, you must have a printer attached (either directly or via a network) to your computer.

To print an e-mail message:

1. Open the message by double-clicking it.

2. From the Toolbar, click the Printer icon (it's the sixth one from the right) to open the Print dialog box (see Figure 4-10).

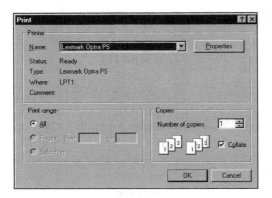

Figure 4-10 Be sure the appropriate printer is selected before proceeding.

3. Select the correct printer (if you have more than one) from the Name drop-down list.

4. Choose the number of pages to print from the Print range options. If there is only one page, only the All option is available. Since the PFC is stored on your hard drive (in the AOL30\Organize directory) you will have a permanent record of e-mail messages saved until you delete them yourself.

5. From the Copies area, select the number of copies to print and whether to collate the pages.

6. When you are satisfied with the settings, click OK to print the message.

Keeping old mail fresh

Occasionally, you may want to keep an e-mail message that you've already read handy for immediate access again. To accomplish this, simply select the Keep As New button in the New Mail window. If you forget to do this, you have to go to the Mail menu and select Check Mail You've Read to open the message again.

TIP **Although it might seem that it should, Keep As New does not extend the life of the message. If you want to save the message beyond the three- to five-day limit set by AOL, you must still change your Mail Preferences. Even though the message is kept as new, AOL considers it as previously read and will delete it in a few days.**

Sending E-Mail

Now that you've got the hang of dealing with your incoming mail, it's time to start sending some of your own. However, before you start gracing the electronic community with your pearls of wisdom, there are a few things that you need to know.

The Address Book

Before you can send anything, whether it's a piece of mail, a package, or an e-mail message, you have to know where to send it. Neither the post office nor the package carrier has the ability to deliver anything unless you provide specific information about the recipient. For starters, who is it going to and where does this person receive mail and packages? The AOL e-mail system is no different. To send an e-mail message, you must first supply a name and an e-mail address.

The AOL Address Book is similar to the typical address book most of us use to keep the physical addresses of friends, family, and business contacts. After you've entered a name in the AOL Address Book, you simply open the Address Book while composing a message, and select the person(s) to whom you want to send the e-mail.

You can start entering names in your e-mail Address Book by following these steps:

1. Select Mail → Edit Address Book... from the Menu Bar to open your Address Book (see Figure 4-11).

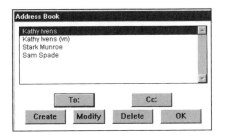

Figure 4-11 Keep all your important e-mail addresses handy with the Address Book.

2. Click Create to open the Address Group form (see Figure 4-12).

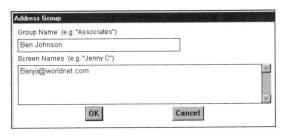

Figure 4-12 The Address Group form can be used for both individual addresses and groups of e-mail addresses.

3. In the Group Name text box, enter the name of the person or the name of the group you want to create. If you often send the same communication to several people, it is easier to create a group and include all their addresses, rather than send a separate e-mail message to each member of the group.

4. Press Tab to move to the Screen Names text box.

5. In the Screen Names text box, include the e-mail address(es) of the individual(s) associated with the group name. Remember, it is only other AOL members whose screen names are their e-mail addresses. Be sure to get precise e-mail addresses from all your non-AOL contacts.

TIP **People with more than one e-mail address have a tendency to "forget" to pick up mail at some of their addresses. If you have a contact who has more than one address, you can include all the addresses in the Screen Names text box and be sure that each message you send to that person is delivered to every address.**

6. When you have entered all the address information and checked its accuracy, click OK to save the entry.

One last note on the Address Book: There is only one Address Book per account. This means that all five screen names, regardless of who is using them, will have access to the same Address Book.

Composing a message

If you've got something to say and someone to say it to, you're ready to compose an e-mail message.

To create an e-mail message:

1. Select the Compose Mail icon (pencil and paper) next to the Mailbox icon on the Toolbar to open the Compose Mail window (see Figure 4-13).

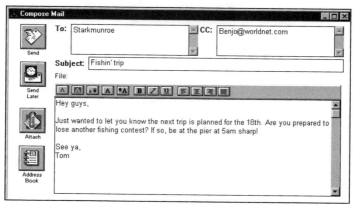

Figure 4-13 Sending an e-mail is as easy as filling out the form and typing in the message.

2. Click the Address Book icon in the bottom left of the Compose Mail window to open your Address Book.

3. Select the name or names to whom you want to address the e-mail by highlighting the name(s) and choosing To:. Every message must have at least one To: recipient. You can also send copies of the message to other individuals by including them using the Cc: button.

4. When you've finished selecting name(s) from the Address Book, click OK to return to the Compose Mail window.

5. Press the Tab key twice to move to the Subject: text box and enter a brief description of the subject matter of the e-mail.

6. Tab to the main message area of the Compose Mail window and type your message.

The following formatting options are available on the message window button bar directly above the main message area. To use the options, first highlight the text you want to format and then click the appropriate button.

🅰 Text Color. There's nothing like colored text to bring a point home (think about red and your checkbook, and you'll see what I mean).

🅰 Background Color. To offset the text even more, you can change the color of the background using this button.

🅰▼ Reduce Font Size. To fit more text in your message (makes for shorter print jobs on long e-mails), use this button.

🅰 Reset Font Size. Use this button to return the font size of the highlighted text to the original default size (10 pt.).

▴🅰 Enlarge Font Size. To increase the size of highlighted text, click this button.

🅱 Bold. For emphasis, it is a good idea to bold some words or phrases.

🅸 Italics. Italics offer a more subtle means of emphasizing textual elements.

🆄 Underline. A third choice for underscoring (sorry, I couldn't help myself) the importance of text is to use the Underline feature.

▤ Align Left. Aligns highlighted text with the left margin.

▤ Center. Aligns highlighted text with the center of the page.

▤ Align Right. You guessed it! Aligns highlighted text with the right margin.

▤ Justify. Aligns the highlighted text with both the left and right margins.

TIP While composing an e-mail message, you can highlight the desired text and right-click your mouse to bring up a formatting shortcut menu that contains all the options on the Button Bar and more. One note of caution — if you send a formatted e-mail message to someone using a different e-mail program, the formatting may be lost.

7. When you've finished typing and formatting the message, click Send to dispatch it immediately or select Send Later to hold it for transmission during a subsequent FlashSession.

X-REF For more information on FlashSessions, see Chapter 3.

Attaching a file

One of the wonders of e-mail is the ability to send not only a simple message but also an entire file to anyone with access to a compatible e-mail system. This means that you can send a copy of your twenty-page speech to your best friend across the country for a last-minute critique before you leap up to the podium and make a complete fool of yourself. If you leave home on a business trip and forget the speech or some other important data file, you can have it e-mailed to you and pick it up from wherever you are (assuming you have a laptop or other computer at your disposal).

To attach a file to an e-mail message:

1. Compose an e-mail message using the Compose Mail window discussed previously.

2. Click the Attach icon to the left of the main message window. This opens the Attach File window (see Figure 4-14).

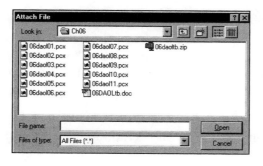

Figure 4-14 The Attach File window enables you to search for and select the file you want to attach.

3. From the Look in: drop-down list, select the hard disk and folder to search.

4. Either type the file name in the File _name_ text box or select the file from the display window, and then click Open to attach it to your e-mail.

5. If the file has been properly attached, a new line appears in the Compose Mail window between the Subject and the main message, indicating the file location and name.

6. If you have selected the wrong file, click the Detach button and repeat the attach file process to get the right file.

7. When you have the correct file properly attached, send your message.

NOTE **Although there are times when you may want to send more than one file with an e-mail, AOL e-mail allows you to attach only one file per message. To overcome this limitation, you can use one of the many compression products (WinZip, PKZip, and so on) available from the AOL software download area to include multiple files in a single Zip file. However, be sure that the person to whom you are sending the file has the ability to decompress the file. Without a compatible compression program, the files are unusable. You should also be aware that many of these compression programs are shareware and as such are provided to you for a limited evaluation period, after which you should either license them or discontinue their use.**

Utilizing E-Mail Extras

Although the bulk of e-mail activity takes place as the exchange of messages and files, there are several other features that make AOL e-mail very handy to have around.

The Gift Reminder

Tired of finding yourself in the doghouse because you can't remember a birthday, anniversary, or other special occasion? Well, AOL is about to rescue you from that unpleasant fate. The Gift Reminder feature (see Figure 4-15) enables you to register names and dates with the service. Then, ten days before the important life event, the AOL Gift Reminder team taps you on the shoulder with an e-mail message letting you know that the time is near.

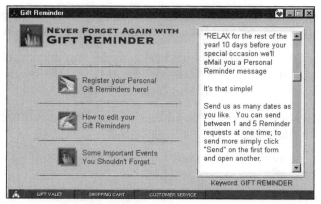

Figure 4-15 Who needs a marriage counselor when you have Gift Reminder?

To use the Gift Reminder service, follow these steps.

1. Click the Keyword button on the Toolbar.

2. Type **gift reminder** in the Enter Word(s): text box and then press Enter.

3. From the Gift Reminder window, select the Register your Personal Gift Reminders here! icon to open the Gift Reminder Service form (see Figure 4-16).

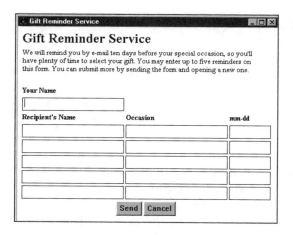

Figure 4-16 Select up to five occasions per form to register.

4. Enter your name and the detailed information for the special occasions.

5. When all the information is entered and correct, click Send.

That's it. You're on your way to becoming the ideal spouse. Ten days before the happy event, AOL will notify you so that you can take the appropriate action (send a card, buy a gift, give yourself up to the authorities, whatever).

Mailing lists

If you've got an interest, chances are that there's a mailing list that covers that topic. Mailing lists are an electronic form of mass distribution of information. They have nothing to do with the direct marketing mailing lists that you are probably familiar with (and tired of being on) that are used to distribute unsolicited advertising. Electronic mailing lists are generally newsletters, magazines, or other vehicles for dispensing information and opinion on a particular subject, and they are transmitted via e-mail. Unlike non-electronic mailing lists, you, the recipient, choose whether you want to be on the list by subscribing and unsubscribing to the list. The AOL Mailing List Directory (see Figure 4-17) contains close to 3,000 Internet mailing lists to which you can subscribe.

Figure 4-17   The AOL Mailing List Directory window provides information on and links to Internet Mailing Lists.

To access the Mailing List Directory, follow these steps:

1. From the Toolbar, click the Keyword button.

2. In the Enter Word(s): text box type **mailinglists** (that's right, it's one word), and then select Go.

3. In the AOL Mailing List Directory window, click the Browse the Directory icon (looks like an open book) to connect to the America Online Mailing List Directory (see Figure 4-18), which is located on the World Wide Web.

Figure 4-18   If you're a mailing list junkie, you'll think you died and went to mailing list heaven.

4. Scroll down (or expand the window) and select Directory Index to see a list of the categories available.

TIP   **If you want to perform a keyword search on the entire database, select Search, fill out the search form, and then click Search to find the matching mailing lists.**

5. After you've obtained a roster of available mailing lists, select the list for further information on the contents and instructions on subscribing.

Pen Pals

Pen pals are not just for kids. They're great for kids, but everyone can enjoy and benefit from a pen pal relationship. AOL understands this and provides a Pen Pal feature that lets you find a pen pal across the street or across the globe. You begin your search at the Digital City Pen Pal or International Pen Pal window (see Figure 4-19).

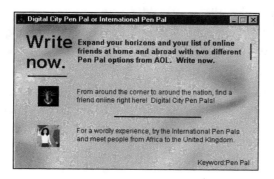

Figure 4-19   You can find a pen pal from Akron to Zanzibar and everywhere in between.

Use the keyword search words **pen pal** to open the Digital City Pen Pal window or International Pen Pal window. From there, select Digital City Pen Pals or International Pen Pals to get more information and find your pen pal.

Play by Mail (PBM) games

Die-hard gamesters, young and old alike, take heart. Now you can play games via e-mail. This means that you don't have to know someone who wants to play or even have the same schedule. You can set up a game to be played as you find the time to e-mail moves or answers to the other player(s). To get involved in PBM games, start at the Play by Mail Forum (see Figure 4-20), which can be accessed by using the keyword search word **pbm**.

Figure 4-20 Find a challenging game to play by e-mail at the Play by Mail Forum.

In the Play by Mail Forum, you can find a game library, message boards to discuss PBM gaming with other members, a conference hall for live chat, and more.

Controlling E-Mail Usage

I want to go on record as stating that I am heartily in favor of free speech. I would also like to state that I am equally in favor of my right to privacy, which allows me to tune out someone else's free speech when I find it dull, inappropriate, or offensive. Fortunately, AOL has given me the tools to do just that when it comes to my e-mail. The tools AOL provides are called Mail Controls, which can be accessed through the Welcome to Mail Controls window (see Figure 4-21).

From this window, you can access the Mail Controls themselves, the Mail Controls-related message boards, Mail Controls Help files, and Parental Controls. One nice thing about the Mail Controls is the fact that the primary account holder can adjust the controls individually for each screen name.

Figure 4-21 Take your e-mail destiny in your own hands with Mail Controls.

To establish the Mail Controls, follow these steps:

1. From the Toolbar, click the Keyword button.

2. Type **mail controls** in the Enter Word(s): text box. Then press Enter to open the Welcome to Mail Controls window.

3. Select Go to Mail Controls to open the e-mail Parental Controls window.

4. Choose a screen name for which you want to change the mail controls, and then click Edit to open the Mail Controls window (see Figure 4-22).

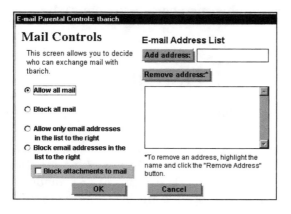

Figure 4-22 Mail Controls allow you to determine who sends and receives e-mail.

The following Mail Control options enable you to tailor e-mail access to suit the needs of each screen name user:

* **Allow all mail**. This is the default, which allows access to all e-mail features.

* **Block all mail**. The complete opposite of the default, this option allows the user absolutely no access to e-mail.

* **Allow only e-mail addresses in the list to the right**. Used in conjunction with e-mail Address List (to the right), this option allows you to restrict the user to e-mail communication with only those addresses you choose to include on the list.

* **Block e-mail addresses in the list to the right**. If you're concerned that a user is "hanging out with the wrong crowd," you can decide to allow e-mail access to all but members of that group. However, remember that changing your screen name, which is your e-mail address on AOL, is as easy as using Velcro

* **Block attachments to mail**. To allow the exchange of e-mail but not the ability to send attachments, select this option. Note that this option can be used with any of the previous options.

* **Add address:**. Enter the e-mail address to be added to the list and used in conjunction with the Allow only and Block e-mail options. Enter the correct e-mail address and click Add address to include the e-mail address on the list.

* **Remove address:**. Also used in conjunction with the Allow only and Block e-mail options, use this option to remove an address from the list.

5. Select the appropriate settings for this user and click OK to save the changes.

6. Repeat this process for each screen name you want to set Mail Controls for.

BONUS

As you discovered early in this chapter, e-mail can be useful for more than simply exchanging messages and files. Although not actually a part of e-mail, AOL's News Profiles feature takes advantage of the e-mail system to provide you with continuous updates of current news happenings.

News Profiles

With the amount of news resources available on AOL, you could easily spend half your day reading up on all the events that are of interest to you. In reality, a good deal of your time would be spent not reading but searching for the items you're interested in. For those of us who cannot spare hours searching for the right news but still want to be well informed, AOL provides News Profiles.

News Profiles are user-defined sets of search criteria that AOL uses to find news articles that match your interests. The articles are then saved to your mailbox for you to read at your convenience. Each screen name can have as many as five profiles, each of which can save up to fifty articles a day (up to the 550 message capacity of each mailbox).

To create News Profiles:

1. Click the Keyword button on the Toolbar.

2. Type **news profiles** in the Enter Word(s): text box, and then press Enter to open the News Profiles window (see Figure 4-23).

Figure 4-23 The only thing better than News Profiles is coming home after a long day at the office and having your mate bring you your slippers, a glass of burgundy, and the daily paper, all while dressed in the new thong you bought him for his birthday.

3. Click the Create a Profile icon to the right of the News Profiles window. This brings up a stepped series of forms to fill out.

4. Fill out the Step 1 form with a title for this News Profile and the number of articles you want to save each day, and then select Next to move to Step 2.

5. In the Step 2 form, you include the words and phrases you want AOL to use in its search for matching articles. Use commas to separate words and single quotes to enclose phrases. When you're through, click Next to move to Step 3.

6. Step 3 provides you with the ability to specify words or phrases that must be in the article in order for it to be saved to your mailbox. Regardless of the conditions you enter in step 2, unless the information designated in step 3 is also found, the article will not be saved. You may choose to leave this blank. To move to Step 4, click Next.

7. Step 4 is actually the flip side of Step 3. Here you can stipulate words or phrases that will cause an article to be excluded if it is found to contain them. Again, you can choose to leave this blank. Click Next to move to Step 5.

8. Step 5 affords you the opportunity to elect which AOL news sources are searched for the criteria you established in the earlier steps. You can select any or all of the four categories: General, Business, Entertainment, and Sports. If you change your mind, you can also remove the sources from your list. Click Next to move to the Summary.

9. The Summary window lists the choices you have made and offers you the option of accepting them by clicking Done or changing them by selecting Prev.

10. When you are satisfied with your Profile, click Done.

If you want to change a previously created News Profile, access the Profile Manager by clicking Manage Your Profiles in the News Profiles window.

Summary

As you can see, e-mail by itself could be billed as a miracle of modern technology. When you throw in all the additional functionality it provides through such features as Mailing Lists, Pen Pals, and News Profiles, it becomes an indispensable tool in your electronic tool chest.

COMMUNICATING ONLINE

IN THIS CHAPTER YOU LEARN THESE KEY SKILLS

CHATTING   PAGE 111

USING INSTANT MESSAGES   PAGE 124

5

Y ou can interact with other AOL users in *real time*, which means there is no time delay between your message and the other users' responses. This direct interaction is the same as talking to a person who is in the same room with you or talking on the telephone to someone. In contrast, when you use e-mail for messaging, you have to wait for the recipient to log on, read the message, reply to it, and then mail the reply to you. Then you read the response, replyto it, and so on. Of course, for real time interaction, the other user must be logged on at the same time you are.

The two main vehicles for interacting directly with other AOL users are chat rooms and Instant Messages. This chapter explains how to use both these features.

Chatting

A t large parties, there are always multiple conversations going on. A small group over in the corner is having an earnest discussion about politics. In front of the buffet, several groups (each of them involving two or three people) are chatting; the conversations are interesting exchanges about books and movies. In another corner, a couple is having an animated discussion that looks as if it might be an argument, so everyone steers clear of that area. There's frequently one person who's loud, opinionated, and sometimes obnoxious. He or she is not talking to anyone in particular, just butting into other people's conversations with loud comments or bellowing to the room in general without seeming to notice that nobody is responding. A bunch of kids (young teenagers) are around too, and mostly they keep asking each other "how old are you?" A couple of people keep touring the room, saying things they think are provocative to all others (an incorrect opinion). And, sometimes there's someone who thinks it's amusing to wander around making rude sounds.

Welcome to an AOL chat room.

Understanding chat room types

There are several types of chat rooms scattered around the AOL "building."

* AOL chat rooms are gathering places that are created and maintained by AOL.

* Member Rooms are created by AOL members as they find each other and decide that some common interest warrants a room. They, too, are organized by category.

* Private Rooms are also created by AOL members and are temporary gathering places used by members who invite others to join them. Because there is no public indication that the room exists, you have to be invited to enter.

Most people use the general AOL chat rooms, which are the main focus of this chapter.

Touring the rooms

If this discussion has whetted your appetite, enter a chat room and check it out, participate, and enjoy yourself. To get there, use one of these methods:

* Click the People Connection icon on the AOL Toolbar.
* Click the People Connection button in the Welcome window.
* Click People Connection in the Channels window.
* Use the keyword **People Connection**.

You immediately go to a chat room; it's a Lobby in the Town Square (see Figure 5-1).

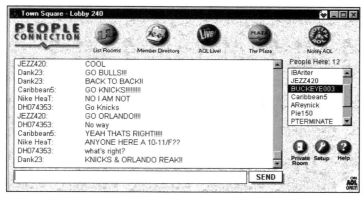

Figure 5-1   The first chat room you enter is AOL's random choice for you, but you can move to another room.

The Lobbies are like lobbies in large buildings — some people are there because they're on their way to somewhere else, and others hang around to talk to folks. You don't have to stay in the Lobby you start in, you can go to another Lobby or move on to a chat room that is devoted to a specific topic. There are plenty of other chat rooms available; those choices are discussed in the following sections.

Understanding categories

The most important icon in the People Connection window (which is usually called the Chat window, so that term will be used from now on) is the List Rooms icon. It's your escape hatch when you want to find a better chat room (you can define "better" any way it suits you). Click the List Rooms icon to see your choices (see Figure 5-2).

Figure 5-2   The category list is on the left. The chat rooms on the right are attached to the selected category.

After you decide what type of conversation you are looking for, you can move to other chat rooms using this window. Be aware that it's the norm to enter a room and find the conversation unrelated to the category assigned to the chat room. Sometimes, however, you get lucky. You might enter a chat room that's supposed to be dedicated to discussing antiques and find that it actually is filled with people discussing antiques. Just don't expect it.

To change the chat room listings (on the right), double-click a category. The new listings reflect the rooms assigned for that category.

Notice that the category list shows rather general topics. The next few sections review the choices so that you have an idea of what to expect.

TOWN SQUARE

Town Square is named after the small-town habit of people to gather in the center of town (where there was frequently a "square" of some type, containing trees or statues or a cannon or a courthouse) and chat. The conversations were about local gossip, politics, opinions on entertainment events, and probably every other subject in the universe.

For that reason, all the chat rooms in Town Square are generic in nature. Most of the rooms are named Lobby followed by a number (the last time I checked, Lobby 926 was the highest number). There are other generic names such as The Meeting Place, the Saloon, and several with the word Chathouse in them. After the first occurrence of the name, duplicates have a number after the name.

ARTS AND ENTERTAINMENT

The chat rooms in the Arts and Entertainment category are designed for discussions about books, music, movies, games, and any other similar topics (see Figure 5-3). Some of the entertainment listings are quite specific — there are chat rooms for Red Dragon Inn and Spacefleet (I couldn't tell from the conversation what that is).

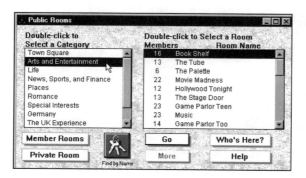

Figure 5-3 Read any good books lately?

LIFE

It's an all-encompassing word, but the majority of chat rooms in the Life category point to the way people define themselves, rather than their interests (see Figure 5-4). Here, too, there are duplicate names for chat rooms, apparently because there are so many teens, divorced people, folks over forty, senior citizens, and people seeking Christian fellowship conversations.

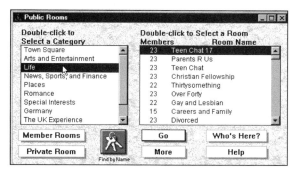

Figure 5-4 Find your soulmate in a chat room.

NEWS, SPORTS, AND FINANCE

Now here's the stuff of argumentative conversations. The topics are guaranteed to bring out opinions and heated discussion (see Figure 5-5). There seem to be a majority of chat rooms dedicated to sports, so that must be the most popular subject. I found a couple of chat rooms for people whose politics are leaning to the right, but none to the left. I have no answer to that riddle.

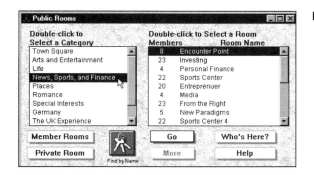

Figure 5-5 Predict the winners for sports and elections and then argue about why it turned out the way it did.

PLACES

There's hot news in the old town tonight, and it would sure be nice to talk about it with somebody. Double-click Places and then head for home. The places referred to here are cities and states. They aren't in alphabetic order, so you'll have to scroll down to find your home (see Figure 5-6). Of course, nothing stops you from visiting another city and learning about its local news and getting to know its people. Some cities have multiple chat rooms.

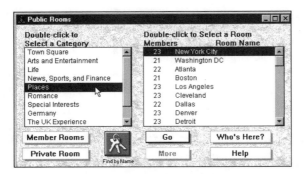

Figure 5-6 Head for home or travel to another place for virtual conversation.

ROMANCE

Poetry, flowers, a stolen kiss, the murmuring of sweet nothings — very little of that seems to exist anymore. "What's your sign," "Let's go Dutch," and "Can I have your cellular number" are lines you hear today. Whatever your taste in the fine art of forming relationships, find the romantic category that fits your whim. A wonderful grandma named Catherine I knew long ago used to tell me "There's a lid for every pot." Maybe the other half of your kitchenware is in one of these rooms (see Figure 5-7).

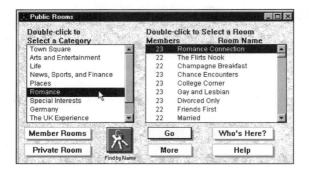

Figure 5-7 Visit the right place and maybe you'll meet the right person.

SPECIAL INTERESTS

There's a little of everything here: hobbies, religion, the fine and creative arts, and psychic predictors (see Figure 5-8). Don't just visit the things you know about (although it's fun to discuss the subject with others), use some of these rooms as a way to broaden your horizons.

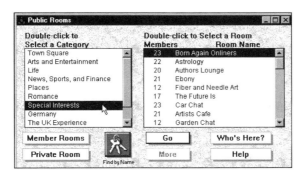

Figure 5-8 There's something for everybody here.

OTHER COUNTRIES

There are chat rooms for other countries (at the time of this writing, Germany, France, the United Kingdom, and Canada were represented). If the country you want to visit isn't English-speaking, you'd better know the language because you won't find much English there. Of course, in the United Kingdom, they say that about the United States.

Entering a chat room

After you've decided on a category (and double-clicked it), scroll through the chat rooms on the right side of the window. When you see a chat room that piques your interest, you can check things out before you go in. Check the number of people in the room. The number is displayed to the left of the name. Chat rooms have a limitation of 23 people, so it's a waste of time to pick a room that's already full.

TIP If you pick a room that's full, AOL displays a message telling you it's full and asking if you want to be sent to a similar room. Answer Yes to let AOL choose a chat room for you, or answer No to select one of your own.

Then, you might want to see who's there. Click Who's Here? to see a listing of screen names (see Figure 5-9). I usually avoid a room filled with people who have names such as Killer because I think the conversation won't be to my taste.

Figure 5-9 Who knows, you might see the name — or nickname — of an old grade school chum.

When you find the chat room you want to visit, double-click its name and you're there. The first thing you see is a message from OnlineHost telling you the name of the chat room you entered. OnlineHost is actually a computer, so you won't find anyone in the room by that name. Then, do whatever is comfortable for you:

* Sit back and watch the conversation for a minute before deciding whether you want to join in (this is called *lurking*) or leave for another room. See the following section called "Following the conversation" for some tips on making sense of things.

* The polite thing to do is to say hello to everybody in the room when you enter it. Just say "hi" to tell people you're there and ready to chat. See the section called "Joining the conversation" later in this chapter for instructions.

TIP If you decide to lurk, you may not get away with it for long. There are a lot of friendly people on AOL, and somebody might notice you and offer a greeting. Just respond with a cheerful hello.

Following the conversation

When you first enter a room, the people who have been there awhile have established some topics of conversation. Note the use of the plural *topics;* there is rarely one topic being discussed. Trying to follow the conversation isn't the easiest thing in the world — individual people are responding to other individual people. Sometimes people make following the conversation easy for you by beginning each line with the name of the person they're addressing. Sometimes they don't, and you have to try to figure it out for yourself by reading the content of the messages. It's like a telephone conference call without any rules, and everybody is talking at the same time. You can try to follow along by looking at Figure 5-10.

If you get stuck, here are some hints:

* A couple of people are helping someone who is trying to use AOL for a genealogy project.

* One person had a serious medical encounter that resulted in a near death experience and that other people are interested in learning about.

It's like playing Where's Waldo, isn't it? Of course, there are a couple of other messages mixed in, and some of them are not connected to the two main threads.

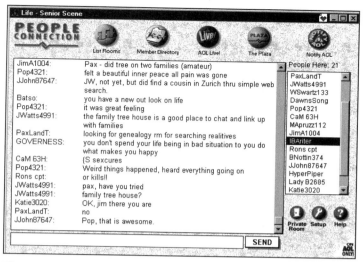

Figure 5-10 Can you follow the threads of conversation?

Joining the conversation

Entering a comment is easy. The bottom of the chat room window has a horizontal space which is your text entry box, and just to the right of it is a Send button (see Figure 5-11). Click in the box to place your insertion point there, and then start typing. Press Enter or click Send to transfer your text into the room. You can change your text as much as you want as long as your cursor is still in the box; nothing is final and nobody sees it until you press Enter or click the Send button.

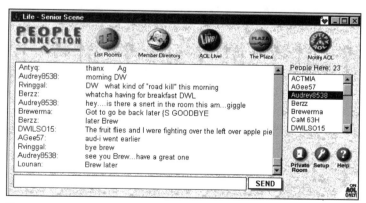

Figure 5-11 Type your contribution to the conversation and then send it into the room.

There is a limit to the characters (including spaces) that fit in the entry box. If you're trying to enter a message that exceeds 93 characters, send the first line, and then enter the next line and send that. If you type quickly, you might even get the two lines to appear in the chat window contiguously.

Finding member rooms

When you're exploring the chat rooms, don't forget to look at member rooms. To see them, first click the List Rooms icon in the Chat window. When the Public Rooms list window appears, click Member Rooms (see Figure 5-12).

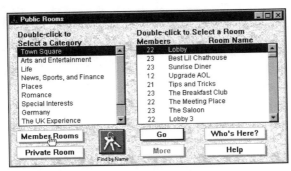

Figure 5-12 Click the Member Rooms button to find more chat rooms.

The listings are the same in the Member Rooms area as those in the Public Rooms area, and you can follow the previous instructions for selecting categories and rooms in the Public area (see Figure 5-13).

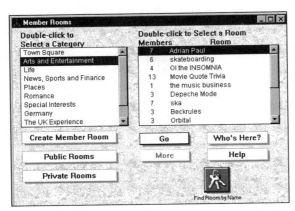

Figure 5-13 Choose your category and then find an interesting room.

You'll find that the member room feels familiar and comfortable. Everything is the same as a public room, except sometimes there are house rules. For instance, public trivia rooms are free-for-alls, but the private trivia rooms are less chaotic and have rules about who can ask questions and when. Sit back and watch for a moment. If you can't figure out the rules by watching, feel free to ask if there are rules.

If you've toured all the member rooms and you think there's a screaming need for a new topic, you should think about creating a new member room. It's quite easy to do.

Here are the steps:

1. If you are in the public chat rooms, click List Rooms and select Member Rooms (if you're already in Member Rooms, click List Rooms).

2. Select the category you want to use for your new room from the list on the left side.

3. Click the Create Member Room button.

4. Enter a name for the room. Make it something that will attract other users (see Figure 5-14).

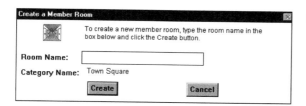

Figure 5-14 Think up a name that will attract other users so that you'll have some company in this room.

5. Choose Create, and voilá, a new room is born.

Go into the new room and wait. Other people will show up. Bring something to read or a crossword puzzle to do; it may take a while for other AOL users to find you. If you chose a really interesting room name, you may come back later to find that it's full and you can't even get in.

Using private rooms

Shh! It's a secret! If you know about a private room, you're part of a select group. Private rooms are not listed anywhere. The only way you can enter one is to know its name, and the only way to know its name is to have been let in on the secret by another user. People use private rooms to chat together without worrying about anyone else invading their space.

To go to a private room, click List Rooms and then choose Private Room. Enter the name of the private room and click Go. You're there.

You can also create a private room from the same Chat window. Instead of entering the name of an existing one, invent a name. Then invite others to join you. Use e-mail and Instant Messages to issue invitations (entering a chat room and typing **Hey everybody, come over to my room** kind of kills the whole point). See the section called "Using Instant Messages" later in this chapter for more information.

Learning the lingo

Experienced chatters use a lot of shorthand in their conversation. It saves typing, time, and characters (remember, there's a limit). If you ask what a shorthand phrase means, you'll be informed by a few nice folks (and made fun of by a few not-so-nice folks). It's easier to start off knowing the basic shorthand phrases, so here are some of them:

LOL = Laughing Out Loud

ROFL = Rolling On the Floor Laughing

AFK = Away From Keyboard

BAK = Back At Keyboard

BRB = Be Right Back

WTG = Way To Go (used in trivia rooms for a correct answer)

BTW = By The Way

IMHO = In My Humble Opinion

IMO = In My Opinion (if you're not humble)

LTNS = Long Time No See

<w> = Wink

<g> = Grin

{} = Hug

* = Kiss

: -) = Smile

: -(= Frown

You will notice other terms and symbols that are peculiar to particular rooms, but you'll soon become comfortable with this cryptic online lingo.

Sounding off

If you have a sound card, you know that when your sign-on process ends, you hear a voice say "Welcome" (sometimes followed by "You've Got Mail" — which is grammatically incorrect, by the way). Your AOL software came with some sound files, and those files are being played.

While you're in a chat room, you can send and receive sounds using the same files that produce your AOL source messages or any additional sound files you put into your AOL directory. To send the familiar AOL "Welcome" sound, type **{S Welcome}** in the text entry box, and then press Enter. Notice the format for this command (the technical term for a command's format is *syntax*), which is a left curly bracket, a capital S, the name of the sound file, and then a right curly bracket. In this case, the name of the sound file is Welcome.

There are many sound files available from AOL (chat room people send them to each other via e-mail). You can search AOL for the word sounds and then download the ones you want. The files all have a .WAV extension.

Many of the sounds are annoying to some people (me, for example), and using them constantly is likely to result in some nasty comments from your roommates. So, use them for fun, but don't use them to the point of being obnoxious.

 X-REF Read Chapter 2 for information about downloading files from AOL.

Avoiding snertiness

People who are obnoxious and disruptive in chat rooms are called *snerts*, and being called a snert is the ultimate insult in the world of AOL chatting. The origin of the word is Snot-Nosed, Egotistical, Rude Teenager (which fits the description of most snerts), but the term is now used to describe anybody who is generally obnoxious.

Avoiding snert-like behavior is a two-sided street. You should avoid being an annoying snert, and you can stop being annoyed by a snert who is in your chat room.

There aren't any computer book instructions to tell you how to avoid being a snert — that's up to you. But I can tell you how to avoid letting a snert's behavior ruin your time in a chat room.

IGNORE THE SNERT

There's a clever device in AOL chat rooms that makes it possible to turn off the contributions of any roommate.

Here's how it works:

1. In the members list to the right of the chat area, find the offender's name and double-click it.

2. When the member's info window displays, click Ignore (see Figure 5-15).

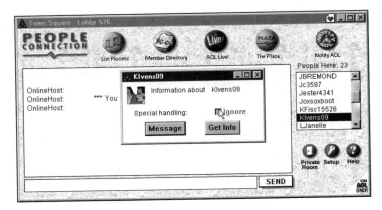

Figure 5-15 Ignore all snerts.

GET HELP FROM AOL

You can also get help from an AOL Guide. These people are trained to make sure that everybody who uses AOL lives up to the TOS (the Terms of Service statement you agreed to live by when you signed up). If people fail to meet the standards of the TOS, the Guides have authority to take corrective action. They usually start dealing with snerts politely; however, if that doesn't work, they have all kinds of power to take stronger measures. To get a Guide, you have to page one. Use the keyword **Guide Pager**, and a Guide will enter the room in a minute or so.

You can also page a Guide if you're being harassed by somebody sending you annoying, threatening, or disgusting Instant Messages (see the following section called "Using Instant Messages").

TIP Paging a Guide is like dialing 911; it's for real problems, a total disruption of a chat room, or a seriously bad Instant Message. Make sure the problem is a TOS offense before paging.

Using Instant Messages

Any two people who are signed on to AOL at the same time can converse in real time without going to a chat room. The device that makes this possible is called an *Instant Message*. Veteran AOL users call an Instant Message an *IM*. In fact, they've made a verb out of the expression. You'll see people in a chat room saying "so-and-so IMed me" or "I was busy IMming."

An IM takes place in a little box in the corner of your screen, so you don't lose sight of whatever you're doing in AOL during an IM encounter.

IMs can be very handy. In fact, the two authors of this book used this feature to communicate as it was being written.

Sending an IM

To send an IM to another AOL user, follow these steps:

1. Press Ctrl+I, which brings up the Instant Message window (see Figure 5-16).

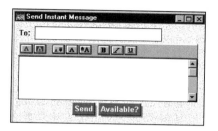

Figure 5-16 The message window is small, so keep it short.

2. Enter the recipient's screen name in the To box at the top of the window.

3. Press Tab to move to the message area, and then enter the text of your message.

4. Click Send.

If the recipient is online, the message is sent immediately. If not, you're informed of that fact (see Figure 5-17).

Figure 5-17 If your friend isn't online, you can still send e-mail. Meanwhile, click OK to clear the message.

TIP If you have a Buddy List and a buddy who is online, you can highlight the name of the person you want to IM and click the IM button. Your buddy's name is filled in automatically, and you can just start entering the message.

Replying to an IM

Here's the plot: I'm working in AOL, gathering information for this book. My co-author is doing the same thing. Suddenly, I hear a set of tones from my sound card, and a little window opens in the corner of my screen (see Figure 5-18). It's a message from Tom, and I head for the Respond button to begin writing a reply.

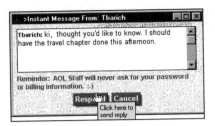

Figure 5-18 IMing is easier than dialing the phone and calling.

Clicking the Respond button opens a message area where I can enter text (see Figure 5-19).

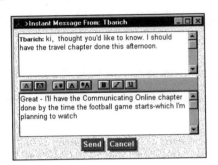

Figure 5-19 I use the bottom message area to write a reply to Tom.

When I click Send, the text is sent to Tom and at the same time is moved to the top window, clearing the bottom window for my next note (see Figure 5-20). When Tom replies, I'll see the message in the upper window and can type my response in the lower window.

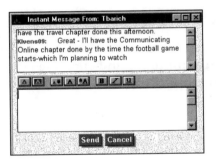

Figure 5-20 When there's a response, two windows are established to facilitate back-and-forth communication.

You can go on this way for a while, depending on how much you have to say to the other person. Of course, if you're not a good typist, this can be a pretty uncomfortable way to communicate (most authors type fast and easily, so for us this wasn't a problem).

TIP Instant Messages are only good for short notes because the IM window holds less than 10 full lines of characters. You can resize the window to see more of a long message and avoid scrolling.

Reporting IM scams

Unfortunately, some people use Instant Messages to try to fool you into giving out your password. Before AOL went to flat-rate pricing, it was profitable to get someone's password because a thief could spend many happy hours on AOL, running up the victim's credit card bill. Today, having somebody's password doesn't save you money, but it sure makes it possible to wreak havoc in someone else's name.

The people who try to scam you into giving them your password are clever enough to make it look as if you really should reveal that information (see Figure 5-21).

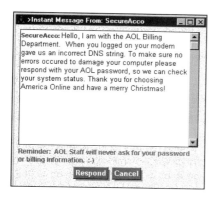

Figure 5-21 This looks terribly official, but it's a scam.

You have only two choices for dealing with an IM like this: click Cancel to ignore it, or take steps to report it. Never choose to answer.

To report the scam (which is the right thing to do), follow these steps:

1. Highlight the text in the IM by placing your mouse pointer at the top or bottom of the message and then holding down the left button while you drag your mouse across the text. Release the button, and the text is highlighted.

2. Choose **Edit** → **Copy** from the AOL Menu Bar.

3. Use keyword **Guide Pager** to bring up the I Need Help window (see Figure 5-22).

4. Click Password to report this IM password solicitation.

5. The Report Password Solicitations window displays (see Figure 5-23).

6. Choose **Edit** → **Paste** from the AOL Menu Bar to paste the text you copied earlier into the form.

Figure 5-22 AOL Guides are ready to help when untoward events occur.

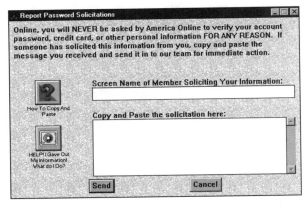

Figure 5-23 AOL has a form for a password solicitation report, and it's easy to fill out.

7. Click in the Screen Name text box and enter the name of the person who solicited your password.

8. Your report is ready to go to AOL (see Figure 5-24); just click Send to report this event.

TIP   **If you do give your password out accidentally, click the button marked Help! I Gave Out My Information! AOL will help you change your password on the spot.**

Shutting Off Instant Messages

If you don't want to receive Instant Messages at all, from anyone, you can turn off the feature. To do this, follow these steps:

1. Use Ctrl+I to bring up the Instant Message window.

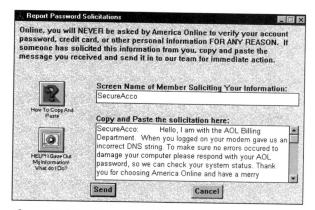

Figure 5-24 After everything is filled out, send your report.

2. Enter **$im_off** in the To field (the recipient).

3. Enter anything you wish in the message area, you must enter at least one character.

4. Click Send.

Hereafter, if anyone tries to send you an Instant Message, he or she will be notified that you are not willing to receive them.

To turn Instant Messages back on, follow the same steps, except enter **$im_on** in the To field.

TIP AOL personnel can always send you Instant Messages, even if you have turned off the feature.

BONUS

There are additional chat rooms scattered throughout AOL. For instance, there are special interest rooms in the Plaza. Click the Plaza icon in the Chat window to meander over and see what's there (see Figure 5-25).

In the Plaza, there are special events such as lectures and seminars. Click the AOL Live icon in the Chat window (or use the keyword **Live**) to see what's happening (see Figure 5-26).

Figure 5-25 For specialized chat rooms and other forms of interactive communication, try the Plaza.

Figure 5-26 All kinds of special events go on in AOL.

Click Coming Attractions to see what's coming up. The subjects encompass anything you could be interested in, and you can examine the choices by date or by category.

Don't forget about message boards in AOL areas. Many special interest sites have message areas where you can leave questions or comments and read those of others. It's frequently an easy way to learn more about the subject.

Summary

The ability to communicate in real time with other online users is a remarkable feat. It carries some responsibilities, however, in terms of your behavior. The more that people abuse the Terms of Service and common decent behavior, the less fun AOL is for everyone.

You're about to take a whirlwind tour of all the AOL high spots. You'll travel to cities, libraries, museums, and even into classrooms. You'll learn where to go to find information about computers, personal finance, and today's headlines.

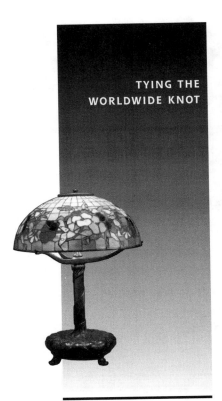

Imagine being able to negotiate a contract, collaborate with a photographer, and collect material for a book, all without leaving your office. Imagine also that the book is a pageant of the world's cultures, an excursion through many lands, and historical periods. Such a book is *Wedding Traditions from Around the World*, a work in progress by Boston-based Diana La Vigne.

Ms. La Vigne has used her AOL prowess for every facet of the book, from hammering out the contract via e-mail with collaborator/photographer Israel Talby, to soliciting information from AOL's multi-cultured membership, to visiting online libraries. "AOL offers a huge pool of users who are able to offer information just for the asking," she said. "I post requests for information on a certain country's wedding traditions, and many respond."

Early in the project, she was concerned that the information she might gather online might be too personal, but she discovered otherwise. "I found the e-mail I received came from knowledgeable people," she said. "I have a world of resources, and my direction changes daily due to the input of AOL users."

Ms. La Vigne initially looked at AOL as a partial communications solution for an onerous schedule: "With e-mail, I can return messages when I find time in my schedule. If I were held to accessing information only during business hours, this book would take twice as long! Now I can develop my project in the most productive way possible."

How did she come to choose America Online, when one can get e-mail service practically from any corner newsstand? "I selected AOL because of the name recognition and the fact that I wanted to establish an e-mail address that was easy to recall," she said. Ms. La Vigne estimates that she receives 20–50 e-mail messages per day.

She maintains her working relationship with the book's photographer, who lives in Israel, via e-mail, as well. "We connect every other day via e-mail to update our information. He is halfway around the world, but we are able to keep in touch and on pace! We have built a great working relationship via the Internet. The bulk of our relationship has been via e-mail."

Besides direct questions, Ms. La Vigne uses the service to glean background information about the countries whose wedding traditions she is writing about. The International channel and Religious Beliefs section have helped her understand other cultures and religions.

CHAPTER SIX

TRAVELING
WITH AOL

IN THIS CHAPTER YOU LEARN THESE KEY SKILLS

C'mon, admit it — you've always wanted to take a romantic cruise around the Greek Islands. Or perhaps you've dreamed about a safari through Kenya or an adventure on the Amazon. No matter what your travel experience, chances are that there are places you'd like to visit and sites you'd like to see. Even if it's just a short family vacation a couple of hundred miles from home, the success of any travel plan can be greatly enhanced by proper planning and preparation. Using AOL's travel area to get ideas and advice on travel locations and ways to get there is a great way to begin any trip.

You can find lots of information on commercial travel services, including pricing and schedules. Tips for saving money, enjoying yourself, staying out of trouble, and bringing the right clothing are available both from the experts and from fellow travelers. Of course, the weather is important no matter where you're going. What's a ski vacation without snow, or beach vacation without sun? AOL lets you check out the weather forecasts around the corner or around the globe.

Using Travel Resources

AOL has almost as many travel resources as the world has travel destinations. Okay, so maybe that's a slight exaggeration, but there's no denying that the service has extensive information covering all types of travel. Whether your travel is for pleasure or business, a stop at the AOL travel area can make your journey a little easier, more economical, and a lot more pleasant. Finding the information you need is a snap when you utilize AOL's travel resources. To use these resources you must access the Travel channel (see Figure 6-1):

Figure 6-1   The Travel channel is your jumping off place for destinations near and far.

* If the Channels window is open select Travel, otherwise,
* If the Channels window is not open, click the Keyword button on the Toolbar. Then, enter **travel** in the text box and click Go.

Finding the right place

Unless you're traveling for business or have a long-awaited dream vacation to take, you often decide to travel before you decide on a destination. Most of us have to work for a living, and one of the few benefits (aside from the regular paycheck) is the annual vacation time that you accrue. All too often, that vacation time is used to paint the house, remodel the kitchen, or just turn off the telephone and stay at home catching up on the work that's getting out of hand at the office.

However, when you finally decide to take some time and travel, you want it to be time well spent. A critical factor in making that decision a reality is choosing the right destination. Unfortunately, relying on travel posters, cocktail chatter, and memories of childhood vacations can often lead you astray. A little research, on the other hand, can go a long way in helping you choose the right vacation spot.

INTERESTS AND ACTIVITIES

One way to select a location is by taking your interests or the interests of people in the group you're traveling with into consideration. If your group is composed of downhill skiing fanatics, chances are that you are going to want to go someplace with mountains and snow. If you're an archeology buff, ruins of ancient civilizations are a must. Whatever your interests, AOL can help you find the right place to pursue those interests.

FANTASIZE

A single mouse click is your ticket to the Travel channel's Fantasize area (see Figure 6-2), where you can find lots of information on hobby- and interest-related travel.

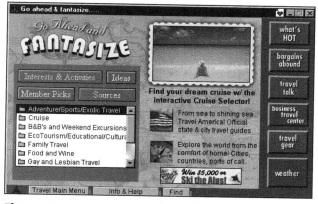

Figure 6-2   Select Interests & Activities to find the travel location that suits your interests.

The first stop is Adventure/Sports/Exotic Travel:

1. From the Fantasize window, select Interests & Activities.

2. Double-click Adventure/Sports/Exotic Travel in the display window.

If your idea of a good time ranges between playing a relaxing round of golf and jumping off a 3,000-foot cliff with nothing more than a parachute and a prayer, this is the place for you. This section of the Travel channel offers information on every outdoor activity you can think of. There are scores of biking tours, golfing tours, ballooning, mountaineering, scuba diving, and skiing tips to choose from (just to mention a few). One of the best links in this area is Outdoor Adventure Online (OAO). In the Adventure/Sports/Exotic Travel window, double-click Outdoor Adventure Online to open the OAO window (see Figure 6-3).

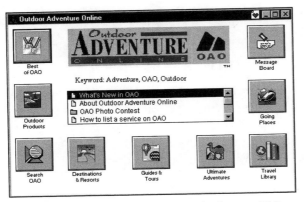

Figure 6-3 From the mundane to the insane, OAO covers everything you can do in the great outdoors.

Outdoor Adventure Online features include:

* **Best of OAO**. Here you can find OAO top picks for outdoor vacation destinations, companies, tours, and resorts.

* **Outdoor Products**. Catalogs of outdoor gear for sale.

* **Search OAO**. A handy keyword search feature to help you find information fast.

* **Destinations & Resorts**. An abundance of information on campgrounds, resorts, ranches, and more.

* **Ultimate Adventures**. Not for the faint-hearted. Rafting down the Zambezi river, climbing the Matterhorn, and leaping off Venezuela's Angel Falls with a parachute are a few of the adventures available here.

* **Travel Library**. Information on outdoor magazines, books, maps, and more is found in the Travel Library.

* **Going Places**. General travel information, including passport, ticket, and tourist information.

* **Message Boards**. Lots of AOL member feedback on adventure travel.

ECOTOURISM

Are you a nature lover? If so, stop in at the EcoTourism/Educational/Cultural Travel area of Interests & Activities. What better way to vacation than combining sightseeing and learning to make the most of your holiday resources. Check out the CultureFinder, America's Favorite Zoos & Aquariums, Cruises for Nature Lovers, and Eco-tours & Safaris.

FAMILY TRAVEL

Finding a vacation spot that's right for the whole family can be challenging. One way to get the whole family working toward a common goal is to do your research in the Family Travel area of Interest & Activities. In addition to a wealth of information on Disney World, the Family Travel includes:

- **Family Travel Network**. Places to go with the kids, tons of tips about traveling with kids, message boards with input from fellow AOL family travelers, and lots more.

- **Family Travel (Parent Soup)**. Educational Vacations, Exploring the Great Outdoors, Family Vacations, and Water Vacations should give you enough options to suit every member of the family.

- **Family Cruises**. Cruises for families, tips for cruising with kids, and information on children's facilities provided by various cruise lines.

- **Web: Search for Family Travel Information**. A direct link to the WebCrawler search engine and some WebCrawler Family Travel Reviews.

FOOD AND WINE

If, like Napoleon's army, you travel on your stomach, this is the place to start your vacation planning. Here you can find restaurant reviews, dining guides, and Wine Country Vacations.

GAY AND LESBIAN TRAVEL

Discover the ongoing events, popular destinations, and travel companies that provide members of the gay community the opportunity to enjoy vacation time to its fullest. In the Over the Rainbow area of Gay and Lesbian Travel, you can find travel tips, insights on the gay scene worldwide, and special vacation packages that cater to gay and lesbian clientele.

ROMANCE/HONEYMOON TRAVEL

It doesn't matter whether you're eighteen or eighty, there's always room for romance. And how better to fan the flame than by traveling to a romantic spot and spending some time alone with the one you love? If you're planning a first, second, or third honeymoon, you might want to stop at the Romance/Honeymoon Travel area and get a few ideas:

- **Bed & Breakfast Guide by Lanier**. There's nothing like a small, cozy bed and breakfast to rekindle romance in any relationship.

- **Honeymoon Getaways in High Gear**. Lots of information on getting hitched and getting away. It even offers tips on how to elope.

- **Picture Album: Romantic Locales**. It's always a good idea to look before you leap.

- **Romantic Cruising**. In addition to detailed information on the major cruise lines, you'll find the top ten romantic cruises and advice on getting married on-board as well as honeymooning.

WEB PATH ➡ ✳ **Search the Web for Honeymoon Information**. A direct link to the WebCrawler search engine and Honeymoon Travel Reviews.

PORTS OF CALL

If your idea of the perfect life is retiring at 35 and spending the next 50 or 60 years visiting as many places on the globe as you can reach, it will not be the activities but the destinations themselves that draw you. The ideal place for globetrotters to start — apprentice and professional alike — is in the Travel Channel's Research & Plan area (see Figure 6-4).

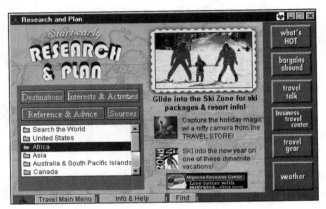

Figure 6-4 If you're afflicted with wanderlust, don't miss the Research and Plan area.

For travel information on every world location from American Samoa to Zimbabwe, check out the Destinations area of Research and Plan. Broken down by continent or world area, practically every piece of dry land is covered. You can find bed and breakfast, city, passport, tour, and vacation package information. As a world traveler, you should also keep up on the economic and political conditions in the places on your itinerary. You can find that information here, too.

Finding the right price

In reality, it's actually pretty easy to find the ideal vacation spot or package. The problem generally comes in trying to plan the vacation that is equally agreeable to your tastes and your budget. Unless you have too much money and can't figure out how to get rid of it, I suggest spending a little time researching the Travel Channel for price as well as location. There are a multitude of ways to stretch your vacation dollar with little or no sacrifice. To get started, click the bargains abound button on the Travel Channel's main menu.

GREAT DEALS

Be sure to check out the profusion of parsimonious pickings (sorry, I tend to wax poetic when I think about saving money) available in the Great Deals area. Among the many offerings, you find:

* **Arthur Frommer's Secret Bargains**. The best-known travel expert gives you the low-down on bargain vacations.

* **Bargain Box**. One of a kind and limited availability specials on airline tickets, cruises, and more. It's worth a quick check no matter where you're going.

* **Dynamite Deals for Families**. A lot of kids' free stuff here, including airline tickets, ski passes, and gifts.

* **Ship Shop Cruise Bargains**. A little smart shopping and you may end up with your dream vacation at dream price.

MONEY-SAVING CLUBS

This area features discount dining and travel offers as well as a link to the AAA (American Automobile Association).

Finding the right advice

Even the most well-seasoned traveler can be caught unawares unless he or she does a little research on a never-before-visited destination. In addition to finding advice on local sightseeing, shopping, and dining, there are a number of other important items that are easy to overlook. However, if you look in the right place on the Travel Channel, you can find travel tips and advice on every subject imaginable. Many of the things you take for granted at home have the potential to create havoc on a vacation.

Take electricity, for example. It's obvious that all except the most remote rural areas of the world have electricity. So far so good. The problem lies in the fact that many countries, particularly those in Europe, use 220-volt electrical outlets, not 110-volt as we do in the United States. Consequently, if you're heading for one of those countries, none of the handy little electrical appliances (hair dryer, shaver, and so on) you've thrown in your overnight bag is going to work unless you also threw in some voltage converters.

TRAVELER'S RESOURCE CENTER

Aptly named, the Traveler's Resource Center, which can be found in the Tips & Strategies area of *Bargains Abound*, offers tips and advice on everything the well-prepared traveler needs to know. There are too many to list them all, but here is a sampling of what you can find:

* **Advisories from the U.S. State Department**. Travel warnings and updates about conditions around the world. The State Department database contains Consular Information Sheets on all countries with which the U.S. has diplomatic ties. In addition to embassy contact information, the Consular Information Sheets contain a description of the country, entry requirements, information on crime statistics and medical facilities, and more.

* **Electricity Around the World**. A listing, by country, of the electrical voltage and outlet types used in countries around the world.

* **Exchange Rates**. It's difficult to get by in a foreign country if you don't know what your money is worth in the local currency. The Exchange Rates area provides a handy conversion table for most of the world's major currencies.

* **Packing Tips**. Advice on everything from the appropriate luggage to shoes, toiletries, and packing methods.

* **Passport Information**. Everything you need to know to get a passport — including how to get a quick passport for emergency travel.

* **Telephone Tips for Travelers**. Here you find some good tips on how to not get ripped off when phoning home from abroad.

* **Weather - International & U.S. Cities**. There's nothing worse than running around in the rain trying to buy an umbrella.

TRIP PLANNING (AAA)

When it comes to trip planning, who is better qualified than Triple A? All those years of experience are now available online at the Trip Planning area of *Bargains Abound* Tips & Strategies. Some of the helpful hints and tips you can find there are:

* **Car Care Tips**. Selecting the right fuel, how often to change your oil, taking care of your battery, and winterizing your car are just a few of the subjects covered.

* **Construction Hotspots**. When you're traveling through the U.S. or Canada, be sure to stop here for the latest updates on construction tie-ups to avoid.

* **Traffic Traps**. Interstate travelers should scan this advisory before heading out. AAA highlights any communities or areas where entrapment or strict enforcement of traffic laws is done primarily for financial rather than safety reasons. Included are places that have sudden speed reductions, obscured traffic signs, unreasonably slow speed limits, and so on.

* **Scenic Drives**. If you're just out for a Sunday afternoon drive or a cross-country trip, it's always nice to enjoy the scenery. Check here for the most scenic route to wherever you're going.

EXPERT OPINIONS

If you want to know what the travel experts have to say, plan a layover at the Expert Opinions area in the Fantasize/Ideas section of the Travel Channel. Everything from top cruise picks to tips on traveling with children and a lot in between can be found here.

Keeping Up with Travel News

Whether you're planning a trip or just dreaming about one, it's a good idea to keep abreast of the latest in travel news. New tours, vacation packages, and prices are always popping up. Fortunately, the Travel Channel has a number of online travel magazines and mailing lists.

* **Travel Magazines & Newsletters**. Found in the Fantasize/Ideas area, the Travel Magazines & Newsletters area contains a number of online travel magazines including the Backpacker Magazine, the Boating Magazine, American Express' Travel & Leisure, and more.

* **The Independent Traveler's Mailing List**. If you want to know about upcoming travel chats and pertinent travel news, sign up for the Independent Traveler's e-mail list.

* **The Cruise Critic E-Mail List**. To be alerted to upcoming cruise chats and cruise bargains, sign up for the Cruise Critic's mailing list. From the Fantasize/Interests & Activities menu, select Cruise, select Cruise Critic (Complete Cruise Information), and then click the question mark (Frequently Asked Questions). From the list of Frequently Asked Questions, choose Join our Mailing list for FREE Newsletter!, fill out the form, and then send it.

* **Passport Newsletter Online**. An upscale online newsletter with reviews of "off the beaten path" world dining, lodging, sightseeing, shopping, and cultural resources.

* **Inside Flyer Online**. This online rag (figuratively speaking) is dedicated to keeping you up to date on all the various frequent traveler programs currently in existence. You can find the Inside Flyer Magazine in the Sources area of Fantasize.

TIP It is also a good idea to check out the regular AOL news services periodically to keep up on political or natural upheavals around the world that might affect your travel plans.

Sharing Member Experiences

The only trouble with relying on the experts is that they often see things from a different perspective. All too frequently, they are traveling first class when your needs are economy. The other problem with well-known travel experts is that they are often recognized and treated to a higher level of service than the average traveler. If you'd like to find out what the real story is, you might want to spend some time browsing through the travel message boards and participating in some of the travel chats.

Message Boards

The Travel Message Boards afford members of the AOL community an opportunity to share their travel experiences, good and bad alike. In addition to being able to read about other people's experiences, you can also contact them directly and ask specific questions that have not been answered in their postings. To make them even more helpful, the Message Boards come in four flavors: Domestic, International, Interests & Activities, and Travel Issues & Tips (see Figure 6-5).

Figure 6-5 Discover how fellow AOL members have fared in their travel adventures.

Chat sessions

Although the Message Boards give you the opportunity to browse leisurely through other members' experiences, it is sometimes a slow and frustrating process to find the information you seek. Participating in a travel chat session provides you with immediate feedback and the chance to pose your questions to everyone in the room. Chances are, someone's bound to have an answer — or at least an opinion. To find out when travel chat sessions are taking place, check the Chat Schedule in the Travel Channel's Travel Talk area.

BONUS

Much of the travel information found in the Travel Channel's general areas is appropriate for both the leisure traveler and the business traveler. However, there are unique challenges faced by the business traveler that require more tailored information. To accommodate the special needs of the business traveler, AOL has constructed the Business Travel Center (see Figure 6-6).

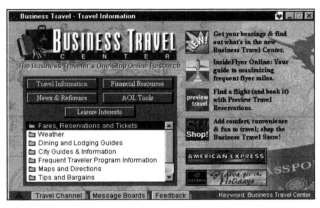

Figure 6-6 Don't leave home without checking the Business Travel Center.

The Business Travel Center provides resources to make your travel plans for business as smooth and effortless as possible.

* **Travel Information**. Stop here to find general travel information. Reservations, weather, dining guides, maps, and directions are just some of the things you can find in Travel Information.

* **Financial Resources**. Everything the traveling business person needs to keep in touch with the world of finance — from Wall Street quotes to currency conversion.

* **News & References**. When I travel for fun and relaxation, I generally try to avoid the news as much as possible. Not so on business. The business traveler can't afford to be uninformed. The News and References area provides world, business, sports news, and more.

* **AOL Tools**. When traveling for business, you can take advantage of many of AOL's features to make your trip more productive. The worldwide listing of access numbers lets you sign on wherever you are. Setting up your own news profile can save you a lot of time looking for pertinent news information, especially when time is limited.

* **Leisure Interests**. All work and no play not only makes you dull, it also makes you a dullard. Grabbing a little leisure time on a business trip can rejuvenate you and minimize the stress of traveling and conducting business at the same time. So, for the sake of keeping yourself sharp and at your peak, it might be a good idea to check out the leisure activities available wherever you are traveling.

Summary

Whether for business, for pleasure, or just to get somewhere else, everyone travels at one time or another. With the proper planning and preparation, the journey can be pleasant and rewarding. Without it, a trip can become your worst nightmare. AOL's Travel Channel offers all the tools and advice you need to make your travel plans a dream.

GETTING THE NEWS

To keep up with what's going on in the world, you can subscribe to a lot of newspapers and magazines — or you can use AOL. The choice is easy: AOL is cheaper, and you won't have to buy an additional trash can or recycle bin to dispose of all those periodicals after you've read them.

This chapter shows you how to get to the news of the day. The content changes as the day goes on because the AOL news summary feature keeps on top of things as they happen. The news of the world is at your fingertips (well, at your mouse pointer). In addition, you'll learn how to access other news features such as weather and sports. You'll also get directions for visiting the AOL Newsstand, which has many newspapers and magazines you can read. Of course, because it's so easy to access periodicals this way, you probably won't be subscribing to as many magazines as you might if you didn't have AOL. Hopefully, that won't ruin your chances to win big when Ed McMahon comes calling.

Getting Today's Headlines

For a quick way to see what's happening and decide which events you want more information on, choose Today's News from the Channels window, and then enter the keyword **News** or click the Today's News icon on the Toolbar (see Figure 7-1).

Figure 7-1 The Toolbar has an icon for quick access to the latest news.

The Today's News window opens (see Figure 7-2) and displays six mini-windows representing different categories. You can visit any or all of these categories:

* U.S. & World News
* Politics
* Weather
* Sports
* Business
* Entertainment

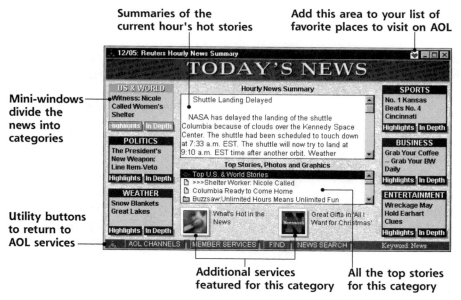

Figure 7-2 Head straight for the mini-window category that interests you.

AOL provides a couple of choices for you as you explore these categories so that you can keep up with what's happening in the world. Each mini-window has a headline for one of its stories, and then it offers two choices:

* You can click Highlights in any category to see the stories that have been selected for that category.

* You can click In Depth to see other stories and other sources for stories connected with the category.

Selecting Highlights actually gives you two choices: you can view a summary of the important stories for the category, or you can choose to see the entire story and any related stories from additional news sources.

Getting the Highlights

To see highlights of all the stories in a category, follow these steps:

1. Move to the category and click Highlights (in this case, I've chosen the Politics category). The middle section of the Today's News window changes to reflect your choice (see Figure 7-3).

Figure 7-3   Scroll through the stories for a summary of the important news events in this category.

2. The top half of the middle part of the Today's News window contains the summary version of the stories in the category you've chosen.

3. Use the scroll bar to move through the stories. Grab a cup of coffee and enjoy your online newspaper.

4. Click Highlights in a different category to follow your other interests. The middle of the Today's News window changes to reflect your new category choice.

TIP   You don't have to go through any steps to exit the first category, merely clicking the Highlights button in a different category moves you to the new selection.

Getting the whole story

If the summary version of a story whets your interest as you look at the news highlights of the category you chose, you can get more information about the story. These additional details are available in the bottom half of the center of the window.

Getting a story isn't always a straightforward process, and different categories work different ways. For example, in the Political News Summary, some of the stories I browsed through have equivalent headlines in the bottom box (see Figure 7-4), but some don't.

Figure 7-4   There's a file with the full story to match this summary news item.

Double-click the item in the bottom box to see more information than the summary article provided (see Figure 7-5).

The bottom box has a variety of stories (some of which are not connected to the summary stories in the top box but are additional stories for the category). It also has other elements such as photographs and cartoons; you can view them to gain additional knowledge about the news in the category. You can also read commentary — some columnists provide AOL with their observations and remarks.

Each category also has two featured services that you can access either to get more information or to learn about special utilities you can get through AOL (not everything is free). Click the icon for the feature you'd like to explore. Like the news headlines, these icons change regularly throughout the day.

Displaying the news ticker

In the US & World mini-window, if you scroll through the Top Stories box (the box at the bottom center of the window), you'll see an entry named +++*AOL NewsTicker*++. Double-click it to put the ticker on your screen (see Figure 7-6).

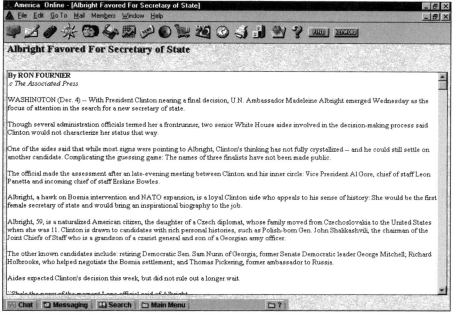

Figure 7-5   The entire original story is available. Maximize the window to make it easier to read.

Figure 7-6   The ticker rolls headlines past you just as if you were standing in Times Square in New York City.

When you see a headline that seems interesting, choose Read This Story. You can also choose ticker headlines from other sources by choosing Show Options (see Figure 7-7).

You can, in fact, open multiple tickers and have them on your AOL screen while you travel through your favorite AOL places. When a headline appears that catches your eye (and your interest), you can read the story. Because the news is updated hourly, if you spend a lot of time on AOL you won't miss major events.

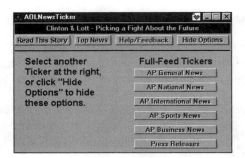

Figure 7-7 Open another ticker to see headlines from a different source.

Getting in-depth coverage

The news summaries you see on AOL are provided by Reuters, a news gathering service that has been around for a long time. Reuters actually existed before AOL, and it continues to provide general news services to newspapers and magazines in addition to AOL. Other services, magazines, and newspapers are also available to you.

Click the In Depth button on the category you want to explore to see a plethora of additional choices. Like the news, the specific choices in the In Depth window change from day to day (or hour to hour) as the category is updated to reflect recent events.

US & WORLD NEWS IN DEPTH

A news junkie could spend half the day on the In Depth coverage of the latest news around the country and the world (see Figure 7-8).

Figure 7-8 The choices are mind-boggling as you explore today's news around the world.

Click an arrow to focus on its category. For most of the categories, a list of stories displays (see Figure 7-9).

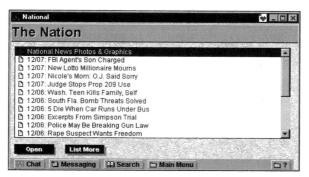

Figure 7-9 Choose the story files you want to open to keep yourself well informed.

Open a story file by double-clicking it or by selecting it and then choosing Open.

In addition to the categories for story files, you can get the crossword puzzle from The New York Times. You can also see the commentary on the Op-Ed pages of publications.

TIP To do The New York Times crossword puzzle, you have to download it. You'll first need to download software from AOL that gives you the ability to save, display, and print the crossword puzzle. The software is called Across Lite, and the easy directions for downloading it and installing it on your computer are available when you select the crossword puzzle category. Don't forget to read and follow the instructions for registering the software.

Once you have the puzzle, you can work on it on-screen. Or, you can print it and go at it with a pen. (If you're timid or insecure, you can use a pencil, but personally I find it a matter of pride to do the puzzle only with a pen, since I was brought up in a household of people that yelled "chicken" at you if you approached a crossword puzzle with a pencil.)

You can also choose one of the icons on the right side of the window to visit other areas and read the news as reported by them: The New York Times, ABC News, The Congressional Quarterly, Newsweek Magazine, and a list of Internet sites.

POLITICS IN DEPTH

To make sure your cocktail-party-chatter skills are kept well honed, keep up with the political scene. Choosing In Depth on the Politics mini-window brings you plenty of choices for stories and opinion (see Figure 7-10). There's usually a poll going on or a debate raging, and you can select the appropriate icon to join in.

Double-click a story file to read about the latest political happenings so you know who's doing what to whom, who's a threat to others, who's in, and who's out. Then you can put it all together for your next argument with the kids. (Have you noticed that many of today's kids are more conservative than their parents? It used to be the other way around!)

While you're in the Politics forum, don't forget to take a look at today's political cartoon (see Figure 7-11).

Figure 7-10 The politics forum gives you the facts to back up your opinions when you enter the perilous world of political discussions.

Figure 7-11 Sometimes I find a political cartoon that tickles me because I can relate to its subject matter.

BUSINESS IN DEPTH

Even if you're not in business for yourself, keeping up with business news makes it easier to consider your financial options. You may be thinking of purchasing a home or refinancing your home, and it's a good idea to find out which way interest rates are headed so you can time it properly. And, of course, if you invest in the market directly or through funds or pension plans, you'll want to keep an eye on your investments.

When you click In Depth in the Business mini-window, the Business News window opens, displaying a list of categories and some icons to get you to other business topics (see Figure 7-12).

Figure 7-12   The Business News window has stories, resources, analyses, and stock quotes available at a click of the mouse.

Choose Industry News if you're following a particular type of company. A list of categories displays, and you can catch up on what's happening for the industry types of your choice (see Figure 7-13).

Figure 7-13   See what the competition in your industry is up to, or check to see what your company is doing that's making news.

The Personal Finance Channel is chock-full of business news that's aimed at individuals instead of corporations (see Figure 7-14). To get there, just click the pig (it's really a piggy bank) on the upper-right side of the Business News window.

TIP   If you're interested in visiting the Personal Finance area, you don't have to go through Today's News to get there. It's a discrete AOL area that you can access with the keyword Finance. It also has its own button on the Channel window.

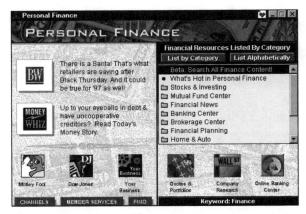

Figure 7-14   The stuff for regular people instead of corporate financial folks is found in the Personal Finance section.

Check out the Motley Fool by clicking that icon in the Business News window. This is a way to learn about investing and investments, but the whole area has a twisted view. The humor ranges from subtle to slapstick (okay, silly), but there's information available that you might want to see before making decisions based on more information from less humorous sources.

ENTERTAINMENT IN DEPTH

Everything you want to know about show biz is right in front of you when you take an in-depth look at the Entertainment category (see Figure 7-15).

Figure 7-15   Gossip, news, schedules, criticism, and more keep you up to date on the entertainment industries.

Check out the Columns icon to get a gander at what the world's best-known gossip mongers are saying today.

WEATHER IN DEPTH

If you want to know more about the weather than your local forecast, there's an entire reference section available when you click the In Depth button on this mini-window (see Figure 7-16).

Figure 7-16 Where is it warm, wet, or dangerous? Check the weather section to find out.

TIP This weather section has plenty of full-color maps you can download or print (a color printer helps), and your school-age child can probably make much use of them.

SPORTS IN DEPTH

Sports fans are gonna love this section! There is more information about sporting events, sports history, sports gossip, and sports commentary than anybody could digest (see Figure 7-17).

If the major sports categories you see aren't enough to satisfy your need for sports information, click More Sports (see Figure 7-18). The listing you see is rather comprehensive; but, if you can't find what you're looking for, just click List More. No sport is omitted. Even cricket results and badminton scores are available!

And that's not all! Believe it or not, there's more, making AOL the next best thing to heaven for a sports fan. See the section called "Browsing Sports" later in this chapter.

Figure 7-17 Get to the In Depth Sports News for everything you could ever want to know about athletics.

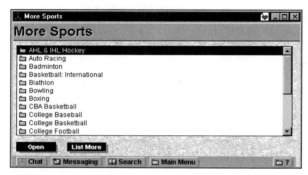

Figure 7-18 Some people have rather esoteric interests, and AOL accommodates them.

Visiting the Newsstand

E very airport has at least one newsstand, where you can find a wide selection of newspapers and magazines to choose from as you buy things to amuse yourself with on the airplane. (Stopping for some good fast food is another airport shopping tradition for people who find a juicy hot dog with mustard and sauerkraut a better alternative than airplane food.)

AOL has a newsstand too, and it's easy to get to:

* Click Newsstand on the Channels window.

* Use the Keyword **Newsstand**.

This Newsstand has icons and listings instead of shelves, but otherwise it's just like any good newsstand (see Figure 7-19).

Figure 7-19 Publications for every interest are available at the Newsstand.

The publications list on the right side of the Newsstand window contains the entire collection of offerings. Featured areas (which change from time to time) are represented by the eight icons around the window.

Browsing the publications list

Although the icons representing featured publications are handy for quick access if you're interested in one of them, the heart of the Newsstand is the list of publications.

The first two items, AOL News Profiles and WebCrawler Search: Newspapers, are special, and you can find more information about them in the Bonus section of this chapter. After that, everything is arranged alphabetically. Unfortunately, this isn't terribly convenient if you're trying to look for all the publications that match your specific interests.

So, as a public service, let's pick out a couple of categories and list the publications that are germane (which saves you the trouble of scrolling through the list over and over when you want to pursue something that intrigues you). The keywords (when they exist) for each publication are included so you can head right for your favorites.

COMPUTERS

Publications about computers are available for every level of interest and proficiency, and you should take a look at a few of them to see which ones provide you with the most information or entertainment (or both).

✴ *Cobb Group Online* (keyword **Cobb**). The Cobb Group is a collection of monthly journals (like newsletters) for specific software applications, operating systems, and computer languages. Each journal contains software tricks and tips as well as general articles of interest to the users of the journal's software. Almost all the popular desktop software packages have a Cobb Group journal.

✳ *Computer Life* (keyword **Life**). Computer Life is a generic computer publication that offers reviews, articles, and general information about or connected with computing.

✳ *FamilyPC Online* (keyword **FamilyPC**). Aimed at family computing (instead of business computing, which is where the majority of computer publications are directed), this is a joint venture of Disney Publishing and Ziff-Davis Publishing. It contains lots of information about multimedia.

✳ *Home Office Computing* (keyword **HOC**). As you might guess, this is a publication that carries articles of interest to people who have home-based businesses in which the use of a computer figures heavily.

✳ *HomePC* (keyword **HomePC**). This is another publication filled with articles and reviews of products for home computing. Special attention to software for kids helps fulfill this mission.

✳ *Mobile Computing* (keyword **mobile**). This magazine has been around for a while with the name *Mobile Office*. It specializes in articles and reviews that are of interest to people who keep in touch from remote sites.

✳ *PC World* (keyword **Pcworld**). A well-known and well-respected general computer magazine, *PC World* has articles, columns, reviews, and plenty of special features.

✳ *Windows Magazine* (keyword **WinMag**). Devoted to Microsoft Windows, this magazine offers users of Windows 95 and NT plenty of information. You'll find reviews, analyses, columns, news, trends, and many helpful tips and tricks. Even the technically advanced will find new information.

After you've checked out these publications, double-click the entry named Computing's Magazine Rack. It's a whole new section of the computer shelves in the Newsstand. In addition to the publications discussed here, there are plenty of additional periodicals listed (see Figure 7-20). Some of them are the business/computer sections of general magazines, and others are computer magazines that don't have an AOL site for their online editions (choosing one of those magazines takes you to the World Wide Web).

KIDS

There's plenty of informative, helpful information in the Newsstand for kids (and for parents, of course).

✳ *DC Comics Online* (no keyword). The kids, naturally, will have a great time here. They'll definitely ask you to order subscriptions. After you've handled that issue, send the kids away and browse this area for yourself. Remember the old superhero comics of your childhood? Or even your parents' childhood? You can take a nostalgic walk through those memories on this site and run into Batman and Robin. Make sure you visit *Mad Magazine* (see Figure 7-21).

Figure 7-20 The Computer Magazine Rack has magazines, reference publications, and articles.

Figure 7-21 Alfred E. (What, Me Worry?) Neuman is alive and well on AOL and even accepts messages.

* *Disney Adventures Magazine* (keyword **Disney**). Written for the elementary through junior high school age group, this publication has stories, sports, comics, and puzzles.

* *Family Life* (keyword **FamilyLife**). This site has projects for kids and parents in addition to articles, advice, and entertainment reviews. There's even an online newsletter you can subscribe to (it arrives via e-mail).

* *Highlights* (no keyword). That familiar periodical from everybody's school days is online. After you're welcomed by a chorus of kids' voices, you can browse through the features (with the kids, of course). There's plenty of interactive stuff for the kids to do; they can even write their

own stories, upload them, and then see them online later (easy directions are right on the site).

* *Marvel Comics* (keyword **Marvel**). Spiderman awaits, and so does The Danger Room (enter at your own risk). There's a trivia contest and lots of great, scary, graphics.

* *Nickelodeon Magazine* (no keyword). After Nick the dog barks a welcome, explore this site to find lots of things kids like to do and read about. There's some dripping green slime with appropriate sound effects, but apart from that, parents will be just as fascinated.

* *Seventeen* (no keyword). A perennial favorite for many years (this publication is as old as I am), this magazine has changed a bit since I last saw it. "Choosing long gloves for your prom dress" has been replaced with stuff that's a bit more sophisticated (relationship stuff), but I guess that's the way it goes.

* *Parenting Magazine* (keyword **ParentingMagazine**). Okay, it's a stretch to mention this one in a section on kids, but it's for parents and it's about raising kids. There's no such thing as having too much help in the raising kids department (well, except for your mother-in-law), so after the kids are asleep, browse here.

HOBBIES AND INTERESTS

There's an abundance of good reading for people who are looking for special interest publications.

* *American Astrology* (no keyword). What's Your Sign?

* *American Woodworker* (keyword **woodworker**). Project, tool reviews, and lots of shop talk.

* *Backpacker Magazine* (no keyword). Trail maps and a barking (or maybe it was howling) animal.

* *Bicycling Magazine* (keyword **Bicycling**). Articles, product reviews, and info about races.

* *Big Twin* (no keyword). Neither the identical nor fraternal varieties, it's a Harley motorcycle magazine. The HOG pen beckoned but I resisted — you might want to check it out.

* *Boating Online* (keyword **Boat**). Boats, weather conditions, and plenty of articles about fishing.

* *Crafts Magazine* (keyword **Crafts Magazine**). Country, fabric, floral, kids, and every other craft you can think of.

* *Cycle World* (keyword **Cycle World**). For every roaring biker — the cycle in this title means *motorcycle*.

- *Flying Magazine* (no keyword). The sound of a roaring jet introduces articles about every type of plane.
- *Karate International Magazine* (keyword **Karate Int**). Articles, columns, and Bruce Lee tributes.
- *Popular Photography* (keyword **PopPhoto**). One of the oldest and best special interest magazines now has an AOL online version.
- *Runner's World* (keyword **Runner's World**). Product reviews, articles, features, and news about running events.
- *Scuba Diving Magazine* (keyword **dive**). Dive in (sorry, couldn't resist) if this is one of your interests.
- *Sew News* (keyword **Sew News**). This will keep you in stitches (sorry again, couldn't resist this one either).
- *Soap Opera Digest* (keyword **SOD**). The online version of the magazine you pick up and read while you're in line at the supermarket (and occasionally buy).
- *Travel & Leisure Online* (keyword **T&L**). The online version of one of the best-selling travel periodicals with stories about places, people, and prices.

REGULAR STUFF

The Newsstand also carries a full selection of generic magazines and business periodicals. And, you'll find *Consumer Reports* (keyword **Consumer Reports**), religious magazines, and health publications.

Browsing Sports

For the real sports fan (you know, the folks that spend big bucks on giant TV screens because it's like being there), there's so much information on AOL that there's a real chance you'll overdose and decide to spend some time pursuing other interests (I know, it'll never happen). To move to the ultimate world of sports information:

- Click Sports in the Channels window.
- Enter the keyword **Sports**.

When you arrive, you face a mind-boggling variety of choices, all of which are connected to sports (see Figure 7-22).

Because the array of items is so vast, you're probably confused. So let's take a logical approach and spend some time in this area in a sensible way.

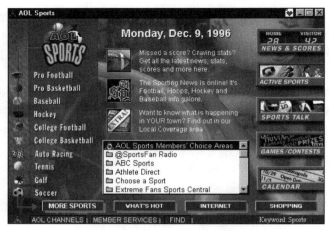

Figure 7-22   The choices are enormous, and the opening
screen is just the tip of the iceberg.

Getting the scores

The first thing many people want to do is check the scores. There may be an icon
for a featured area that has scores (the featured area icons in the center of the
window change from time to time), and you can click there. Or, choose the sport
of interest from the list on the left side of the window to open a window that is
sure to have scores (see Figure 7-23).

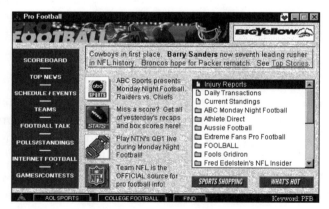

Figure 7-23   It looks as if there are enough scores, stats,
and details available to satisfy even the
most fanatic sports fans.

Of course, if it's the wrong season (it's winter as I write this, so I'm following
football, basketball, and hockey), the sport's window won't have scores; however, there will be plenty of news, gossip, trivia, and predictions.

Move to the scoreboard window (see Figure 7-24) to see the results for recent
games.

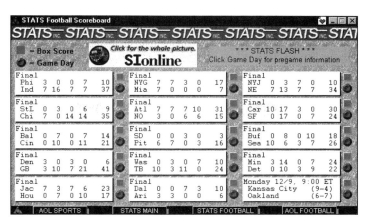

Figure 7-24   All the scores at a glance!

Click the Box Score icon (the red square) next to any game to see complete stats about the game, the way the scoring occurred, and any other important statistics that were accumulated during the game.

Browsing the sports newsstand

Double-click the Newsstand entry in the list box in the Sports window to visit the AOL Sports Newsstand (see Figure 7-25).

Figure 7-25   The shelves of this newsstand hold magazines and newsletters for all sorts of sports — including mushing and heckler snowboarding!

Featured newsstand items are represented by large icons on the window, and they change from time to time. Scroll through the list box for a complete catalog of periodicals.

Using the sports features

There's a lot of inside information about athletes and sports in the AOL Sports Stars Online area. Double-click the Sport Stars Online listing in the main AOL Sports window to get to this window (see Figure 7-26).

Figure 7-26 Personal profiles, commentary, and photos are yours with a click of your mouse.

Having access to information about athletes and their achievements on and off the playing fields makes all these superheroes seem a little more real. If there's anyone you want to know more about, double-click the appropriate Athlete Direct listing. A personal profile window opens, and you can get details on anything that seems interesting to you (see Figure 7-27).

Figure 7-27 Steve Young is one of my favorites — even if he does play for the opposition.

If you want to plan your week, click the Calendar in the main AOL Sports window (see Figure 7-28).

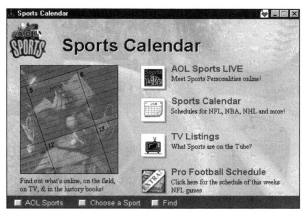

Figure 7-28 This is the place to visit when you need to know what's happening when.

You can check the Sports Calendar to see all the team action or browse through the TV Listings to see when you need to call dibs on the couch and the clicker.

Going Interactive

One of the most interesting side benefits of getting the news and sports from AOL is that every one of the categories offers some form of interactive participation. You can join a chat group and talk to other AOL users who share your interest, or you can check out one of the message boards to read comments and add your own. Sometimes there's a poll to cast your vote in, or there's a debate about a particular hot subject.

 X-REF See Chapter 12 for more information about chatting on AOL.

Different news areas handle interactive participation in different ways. As you work your way through the In Depth choices, you'll find plenty of opportunities to voice your opinion.

For example, while I was reading stories about the financial problems in the Social Security system, I found a message board with interesting comments and suggestions from other AOL users. To add my own thoughts to the debate, I merely had to click Post to bring up a message form (see Figure 7-29).

Every news category has message boards. You can usually find them by choosing In Depth in the category's mini-window.

Try the real fun of interactive computing by joining in on games and contests. They're all over the news and sports areas. Just click and play!

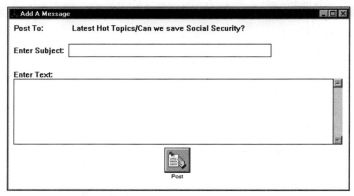

Figure 7-29 You can post a message to air your views on any subject that's being discussed — there are always plenty of debates going on at AOL.

BONUS

As you get comfortable with the news areas and forums on AOL, there are some shortcuts and tricks you might want to try.

Adding to favorite places

Every time you find an AOL area you like, you can add it to your Favorite Places list. The traditional method is to click the heart icon on the window and then answer Yes when AOL asks if you want to add this window to Favorite Places. To save yourself the bother of answering, just drag the Heart icon to the Favorite Places icon on the AOL toolbar (see Figure 7-30).

 Figure 7-30 Make this AOL area easy to get to by dragging the heart icon to the Favorite Places tool.

Searching for news stories

If you have an interest in a particular news story, you might want to read about it in multiple periodicals. Or, you might not want to open multiple AOL resources to try to find this story. Therefore, you'll want a way to search for the story yourself.

When you're in Today's News, a special button named News Search appears on the AOL button bar on the bottom of your window. Click it to bring up the News Search window. Then enter words that describe the story and click List Articles. When the list of articles appears (see Figure 7-31), merely double-click any you want to read.

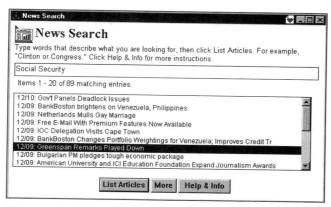

Figure 7-31 Double-click the article you want to read.

There's a certain logic to searching. Here are some tips:

✳ You can use the word "and" to make sure both phrases are included in the search (for example, in the News Search window in Figure 7-34, the search phrase "Social Security and Greenspan" would have narrowed the search considerably).

✳ You can use the word "or" to tell AOL that you'll take either phrase ("Social Security or Medicare").

✳ You can use the word "not" to eliminate articles from the search ("Social Security not Greenspan").

If your search results in a zillion articles, that means you were much too broad in your search phrase (for example, using "congress" as the search phrase will probably overwhelm you with results). Go back and try again with a more specific phrase, or use one of the logical connectors.

The search engine is not case-sensitive, which means that Social Security, SOCIAL SECURITY, or social security (or even SoCIal SecURity) will all bring the same results.

Using profiles to have the news delivered to you

After you've been scanning and reading the news for a while, you might decide that there is a specific topic you want to read about on a daily basis. You can have AOL deliver all the news about that topic to you instead of going after it yourself. The delivery is made to your AOL mailbox, just like e-mail.

This feature is called *News Profiles*, and it's a way to tell AOL to match your interests and send you news articles by e-mail. To make this happen, you just have to create a profile that indicates your interest. You can, in fact, create up to five profiles so you can follow more than one topic.

To create a profile, follow these steps:

1. Go to the Newsstand.

2. Double-click AOL News Profiles in the Publications list.

3. When the News Profiles window opens, click the Create a Profile icon (see Figure 7-32).

Figure 7-32   Pick a subject and decide how much information you can stand to receive about it.

4. Give the profile a name (choose something related to the topic you'll use for this profile) and specify the maximum number of stories you want to receive each day (press Tab to move to that field). Then choose Next.

5. Enter the words or phrases that will appear in any article about this topic (see Figure 7-33). This is a way to get the News Profiles feature to home in on the general topic. Choose Next.

6. In the next window, enter the words or phrases that are required in order to consider the article a match for your interest. This lets AOL narrow the search to only the articles that contain these words. If you want to see everything that matches your words and phrases from the previous window, you can skip this step. Choose Next.

7. The next window is the place to enter words or phrases that will be used to exclude articles (which means if it's in there, don't pick this article). This is an optional choice. Choose Next.

Figure 7-33 Enter text that matches your interests with the articles being searched.

8. Pick the news sources you want AOL to search (see Figure 7-34). Choose Next.

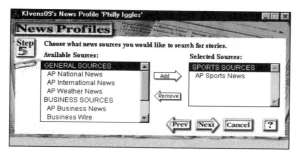

Figure 7-34 Select a source in the Available Sources box and choose Add to place it in the Selected Sources box.

9. AOL displays a message telling you that you've successfully created a profile (see Figure 7-35). Choose Done. Then click OK at the information dialog box.

Figure 7-35 Hooray, a successful effort!

You can repeat the process to create additional profiles. If you want to edit, delete, or temporarily suspend the use of a profile, follow Steps 1 and 2 above and choose Managing Profiles from the Newsstand window. Then follow the simple directions.

Using the WebCrawler

WEB PATH Although AOL has plenty of publications, articles, contributors, and other news resources, there's more available on the World Wide Web. Choose the WebCrawler in the Publications list on the Newsstand to access news resources on the Web.

X-REF More information about using the World Wide Web is available in Chapter 15.

Summary

The news of the day is one of AOL's most powerful features. It's updated constantly throughout the day so you always see the latest headlines. Prior stories are archived so you can go back and see the previous stories. This combination makes AOL a great research tool.

CHAPTER EIGHT

SHOPPING

IN THIS CHAPTER YOU LEARN THESE KEY SKILLS

S hopping can be fun. It's nice to come home with new things or buy something special for someone special. Shopping can also be a nightmare as you search for a parking space, struggle with shopping bags, fight the crowds, and look for a bathroom for a kid who's about to do something embarrassing (that same kid will then demand you find a place to stop for a soda so you can look for a bathroom again in about a half hour). And then, of course, there's the incredible fun of standing in the checkout line.

The best of all worlds can be found on AOL. You can do a whole lot of shopping online while saving yourself the distressing aspects of shopping. This chapter points you in the right direction (actually, multiple directions, because there are plenty of shopping areas) so you don't have to spend time meandering all over AOL to find a place to spend money.

Visiting the Marketplace

The largest shopping center on AOL is the Marketplace. To get there, choose one of these methods:

* Click the Marketplace icon (it has a shopping cart on it) on the AOL Toolbar.
* Choose Marketplace from the Channels window.
* Use the keyword **Marketplace**.

When you first visit, the Daily Goods window welcomes you to your shopping expedition in the Marketplace (see Figure 8-1). After your first visit, you might see advertisements in a window when you choose Marketplace. You can click Cancel to get to the Marketplace window (unless you want to order the merchandise).

Figure 8-1 Learn how to shop in this online mall, and then take a tour of the stores.

You can click an icon and read the information (you'll learn about a great deal of that information in the Bonus section of this chapter), or close the Daily Goods window and head straight for the stores (see Figure 8-2).

Figure 8-2 Think of the opening Marketplace window as the main entrance to a very large mall.

Viewing the Marketplace directory

Click Search to get to the store directory window, which is the easiest way to navigate through the Marketplace (see Figure 8-3).

You have several methods to choose from to get to a store and begin browsing (or shopping). You can scroll through the alphabetical list to find the store you want to visit, and then double-click the entry to get to the store's window. Or, you can click the Category tab to change the list into an index of categories (see Figure 8-4) that are presented in alphabetical order.

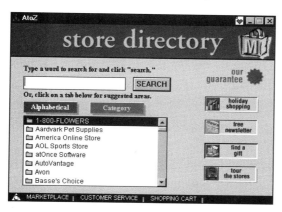

Figure 8-3   By default, the stores are listed alphabetically. You can scroll through the list to find the store you want to visit.

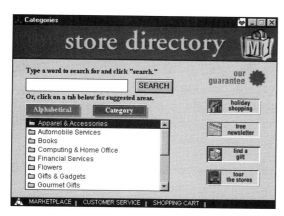

Figure 8-4   Until you've visited the Marketplace often enough to memorize the names of all the stores, it's probably easier to search by category.

You can also search for a product or a type of product. Enter the name of an item in the box next to the Search button, and then click Search to see the stores that carry the product you named (see Figure 8-5).

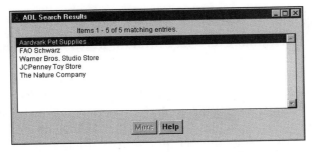

Figure 8-5 Searching for "toys" returned the names of several stores in the Marketplace.

Double-click a store in the Search Results window to visit it. When you finish browsing in that store, close the store's windows; the Search Results window will still be there so that you can double-click a different store. You can continue to return to the Search Results window until you close it.

Visiting stores

After you've selected a store in the Marketplace, double-click its listing to go there (single-click if the store is being featured and is represented by an icon instead of a text listing). Start shopping, or just browse and then visit another store.

Just so you don't have to visit every single store in the Marketplace (although that isn't a terrible idea), I'll offer some suggestions about fun stores to visit.

FOR THE HOUSE

There's an enormous selection of household items at the Marketplace. Here are some places to visit and browse — you'll probably find something you want to buy.

Hammacher Schlemmer (keyword **Hammacher**) is a fascinating place (see Figure 8-6). If you've seen their catalog, you know it's a book you read through as if it were a story, never skipping a page. You can spend as little as $40 or as much as $16,000.

The Sharper Image (keyword **Sharper Image**) is equally fascinating, filled with high-tech items that boggle the mind. Don't you need a laser light projector? Or a battery-operated cat litter box that cleans itself? Oh, wait, I know, you need a dictating machine you can use in the shower.

The Chef's Catalog (keyword: **chefscatalog**) is my idea of heaven because I love to cook and I love kitchen gadgets. All the gizmos and electric doohickeys a chef ever wanted can be found here.

The Nature Company (no keyword) is filled with tools, toys, and assorted items that represent the enchantment of nature. Plenty of unique items make this a place that even kids like to visit.

Figure 8-6 There are always lots of unusual, interesting, and occasionally weird products available at Hammacher Schlemmer.

FOOD

For serious food lovers, there are a wide range of stores to browse in the Marketplace. Start with the Godiva Chocolatier (keyword **Godiva**) because it's always fun to have dessert first. Then visit Omaha Steaks (keyword **Omaha**) and Starbucks Coffee (keyword **Starbucks**). The electronic Gourmet Guide (keyword **eGG**) and Hickory Farms (keyword **Hickory**) have multiple departments for different kinds of food.

Moreover, there are recipes scattered through the food sites (and also in the Chef's Catalog).

CLOTHING AND ACCESSORIES

If your closet and chest of drawers are in need of updating, you have plenty of opportunity to take care of that in the Marketplace. Meander through Eddie Bauer (keyword **Eddie Bauer**), The Reebok Store (keyword **Reebok**), One Hanes Place (keywords **Hanes, L'eggs, Bali, Playtex,** or **Champion**), and J.C. Penney (keyword **JCPenney**).

Also, check out some of the specialty personal items (use the search feature to look up perfume, for example).

BARGAINS

Easy online shopping and bargain prices — what a concept! The Marketplace is full of bargains.

The FreeShop (keyword **FreeShop**) has assembled free offers, free samples, and hugely discounted items from all over. The KidSoft SuperStore (keyword **KidSoft Store**) is the place to go to buy for all those computer-literate children who took to computing a lot faster than you did. Lillian Vernon has her catalog online (keyword **Lillian Vernon**), and if you've been looking all over the place for chocolate body paint, it's at the Love Shop.

For more bargains, click the Big Stores and Outlets icon on the main Marketplace window (see Figure 8-7).

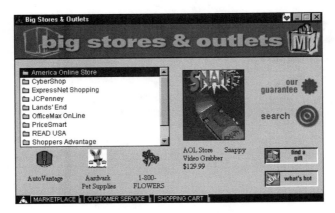

Figure 8-7   There are plenty of bargains available. Just double-click the listing that interests you.

Visit Shoppers Advantage (keyword **Shoppers Advantage**) for some real money savers. This is a members-only store, but joining is easy and inexpensive. You can browse the store without joining, but you can't purchase anything until you sign up.

ExpressNet Shopping (keyword **AmexShop**) is a one-stop store for all sorts of items. Everything you buy is charged to your American Express card. If you don't have an Amex card, no problem; you can apply here.

PriceSmart (keyword **Price**) is an online discount department store, and OfficeMax OnLine (no keyword) offers good prices on office supplies. The Sports Superstore (keyword **Sports SuperStore**) has everything you can think of (as long as you're thinking of sports).

Purchasing from the Marketplace

After you've fulfilled your browsing instincts, you can buy all the things you found that prompted you to think "Hey, I'd like one of those." Purchasing items online is quite easy. The steps to order are similar from store to store, although some stores may ask for special information about shipping or other details.

Generally, however, you can follow these steps:

1. With the product you want on the screen, select Click Here to Order (see Figure 8-8).

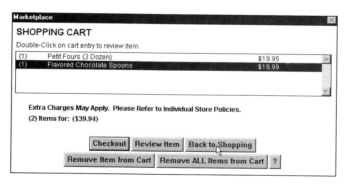

Figure 8-8 Start your order with a single click of the mouse.

2. Answer any questions that are specific to the store or the product (for example, whether this is a gift and you want a message on a card, the size or color you need, and the quantity you're ordering). Choose Continue to move through the windows.

3. When your order is finished, your Marketplace shopping cart opens so that you can see what's in it (see Figure 8-9).

Figure 8-9 This shopping cart does something the ones in the supermarket can't do — it expands to hold everything you want to buy.

4. Click the appropriate choice on the shopping cart window:

✳ Choose Checkout to complete your transaction. You'll be asked for credit card information.

✳ Select Review Item to look at the details about the highlighted purchase.

✳ Choose Back to Shopping to return to the Marketplace.

* Select Remove Item from Cart if you've changed your mind and want to take the highlighted item out of your shopping cart.

* Choose Remove ALL Items from Cart if you've had a serious change of mind and don't want to buy any items.

TIP **You can leave the Marketplace and visit other areas of AOL without checking out. Before you sign off, just return to the Marketplace and click the Shopping Cart button at the bottom of the screen. Then check out.**

Before closing the Checkout window, make a note of the confirmation number of your order (in case you have any problems). And if you're shopping for Christmas, take the shipping cutoff dates with a grain of salt.

Reading the Classifieds

Another shopping area that is worth your time is the classified ad section. To get there, enter the keyword **Classifieds**.

The Classifieds window displays and you're ready to roll (see Figure 8-10).

Figure 8-10 It could be that somebody is advertising a purple bedspread with blue and yellow flowers that your daughter wants so she can complete the decor of her bedroom, now that she's painted one wall red and the other walls black.

You're looking at one of the world's great flea markets — a garage sale on steroids. Let's eliminate some of the confusion by going over the important elements.

First of all, there are two main sections to visit if you want to buy or sell an item. The standard Classified ads are in the Bulletin Boards. The Premier Classifieds are more like real advertisements and are kept in a database that you can search through.

Bulletin Boards

To get to the Bulletin Boards, double-click the listing named BUY & SELL! Bulletin Boards. The Bulletin Board Ads window opens (see Figure 8-11), and you can see the categories.

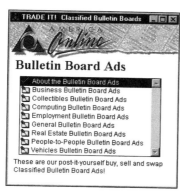

Figure 8-11 The Bulletin Boards are an online trading post where you can buy, sell, or swap items.

Double-click a category that excites your interest and work your way through any additional listings to the category you want to investigate (see Figure 8-12).

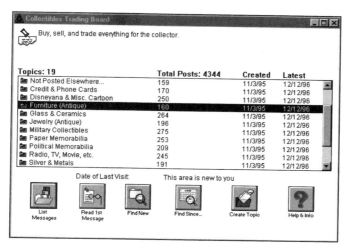

Figure 8-12 Click your way to the right category so that you can begin finding items.

When you arrive at the correct category, double-click to see all the messages about items for sale, as well as requests for items from people who are looking for something to buy.

You are, in fact, not really looking at ads as much as you're reading messages. This is, after all, a bulletin board and in the cyberworld; a bulletin board is a message exchange. People leave messages about items they want to sell. Buyers leave messages in which they explain what they're looking for.

BUYING A BULLETIN BOARD ITEM

If you're interested in an item that's for sale, leave an e-mail message for the seller (his or her e-mail address is posted in the message). After a couple of messages back and forth, you'll probably arrive at a set of terms for price, payment, and shipping.

Use common sense when you buy. Arrange for some kind of C.O.D. delivery instead of sending money in advance. Never send cash. Ask a friend or relative who lives near the seller to visit, inspect, and even pay for and pick up the item.

SELLING A BULLETIN BOARD ITEM

If you have something you want to get rid of, leave a message that describes it in the correct Bulletin Board category. Then wait for the responses.

Use common sense when you sell. It's a good idea to insist on a C.O.D. with a certified check. Ask the seller for the number on that check and the name and telephone number of the bank. Then call the bank to make sure it's real. Instruct the C.O.D. carrier to accept only that check.

Premier Classifieds

Browsing the Premier Classifieds is very much like browsing the Marketplace. You can choose categories to scroll through, or you can use the search function to look for specific items.

To select a category, click the arrow to the right of the Select a Subject box and choose the category that interests you (see Figure 8-13).

The category window lets you narrow your search as you head for the items you need (see Figure 8-14).

Pick a subject, and then double-click the category you want to explore. Continue to double-click items that are of interest. When you find an item you're interested in purchasing, respond to the ad.

TIP   **There is a Respond to Ad button on every item window so you can get in touch with the seller to begin negotiations. Many sellers also place an e-mail address or telephone number within the text of the advertisement. If that occurs, use that method of contacting the seller rather than the respond button.**

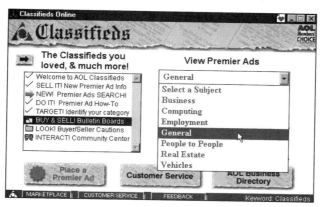

Figure 8-13 A good way to start is to pick the category you want to browse.

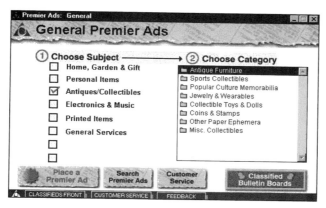

Figure 8-14 When you select a subject, the categories change to match that selection.

To choose a region (if you want to go look at the item), click the arrow to the right of the Select a Region box on the main Classifieds window (see Figure 8-15). If you're not sure where your hometown fits in, choose What Region Am I In, and AOL gives you the right regional category.

If you start your classified shopping knowing exactly what you're looking for, it's probably easier to search for the item directly instead of wending your way through the lists via categories.

At the main Classifieds window, choose Search Premier Ads. When the Search window displays (see Figure 8-16), enter text to describe what you're looking for.

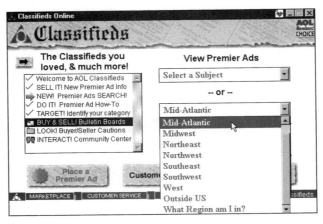

Figure 8-15 Geographical categories are helpful if you want to do your buying or selling in person.

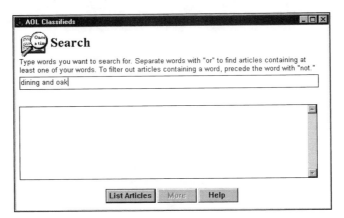

Figure 8-16 Head straight for the item you need without doing any window shopping.

Here are some hints to make your search more productive:

✳ Use the word *and* to make sure that both words are contained in the description of the item. For example, entering **table and oak** avoids all the stuff made out of pine.

✳ Use the word *or* to search for either word. For instance **server or buffet** leads you to that missing piece for your dining room.

✳ Use the word *not* to eliminate a word. For example, **table not oak** results in a search for tables of pine, cherry, mahogany, and so on.

After you enter the appropriate text, choose List Articles. AOL searches for all the matches and presents them. Just double-click an item of interest to see more information about it.

If you have something to sell and you want to use the Premier Ads instead of the Bulletin Board, be aware there's an AOL charge for placing your ad. The charges vary by category, and you can learn the current rates by choosing SELL IT! at the main Classifieds window.

Shopping on the World Wide Web

There's more shopping than the Marketplace and the Classifieds that AOL provides. You can also use AOL to move to the World Wide Web and find more things to buy.

To get there, follow these steps:

1. Go to the Marketplace (use the keyword **Marketplace** or click the shopping basket icon on the Toolbar).

2. Click the Search icon.

3. Select Downtown AOL from the Alphabetical list.

4. Choose Go To Ads - WEB.

Okay, now you may have a problem. Did you see a message like the one in Figure 8-17? Don't panic; read the next section on getting a Web browser. If you don't see a message about browser software, you can skip the next section.

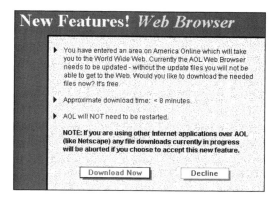

Figure 8-17 This message means that either you don't have the AOL Web Browser software or that the software you do have isn't the current version and needs to be updated.

Getting a Web browser

You can't get to the Web without a Web browser. If you've already browsed the Web through AOL, you can skip this section because you obviously have the browser. Many users don't have the AOL browser because the disk they received in the mail didn't contain it. That's not an error; AOL decided to give you the latest browser software when you visit the Web for the first time.

Choose Download Now to let AOL put the software on your computer.

TIP If you choose Decline, you won't be able to visit the World Wide Web; however, the next time you try to access the Web, you'll see this message again and you can download then.

The software is downloaded, and the progress is noted on the File Transfer window (see Figure 8-18).

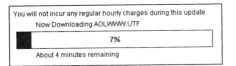

Figure 8-18 It only takes a few minutes to update your AOL software so you can browse the World Wide Web.

After the software is on your computer, you're taken to the Web site you selected.

Browsing the downtown shopping mall

When you arrive downtown (it's a quick trip — much faster than leaving your home to go to the downtown shopping center in your city), you're in the America Online Business Directory (see Figure 8-19).

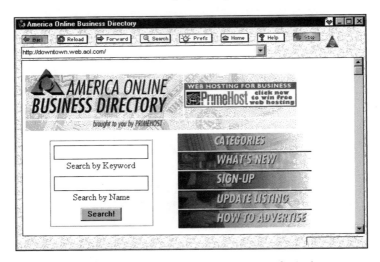

Figure 8-19 Like the AOL Marketplace, you can find what you're looking for by searching categories or by entering a search word.

Don't worry about the name of this AOL window; there's more to buy than business supplies. The businesses referred to are the stores that want you to shop in this online mall. So, start shopping.

＊ If you know the keyword for the store or shopping area you want to visit, enter it in the Search by Keyword box and then select Search!

* If you know exactly what item you're looking for, enter it in the Search by Name box and then choose Search!
* If you want to browse, choose Categories.

Personally, I like window shopping; whenever I'm in this situation, I choose Categories. From there on, it's like the Marketplace. Pick a category, and select the places where you want to shop (see Figure 8-20).

There's no shopping cart when you shop downtown. Each store offers its own method for purchasing goods. Sometimes there's a phone number or fax number to use, and sometimes there's a way to send e-mail to the store and have them get back to you.

Figure 8-20   Yeah, right — dream on!

BONUS

You can buy items all over AOL, not just in the malls and marketplaces. Many of the AOL areas offer items or services for sale. They're usually featured icons in an area's window. You can find them everywhere, even in the news areas.

There are some services in the Marketplace in addition to products to buy, and you might want to browse through them.

* Select Car Pricing Guide from the Alphabetical listing in the Marketplace directory to learn about a service that tells you all the inside stuff about new cars. You can see the dealer's price, projected trade-in values, ratings

on various aspects of the cars, and even a history of the model's collision and injury rates.

* There are lots of financial services available, from brokerages to direct information about purchasing funds.

* Visit the Shopologist, a woman who was born to shop and who lives to shop. She has a service that lets you take advantage of her shopping expertise.

How's your luck? Do you play the lottery and win? When there's an event with door prizes, do you go home with one? Well, keep an eye out for contests in the Marketplace as well as other AOL areas. Sometimes the contests are based on luck, like a raffle, and sometimes it's a real contest and you have to answer a trivia question in order to win.

Summary

Online shopping is a way to get what you need without any of the stress and bother involved in real shopping. You don't have to take the kids (or get a baby-sitter to avoid taking the kids), you don't burn gas, and you don't have to walk through the rain or heat from the parking lot.

Don't forget to read the caveats and the guarantees from AOL and the merchants who sell goods and services.

FINDING STUFF FOR KIDS

9

IN THIS CHAPTER YOU LEARN THESE KEY SKILLS

AOL is full of stuff for children. There are sections that kids can visit and sections that parents can visit to download or purchase items for their children. The AOL areas designed especially (and really, exclusively) for kids are easy to use, and there aren't any youngsters who can't figure the whole thing out in a matter of a few moments. Thereafter, they plunge in and enjoy themselves online.

Most of the areas designed for kids require some reading ability, and it's probably safe to assume that any elementary school or middle school child can handle it all with no problems. For younger children, or children who haven't learned to sound out new words yet, AOL is still a lot of fun. It just takes a little help from Mom or Dad (who should be in the chair next to junior, but who should also keep their fingers away from the keyboard, because letting the kids do it themselves is a great learning exercise).

This chapter takes you on a quick tour of the AOL sites for kids and concludes by helping you gain some control over your children's activities while they're online.

Visiting the Kids Only Area

AOL has an area exclusively for children called Kids Only. I figure you'll want to visit it first before you let the kids romp through it. There are two ways to get there:

* Use the keyword **Kids Only**.
* Click the Kids Only button on the Channels window.

When you arrive, there's plenty to do and plenty to look at (see Figure 9-1).

Figure 9-1 This sure is different from the Dick and Jane books I had when I was a kid.

The Kids Only site is a fun-packed place to visit, but don't be fooled, it's not fluff and silliness. There's plenty of value in some of the activities provided here.

Playing games

Yes, I know, if it were up to you, you'd head right for the reference section and show the kids how to get help for their homework. But let's do it the way the kids would — single-click the Games icon and see what appears (see Figure 9-2).

The full selection of games is in the list box named Play it Now! Double-click the one you want to try. When you go to the games area, you have to redefine your concept of a game. Many of the listings in the Play it Now! box aren't really games, but they're still fun.

For example, double-click Daily Affirmations, and then choose Get Affirmed (the other choice is No, Thanks). A pithy phrase of advice appears (see Figure 9-3); if you want more advice (some phrases qualify more as suggestions than advice), keep clicking Get Affirmed.

Figure 9-2 Having all these games to play online keeps kids off the streets.

Figure 9-3 Hopefully your kids understand humor and don't take things too literally.

There are fortune cookies to read, places to ask for advice (there's even a love counselor), and other non-competitive activities.

Of course, if you're into competitive activities, there are some real games. Sometimes you play others online; sometimes you just play against yourself. For an example of the latter, the Quest Test is a word game (see Figure 9-4). It's like a famous television game except there's nobody with blonde hair turning around the letters and there aren't two other contestants standing next to you.

There are several trivia games available that can be played online. There's Trivia (see Figure 9-5), Sports Trivia, Marvel Comics Trivia, and Nickelodeon Trivia. There's also News Hound Trivia, but it's not played against other people; you just answer questions for the sheer satisfaction of it.

Figure 9-4 An eight-year-old helped me with this puzzle after I guessed a couple of wrong letters.

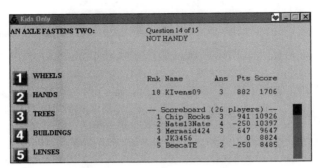

Figure 9-5 Online games go on forever. Each time you join in, you get a chance to score more points than the other players.

There are also online games that are played in chat rooms. They're scheduled for evening hours (probably to eliminate the temptation to cut school), and there's a host, a scorekeeper, and rules. Your kids can check out the schedules and plan to finish homework and chores early to accommodate the game times (see Figure 9-6).

Figure 9-6 We decided to get the dinner dishes cleaned up quickly so we can come back this evening for the Crazy Words game.

You're not restricted to playing online; you can download games to your computer and then play whenever you want. Click the appropriate GameGrabber icon (there's one for Mac Games and one for PC Games) to see what's available (see Figure 9-7).

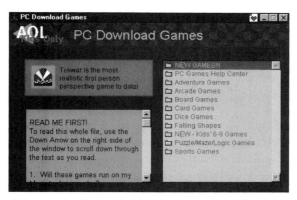

Figure 9-7   Get something for those times the kids whine "I don't have anything to do."

Getting creative

Click the Create icon on the main Kids Only window to move to Kids Only Create, which is filled with artsy-craftsy stuff (see Figure 9-8).

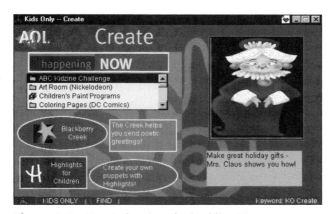

Figure 9-8   Here's the place for budding Picassos.

The happening NOW list box displays the full range of activities. Scroll through it and double-click the activity that looks most interesting. The icons on the window are the currently featured stuff, and they change from time to time.

For those incipient Judy Blumes, there are places to practice creative writing. For instance, Extremely Tall Tales starts a story that you have to finish (see Figure 9-9).

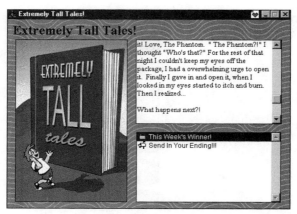

Figure 9-9 What do you imagine could have been in that package?

Extremely Tall Tales has a chat room and message boards so kids can discuss their writing efforts. The same people (ABC Kidzine) run the Express Yourself Café, where kids can send poems, stories, and artwork and get back some gentle hints and tips on making the work better. In fact, ABC Kidzine has a number of entries in Kids Only Create, and they're quite well done in addition to being lots of fun.

Another multiple contributor to this AOL area is Nickelodeon. There's an art gallery (kids can upload their creations), a political poster gallery (more interesting than the stuff on the telephone poles in my neighborhood), and a Nicktionary (kids invent words and explain the definitions). There's also an ongoing interactive story where, at climactic points in the plot, you can choose what the protagonist does. The next part of the story changes depending upon your choice.

Blackberry Creek is a little town in cyberspace, located in Kids Only Create (see Figure 9-10). It's chock-full of creative things to do. There are also message boards and a chat room so kids who visit Blackberry Creek can talk to other visiting urchins.

Remember *Highlights for Children*? I'll bet you read it in elementary school. They're still here, and they have an online presence in Kids Only Create (see Figure 9-11).

The *Highlights for Children* area is really impressive. Besides the stories, games, puzzles, and things to make (all of which also teach by presenting information in an amusing way) there's a message board so kids can talk to each other. Personally, I enjoy the puzzles (see Figure 9-12).

The icons and listings shown in the Kids Only Create window may not be the same when you visit that area. There are occasional changes in the makeup of that AOL section.

Figure 9-10 You never run out of things to do when you're in Blackberry Creek.

Figure 9-11 Each icon leads to another area with more icons, plenty of listings, and so many things to do that there's no chance for boredom.

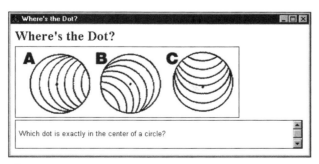

Figure 9-12 Give up? It's B.

Sporting around

Kids and sports are a natural fit, so of course there's a sports section in the Kids Only area. Click its icon in the main Kids Only window to visit (see Figure 9-13).

Figure 9-13   All the action's right here.

The choices are wide and far-reaching, so all kids (and parents) can find something interesting to do.

You can choose your favorite sport by clicking its icon. The list box that displays on-screen has all sorts of information about that sport (see Figure 9-14).

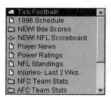

Figure 9-14   Enough scores, stats, news, and schedules to make any fan happy.

Click the More Sports icon to fill your desire to know everything about bungee jumping, soccer, jet skiing, windsurfing, or any other athletic endeavor you can think of.

You should take a tour of all the icons on the Sports window:

* The Stars icon leads to photos, biographies, and interviews of major sports figures.
* The Play It icon offers tips for playing better, covering all sorts of sports (even sports such as dancing and Frisbee in addition to the standard sports). You can also leave a question for Coach Jim, who'll be glad to get back to you with an answer/tip.
* The Games icon has some trivia games, but the main attractions are the polls that encourage you to vote for your favorite players and teams.

This site has plenty of pictures and information that kids can download and then print out to help educate friends about all this data.

Holding club meetings

Kids love clubs — the exclusivity and the feeling of belonging is an important part of childhood. There aren't many kids who can climb into a treehouse, invite a couple of neighborhood kids, and form a club. So, AOL Kids Only provides the clubhouses and the atmosphere (see Figure 9-15).

Figure 9-15   Enter a clubhouse to share information and friendship with kids who share your interests.

Clubs are grouped around interests, and in the Kids Only area, there are some wide interests and some that are more narrow. These clubs may change from time to time, depending on the interests of the kids who sign on, so your Clubs window may look different.

VISIT A CLUBHOUSE

Entering a clubhouse brings up a window like the one shown in Figure 9-16. Except for Pen Pals, all the clubs operate with the same choices.

Figure 9-16   Besides participating in club meetings and activities, you can download files and enter contests.

In the clubhouse, there are plenty of things to do.

* Join the club with a click of the mouse. There aren't any dues, membership requirements, or questionnaires.

* Meet the members in a message forum where you can enter information about yourself, your interests, and your opinion about computing topics.

* Check out the important club stuff to learn how the club rules work (the kids set the rules) and how to participate in the club's direction (the message board).

* Browse the trading post where other kids have uploaded graphics and files for you to put on your computer. When you have something to share, upload a file.

* Visit the chat room when it's open. The club chat rooms have limited hours, and the schedule is available when you click the icon named Club Chat.

The left side of the Club window has an icon for the featured club service. Click the icon to visit — you're usually greeted by some interesting sound effects (see Figure 9-17).

Figure 9-17   There's so much to do in the featured section that there's no chance of boredom.

There's plenty of opportunity for interactive participation — don't forget to sign up for any free newsletters.

FIND A PEN PAL

The Pen Pals section is a message board that has messages from kids who are looking for pen pals. Usually the message is directed at kids who share the same interest, and you'll see sections concentrating on sports, computing, games, and other things kids find interesting. There are also plenty of kids who are looking for pen pals that live nearby, so if you want a chance to meet your pen pal, post a message to someone in your state.

If you don't see pen pals with your interests, leave your own message and announce that you want to talk to folks who think like you do.

START YOUR OWN CLUB

If you have an interesting hobby (it would have to be interesting enough to have that interest shared by plenty of other people), click the Start a Club icon. The rules for beginning a new club are there as well as a reminder about the work you might have to do to get it started. This is a great way for kids to assume responsibility and get the rewards for doing something.

Getting homework help

The homework section of Kids Only is chock-full of reference material and interactive resources (see Figure 9-18).

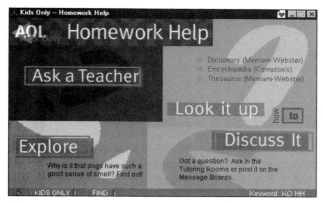

Figure 9-18 There's a learning method to match a child's needs in the Homework Help area of Kids Only.

The basic reference materials are well-known volumes:

* Use the Merriam-Webster Dictionary to check definitions.
* Compton's Encyclopedia offers a couple of methods for finding information: you can go through the Table of Contents or enter a word (or phrase) to search all the contents.
* The Merriam-Webster Thesaurus works by entering a word and then looking up its synonyms and antonyms.

TIP Unfortunately, spelling counts. You can't use the dictionary to check spelling because if you misspell a word you're told it doesn't exist. The dictionary is for definitions only. The encyclopedia and thesaurus also reject words that aren't spelled correctly.

Choose Discuss It to enter a help room. There are four subject rooms and a general help room (see Figure 9-19).

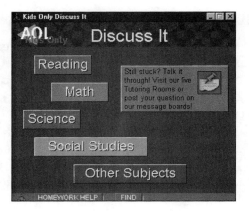

Figure 9-19 You can discuss your homework problems with an expert in one of the tutoring rooms.

The four subject rooms have limited hours (late afternoon into the evening). The room called Other Subjects opens whenever someone wants to enter. These are not chat rooms; they are run specifically for homework help, and teachers or other experts respond to the questions you leave.

The Teacher Pager is activated by clicking Ask a Teacher (see Figure 9-20). The answers tend to come fairly rapidly; it's rare to have to wait more than a couple of hours.

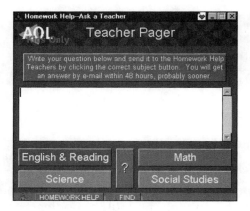

Figure 9-20 Teachers lend a helping hand to the Homework Help section of Kids Only.

It's handy to have this feature, but don't let the young students in your household rely on it too much. Nothing beats the experience of visiting a library and getting to know about (and love) books, whether they're reference books or fiction.

Seeing stars

Choose Shows and Stars to enter the exciting area of show biz (see Figure 9-21).

Figure 9-21 Shows, stars, games, and contests abound.

The Cartoon Network is a plethora of resources for the enduring cartoon characters that kids love. The Jetsons and the Flintstones live here, and — yabba dabba do — you can play games with them, see their histories, and collect pictures.

Ringling Bros. Circus has the Greatest Show on Earth, and it's filled with interactive activities, information about circus characters and animals, and contests.

Nickelodeon has a wide variety of activities and information, and it's always a visit worth making.

Click Characters to see more than you ever wanted to know about every character any kid ever knew about. You can read about characters, download pictures, get advice (Goofus and Galant are constantly trying to help), and talk about it all in a chat room.

Learning by Doing

There are a lot of great sites for kids on AOL that make learning fun. Sometimes, kids don't even realize they're getting educated as they play games, enter contests, and read the stuff that's found behind the bold graphics.

There's news for kids on some of the news sites, or you can just let them wander through the stories and headlines available in the periodicals that appear on AOL.

X-REF See Chapter 7 for more information about getting the news from AOL.

And, there are plenty of sites that are either designed for kids or have lots of stuff that is kid-friendly or kid-useful.

Taking a study break

For all those kids who are on AOL for educational purposes (at least while parents are in the room), there's a study break available. Or, if the studying is taking the traditional form of reading textbooks, there's a brain-settling break available by firing up the modem and logging on to AOL. The area is called Study Break (keyword **Study Break**), so it's easy to remember (see Figure 9-22).

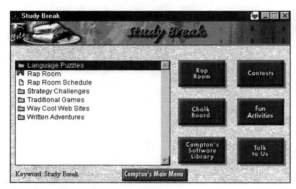

Figure 9-22   It's break time, and the Study Break corner has the diversions you need to clear your brain.

There's plenty to do here, and almost all of it is interactive:

* The Written Adventures listing is a group of games that are a lot of fun, but are pretty tough. (This is a break from studying?)
* The Strategy Challenges and Traditional Games are diversions that can be downloaded to your computer.
* Fun Activities are interesting and challenging things to do. Download the instructions to proceed at your own pace.
* Contests, message boards, and chat rooms round off the site.

The study break is an entertaining, mind-tingling place to visit.

Visiting the reference library

The New York Public Library's desk reference sits in the AOL Reference section, which you can get to by one of these methods:

* Using the keyword **Reference**.
* Clicking the Reference icon on the Channels window.

When you first arrive, the choices seem enormous (see Figure 9-23), but you'll soon become comfortable and work your way through all the features you need.

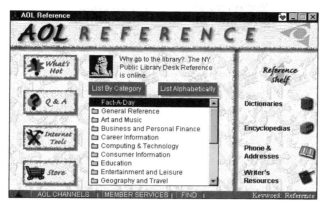

Figure 9-23 Tools that go way beyond the traditional reference books are at your fingertips.

The category listing in the center of the window is an easy way to look for the information you need. If you're not sure what category your problem topic belongs to, click List Alphabetically and see if you can find it that way.

The right side of the window has icons for Dictionaries and Encyclopedias. The plural use of those words is accurate because there are choices for those reference volume types available (including references specifically aimed at kids).

 X-REF For more information about the AOL Reference area, see Chapter 10.

Getting pearls of culture

The Learning & Culture button on the Channels window (keyword **LC**) takes you to an AOL site that contains an almost overwhelming collection of information (see Figure 9-24).

Figure 9-24 This is such an incredible collection of information that I could spend many happy days here.

There is plenty of stuff here for kids, some of it even aimed directly at the younger set. The most obvious places to visit are the items on the Learning list.

* Choose Careers to get a plethora of information about different occupations, résumé writing, retirement planning, and even advice about appropriate behavior at the office.

* Click on Homework Help to enter one of the homework categories, including kids, teens, and college (see the section on homework earlier in this chapter).

* The Courses icon takes you to a wealth of online courses that cover a myriad of subjects. There are lectures, seminars, and even registration fees.

* Click Student Center to reach activity centers for junior high, senior high, and college students. There are also lots of reference volumes available. And, the lockers open to reveal tons of useful information for young people interested in the performing arts.

* Enter the Educator's Network to find teachers who will help with homework. And, there's a collection of Barron's Booknotes (for when you have a book report due and haven't really read the book).

* Click Reference Desk to get to the AOL Reference area (discussed earlier in this chapter).

* The Science & Nature icon takes you to information about the environment, astronomy, math, space, and other scientific subjects. You can visit the Lab to get information via message boards and chat rooms.

The Culture half of the Learning & Culture area has plenty of information that kids will enjoy gathering.

 For more information on the Culture topics, see Chapter 11.

Finding the Fun Stuff

Sometimes kids use AOL just for fun. There's plenty of amusement available, and you'll be surprised at what some young people go for if you give them free rein.

Playing games

Many kids head right for the Games area (see Figure 9-25). You get there by either one of these routes:

* Use the keyword **Games**.
* Click the Games icon on the Channels window.

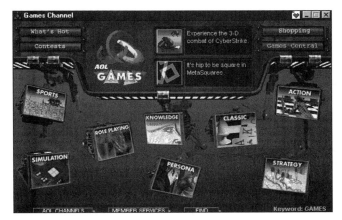

Figure 9-25 The fun's here — c'mon in.

Each icon leads to games in that icon's category. Besides playing games, you can chat, contact the companies that made the games (for support), download games, and buy games.

Relaxing with music

Well, not all music is relaxing to everybody — some of the music kids listen to doesn't exactly put me into a placid and tranquil state. But eventually, almost every kid heads for the music area by one of these routes:

* Enter the keyword **Music**.
* Choose the Music Space icon on the Channels window.

Once there, the choices are encompassing, so everybody's taste can be met (even mine, and I'm pretty fussy). There are icons for different types of music and listings for specific activities related to the world of music (see Figure 9-26).

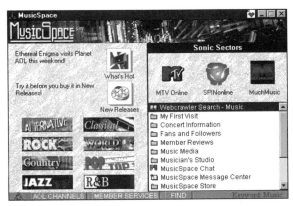

Figure 9-26 Maybe you can get your children to try
something new, like classical music.

In the Music Space, you'll find information about new releases, concert schedules, gossip about performers, chat rooms, message boards, music to download, and music to buy. MTV has a large presence here (which seemed to act as sort of a seal of approval for the kids I showed this area to).

Imposing Controls and Guidelines

One of the important issues for parents is controlling what their kids can see and do while they're online. All online services are free to display whatever they want to, and the market controls what's out there. If there's a market for information, that information will be made available, and the United States Constitution guarantees that freedom. Sometimes, however, that information is something you'd prefer to keep hidden from your children.

Remember that AOL is not the only place your children can visit in cyberspace; they can use AOL to move to the Internet, where there may be a great deal more variety in the subject matter. The Internet is not governed — there's no organization in charge. Therefore, there's no place to complain to, and you'll have to deal with controls either through limiting access to the Internet with AOL controls or by controlling your children's behavior directly.

Also, sometimes children run into situations that might be bothersome or even dangerous. It's important to help them recognize those events and deal with them properly.

This section covers the important issues parents have to know about and explain to their children.

Using Parental Controls

AOL has provided features that let you control the access your child has so that you can limit children to certain areas on AOL. You can use the built-in controls or customize controls for each child.

BUILT-IN CONTROLS

To make use of the Parental Control feature by limiting access with the built-in controls offered by AOL, follow these steps:

1. Make sure you are logged on to AOL with your Master account screen name.

2. Use the keyword **Parental Controls** to reach the Parental Controls window (see Figure 9-27).

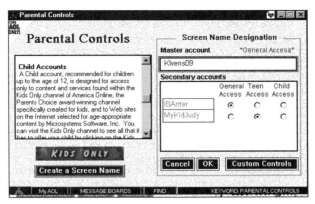

Figure 9-27 Use the Parental Controls window to create limits on your children's access of AOL areas.

3. If you already have a secondary account for a child, select Teen Access or Child Access by clicking the appropriate button next to the child's screen name. Briefly, the controls are:

* **Teen Access** imposes controls only on the Internet Web sites that are reached through AOL. Sites (approved by an independent arbiter) for teenagers (up to the age of 16) and newsgroups that don't permit file attachments are considered safe for this group and are accessible.

* **Child Access** limits AOL visits to the Kids Only channel and all its sub-areas. No Instant Message can be sent or received while the child is online, and no file attachments are permitted for e-mail. Chat rooms that are created by members are not accessible.

4. If the child does not have an account, choose Create a Screen Name and then choose Create a Screen Name from the Screen Names window to get to the Screen Name window (see Figure 9-28).

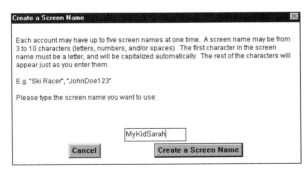

Figure 9-28 To use AOL with controlled access, a child needs his or her own screen name.

5. Enter a screen name for this child and then click Create a Screen Name.

6. Enter a password for this screen name, press Tab and enter the password again, then choose Set Password.

7. At the Parental Control window, select the appropriate access control: General, Teen, or Child. Then choose OK.

8. AOL notifies you that the name has been added to your account. Click OK. The AOL "voice" notifies you that you have mail waiting (if you don't have a sound card and can't hear it, trust me, you have mail waiting). You can go to your mailbox and read a message from AOL about parental controls.

9. Close the Screen Name window to return to the Parental Controls window.

When your child logs on with this screen name, the controls you've imposed are in effect (don't forget to tell your kid the password — or let your children invent their own passwords).

CUSTOM CONTROLS

You can create your own controls if you don't want to use those designed by AOL. To accomplish this:

1. Follow steps 1 and 2 above to get to the Parental Controls window.

2. Choose Custom Controls to bring up the Custom Controls window (see Figure 9-29).

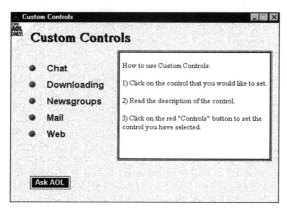

Figure 9-29   Choose one or more areas of cyberspace and impose controls on access.

3. Choose an AOL area to manipulate.

4. Read the description of the area and then click the red Controls button.

5. Select controls for each Screen Name as needed (see Figure 9-30).

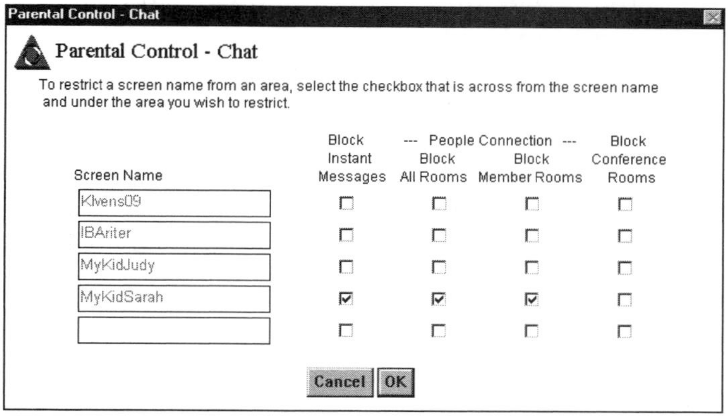

Parental Control - Chat

To restrict a screen name from an area, select the checkbox that is across from the screen name and under the area you wish to restrict.

Screen Name	Block Instant Messages	--- People Connection --- Block All Rooms	Block Member Rooms	Block Conference Rooms
Klvens09	☐	☐	☐	☐
IBAriter	☐	☐	☐	☐
MyKidJudy	☐	☐	☐	☐
MyKidSarah	☑	☑	☑	☐
	☐	☐	☐	☐

Cancel OK

Figure 9-30   Control access to this area by selecting restrictions. If you've used built-in controls, you'll find some restrictions already in place.

6. Choose OK. AOL notifies you that your new settings have been saved.

7. Repeat the process to impose controls for other areas.

The controls you set for a Screen Name take effect the next time that Screen Name logs on to AOL.

Helping kids cope with problems

No matter how many controls you impose on access, kids can run into troublesome situations. E-mail from strangers can be badgering or insulting — or worse. A site that depicts gratuitous violence should be considered as obscene and disturbing as sexually explicit material.

You can help your kids cope with some of the potential or real problems that are a risk in cyberspace. Have a frank conversation that explains what's appropriate and what's not.

✳ Make it a firm rule that your child never provides personal information to any other AOL user. No real names (use screen names that don't reveal your last name), no addresses, no telephone numbers, no school names — nothing that can let another user track down your child.

✳ Make sure your child understands that making arrangements to meet someone in person is never permitted.

✳ Let your child know that if anything occurs in a chat room that makes him or her uncomfortable, he or she should leave the chat room immediately.

✳ Instruct your child not to respond to any message that is disturbing and to notify you immediately if such a message is received.

TIP One of the negative side effects of online communication is that the question "What's in a name?" has no answer. You can't tell anything about a person from a screen name. Even the screen name Mary doesn't necessarily mean you're communicating with a female. There are, unfortunately, predatory people everywhere. Remind your children that just because the contents of a message or the name on a message says there's a nice lady or a little girl trying to communicate, there's no way to know for sure.

In addition to having conversations about these topics, keep an eye on your children as they use AOL. Know where they go; know what they do. If they get annoyed at your "spying," ask them for help. Because most kids believe that most adults don't know their way around computers (and also believe that they're too old to learn), it's usually easy to make your child believe you need help. A simple request such as "Duh... show me what your favorite places are and how you get there and what you do" frequently works just fine.

BONUS

Kids can get into some uncomfortable situations in message boards. Sometimes people get nasty or snotty, or they make fun of people who don't have a high level of knowledge about a subject under discussion. Worse, there are people who just lash out with personal attacks. You can help your children cope with this by learning how to respond (or not respond):

* If a person is continuously nasty and is directing abasing comments at your child (either specifically, or in addition to attacking others), it's okay to ignore it.

* If you have a child who finds it difficult to let things like this go unchallenged, explain that fanning flames keeps the fire going. Sometimes a more subtle confrontation (such as "Feel better now?") quiets things down.

* Make sure your child understands that asking questions is normal and that it's okay to ignore responses that belittle his or her lack of knowledge. A response of "That's why I asked the question" or no response at all is appropriate.

Reporting problems

If your child encounters a serious problem in a chat room, you can notify AOL of it. It requires collecting a bit of information, so it might be a good idea to look at the Problem Report window now, before you have to use it. Then you can be prepared to report a problem when the need arises.

To report problems, follow these steps:

1. Choose People Connection from the Channels window (or click the People Connection icon on the Toolbar).

2. When the People Connection window opens (you'll be in a chat room, and it doesn't matter which chat room you're in), click Notify AOL.

3. The form for AOL notification displays on-screen (see Figure 9-31). Note the steps you take, which are spelled out for you.

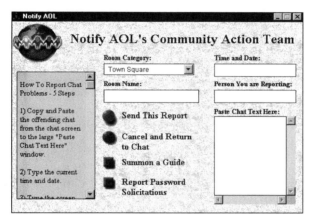

Figure 9-31 Just take it one step at a time when you want to report a problem to AOL.

If a problem occurs, you just have to be sure you've gathered the necessary information, and then you can follow these steps.

You can also summon help or leave a note for AOL by entering the keyword **Guidepager**. This brings up the Guidepager window, which offers a number of alternatives for requesting help (see Figure 9-32).

Figure 9-32 Page a Guide when you want help from AOL because of a disturbing incident.

Parenting

If you are interested enough in kids on AOL to read this chapter, you're probably a parent. There's a great section for parents on AOL you might want to visit. Okay, it's really for moms, but I don't think dads get tossed out. It's called Moms Online (keyword **Moms Online**), and it deals with child raising from infancy up.

There's an online publication (Ma'Zine) that's filled with stories, humor, advice, reviews, and polls. There are chat rooms, message boards, and online shopping sites.

Moms Online is an area in the Families section of AOL (keyword **Families**), where you can find plenty of support for surviving parenthood.

Summary

Kids and online services find each other — they seem to go together. If given access to a computer and modem, most children will learn to use them as if the knowledge were genetic. There's almost no way to prevent kids from wanting to get online and play around with everything in sight. The AOL controls give parents an opportunity to limit what's in sight. What AOL can't control easily is the way children behave once they're interacting with others online. Parents have to guide their children's behavior online the same way they guide behavior in any other social situation.

BROWSING THE REFERENCE STACKS

IN THIS CHAPTER YOU LEARN THESE KEY SKILLS

ref*er*ence (noun) First appeared 1589: one referred to or consulted: as (1) : a source of information (as a book or passage) to which a reader or consulter is referred (2) : a work (as a dictionary or encyclopedia) containing useful facts or information.

Okay, is everyone clear on what this chapter's about? Good. Please pay attention and take notes; there may be a quiz afterward. To start with, that definition of the word *reference* comes from the Merriam-Webster Dictionary, which is part of AOL's extensive Reference Channel.

Whether you're fifteen or fifty, there always comes a time when you need to do some research. There's no question that anyone who is still in school (from grade school up) requires an understanding of, and access to, good reference material. Term papers, special projects, and exams can be fun and rewarding when done with the proper tools. Hmm. You're not buying the "fun" part, eh? How about more fun than catching lizards with your teeth? The bottom line is that whether you're writing a paper for school or a speech for the sales convention, or you're looking into the viability of opening a paper clip plant in Botswana, sooner or later you're going to need a good reference library. It just so happens that the AOL Reference Channel provides a large selection of material on everything from sign language to space travel.

Getting Started

Before delving into the specifics of what the Reference Channel has to offer, it might be a good idea to take a quick tour and get an overview of the type and breadth of material you can find there. The first step is to get to the Reference Channel — simple enough. If you have the Channels screen in front of you, click the Reference button and you're on your way. Otherwise, click the Keyword button on the Toolbar, type in **reference**, and press Enter. Either way, you end up at the AOL Reference window (see Figure 10-1).

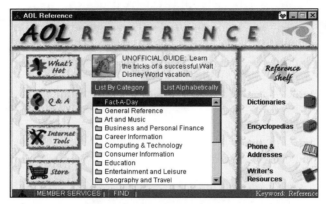

Figure 10-1   The Reference Channel is the best place to start research on any topic.

Displaying lists of resources

In the center of the AOL Reference window, you find the list of resource categories available. This is a quick way to narrow your search for source material. If you are writing a term paper on the fall of the Roman Empire, then head for the History and Religion category. To access a list of sources available in a category, double-click the category listing.

Reference Shelf

The Reference Shelf, found on the right side of the AOL Preference window, provides shortcuts to several different types of general reference resources. Dictionaries (see Figure 10-2) includes links to over nineteen different dictionaries and thesauruses (thesauri, if you prefer).

The Encyclopedias shortcut provides access to three major encyclopedic resources: Compton's Living Encyclopedia, The Columbia Concise Encyclopedia, and the Grolier Multimedia Encyclopedia (see Figure 10-3).

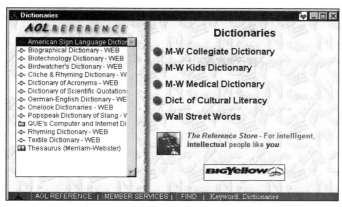

Figure 10-2 Spend some time in the Dictionaries area and go to the head of the class.

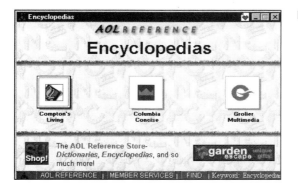

Figure 10-3 These encyclopedias not only present information, they bring it to life.

The Phone & Addresses area (see Figure 10-4), among other things, contains Yellow Page listings, White Page listings, 800 number listings, and a zip code directory.

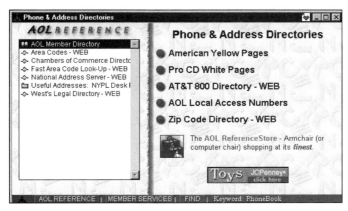

Figure 10-4 Let your mouse do the walking.

Last, but not least, is the Writer's Resources link (see Figure 10-5) that includes lots of good stuff for beginning and professional writers alike.

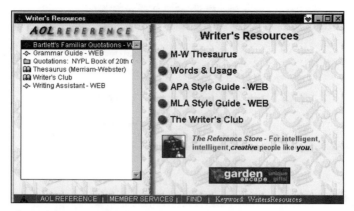

Figure 10-5 A good writer is never at a loss for words.

What's Hot

 What's Hot (see Figure 10-6) is actually a jumble of new and interesting stuff. There's a list of new Web links, the Quote of the Day, a link to sign up for the Reference Newsletter, and more.

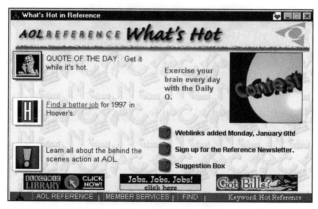

Figure 10-6 It's worth a quick check to see what's new.

Q&A

The Reference Q&A area (see Figure 10-7) includes questions and answers from experts in fields as widespread as money, medicine, and mechanics. You can also find the Reference Message Boards here, as well as a list of Frequently Asked Questions (FAQ) about the Reference Channel.

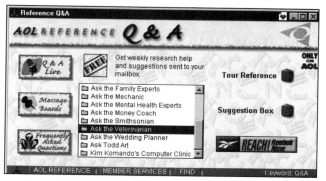

Figure 10-7 Go to Ask the Veterinarian and get your answer straight from the horse doctor's mouth.

Internet Tools

WEB PATH Although there is always a heated debate going on somewhere about the Internet, the one thing everyone agrees on is that it has plenty of information to offer. As a matter of fact, it often seems that it has too much information. In reality, it is not the amount of information that is problematic, but rather the ability to find the information you need. That's where AOL's Internet Tools area (see Figure 10-8) comes to the rescue.

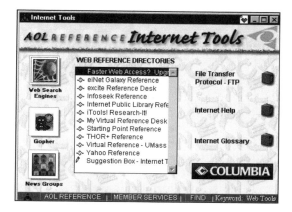

Figure 10-8 Harness the Internet's wealth of reference information with Internet Tools.

The AOL Reference Store

If you're not satisfied with the reference information available online, you can always stop by the AOL Reference Store (see Figure 10-9) and pick up a book, CD, or report from among the many products offered there.

 For more information on shopping on AOL, be sure to read Chapter 8.

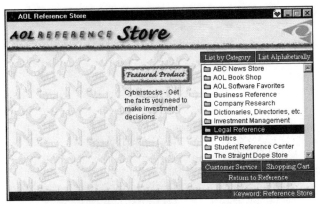

Figure 10-9 You can load your shopping cart with plenty of reference goodies at the AOL Reference Store.

Using the Reference Resources

Because the volume of material available on AOL is so vast, and because the needs of one researcher are usually different from the next, I've decided to cover only three major areas of research. The first is, of course, education. A student without reference material, like a sailor without limes, is bound to be somewhat rickety. The second area of reference resources covered is business. Home reference material is the third category explored.

Hitting the books

The most obvious use of reference material is in the pursuit of education. Everyone who attends school, at one time or another, is given a project that requires research. From the fourth-grader writing a one-page paper on his favorite historical figure to the doctoral candidate completing her thesis on the economic and social consequences of diminishing oil and gas industry activity on Alaskan communities, people require access to reference material. Although their needs may be different, everyone can find useful information on the AOL Reference Channel. Some of the resources that students can find on the Reference Channel include the ones discussed in the following sections.

COMPTON'S EDUCATION CONNECTION

In addition to the Compton's Living Encyclopedia, which can be accessed through the Encyclopedia shortcut of the Reference Shelf, Compton's also provides an area called the Education Connection.

The Education Connection can be accessed by following these steps:

1. From the Toolbar, click the Keyword button.

2. Type in **education connection**.

3. Press Enter to open the Education Connection window (see Figure 10-10).

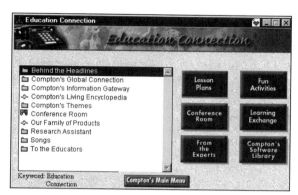

Figure 10-10   The Education Connection is a great educational area for student and teacher alike.

The following are just a few of the useful tools that can be found at Compton's Education Connection:

* **Compton's Global Connection.** A world map with links to information relating to each of the seven continents (see Figure 10-11). By selecting a continent, the user opens a window with links to related Web sites, bulletin boards, and the Compton's Encyclopedia for that continent.

Figure 10-11   The Global Connection is an excellent tool for geography and history students.

* **Compton's Information Gateway.** Here you find a listing of recommended educational Web sites.

✴ **Research Assistant.** This handy tool provides a basic tutorial on how to do effective research. It offers suggestions on how to organize your research and where to find information, and it offers tools to use in compiling your information.

SCIENTIFIC AMERICAN ONLINE

Since its inception in 1845, Scientific American has been one of the leading journals of science in the world. Professional scientists and laymen both can find useful and interesting information here. In addition to current and back issues of Scientific American, you can also access the company's medical publications.

To access Scientific American Online, follow these steps:

1. Click the Keyword button on the Toolbar.

2. In the Enter Word(s): text box, type **SciAm**.

3. Press Enter to open the Scientific American Online window (see Figure 10-12).

Figure 10-12   Keep up with the latest developments in science and medicine at Scientific American Online.

THE NEW YORK PUBLIC LIBRARY DESK REFERENCE

Compiled using the research questions most frequently asked of the New York Public Library staff, this reference tool covers 26 different categories, ranging from first aid to foreign aid.

To open the New York Public Library (NYPL) Desk Reference:

1. From the Toolbar, click the Keyword button.

2. Type **nypl** in the Enter Word(s): text box.

3. Press Enter to access the primary New York Public Library Desk Reference window (see Figure 10-13).

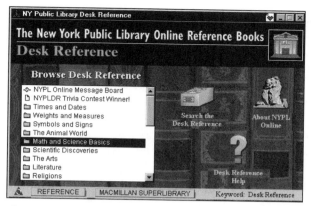

Figure 10-13   You don't have to fight the traffic to use this New York Public Library resource.

Taking care of business

I'll bet that when you finally graduated and got a "real" job, you breathed a sigh of relief. You probably figured that you had escaped the clutches of academia and could relegate thoughts of school to looking forward to future reunions. Well, if you've been working for any length of time, you've undoubtedly realized that nothing could be further from the truth. If you want to get ahead today, you must keep learning and improving your skills, no matter what they are. That means taking classes or studying at home in your spare time.

Then, of course, there are those extra projects. Although they are above and beyond the call of duty, these projects play a significant role in advancing your career. So, far from eliminating the need for access to research material, being a part of the business community means that good reference resources are just as important as ever.

HOOVER'S BUSINESS RESOURCES

Whether you're a potential investor, looking for a job, or need to research the competition, Hoover's Business Resources provides extensive information on business and industry worldwide. With financial and operating data on close to 10,000 companies, this is the perfect place to start your research.

To access Hoover's Business Resources, follow these steps:

1. Click the Keyword button on the Toolbar.

2. Type **hoovers** in the Enter Word(s): text box.

3. Press Enter to open the Hoover's Business Resources primary window (see Figure 10-14).

Figure 10-14 You'll find everything but the CEO's shoe size here.

Among the information available at Hoover's Business Resources, you can find these tools and more:

* **Hoover's Company Information Center.** Type a company name and search any of Hoover's various resources for information.

* **Hoover's Cyberstocks.** A Hoover-sponsored Web page featuring information and news on companies involved in the Internet.

* **IPO Central & This Week's IPOs.** If you want to get in on the hot IPO action, be sure to make a stop here. You'll find a listing of the latest companies that have filed to go public.

* **Plunkett's Almanacs.** Company profiles of the top U.S. employers. Information includes sales and profit ranking, contact information, financial data, and salary and benefit information.

COMPANY NEWS

To stay ahead of the competition, it is important to know what is happening in the business world every day. AOL's Company News area (see Figure 10-15) is a great resource to keep you informed of the latest events in the business community. It provides access to news articles from Reuters (RTR), PR NewsWire (PRN), and Business Wire (BSW) that have been published within the preceding thirty days. To open the Company News window, use the keyword search **company news**.

Not only can you search by individual company, but you can also set up a personal portfolio to automatically capture only the news you specify. In addition to the archives, you can view current market news and perform company research (see Figure 10-16).

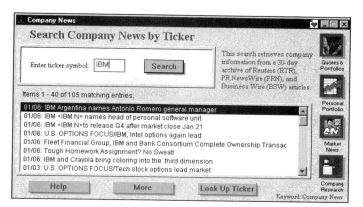

Figure 10-15 Stay on top of your profession by staying on top of the news.

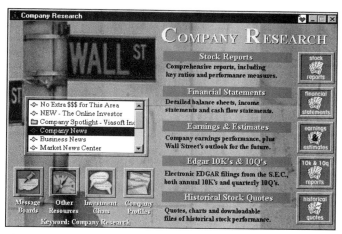

Figure 10-16 Get the bottom line on thousands of companies worldwide.

YOUR BUSINESS

The small business owner is the backbone of this country's economy and has to work just as hard as the big players to stay in the game. Although the needs of the entrepreneurs may differ from those of the corporate giants, they too require good resources. If you run a small business or are thinking about opening one, AOL's Your Business area should be your first stop.

To access Your Business, follow these steps:

1. Click the Keyword button on the Toolbar.

2. In the Enter Word(s): text box, type **your business**.

3. Press Enter to open the AOL's Your Business: Front Page window (see Figure 10-17).

Figure 10-17 If you're planning a new business, do your homework first.

Here you can find information on Chambers of Commerce, federal resources, financing information, marketing tools, and more.

Helping out around the house

Although you generally don't do the kind of extensive research around the house that you do for school or work, there is still a tremendous need for reference resources. It is comforting to have a first aid reference and a poison control listing around when you have small children. Home improvement, personal finances, legal issues, consumer questions, and other such matters arise in the home environment on a regular basis. If you have access to AOL's Reference Channel, the answers to many of those questions are just a couple of mouse clicks away.

NEW YORK PUBLIC LIBRARY DESK REFERENCE — FIRST AID

It is very often the first few minutes of an emergency that are critical to the victim of serious injury. Did you know that bleeding can cause death in as little as five minutes if the source is a large artery? How would you stop the bleeding without causing further injury? What should you do if someone stops breathing? When is it safe to move a health emergency victim? The First Aid section of the NYPL Desk Reference contains the answers to these questions and more.

To access the NYPL First Aid area, follow these steps:

1. From the Toolbar, click the Keyword button.

2. In the Enter Word(s): text box, type **nypl**.

3. Press Enter to open the NYPL Desk Reference window.

4. From the category list, double-click First Aid to open the First Aid window (see Figure 10-18).

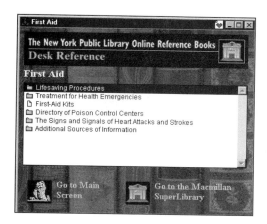

Figure 10-18 Having the right reference tool handy might make a critical difference.

CONSUMER REPORTS

As a nation of consumers, there is one reference no one should be without. That is, of course, *Consumer Reports*. With the phenomenal number of products and the amount of marketing hype surrounding them, it is difficult to make intelligent buying decisions without doing a little research. Whether it's cars, stereos, or home insurance, there's hardly a product that *Consumer Reports* doesn't cover.

To access the Consumer Reports area:

1. Click the Keyword button on the Toolbar.

2. Type **consumer reports** in the Enter Word(s): text box.

3. Press Enter to open the Consumer Reports window (see Figure 10-19)

Figure 10-19 To buy or not to buy? With Consumer Reports, the answer's easy.

NOLO PRESS SELF-HELP LAW CENTER

There are many times when a simple legal question does not require the services of a two-hundred-dollar-an-hour lawyer. But, where do you turn when you need legal advice? If you're on AOL, the answer's easy: the Nolo Press Self-Help Law Center. Here you can find information on estate planning, bankruptcy, real estate, child custody, and other vital issues that often arise on the home front. To avail yourself of the legal resources in the Nolo Press Self-Help Law Center (see Figure 10-20), use the keyword search **nolo press**.

Figure 10-20 Reduce your legal bills by doing your own research.

BONUS

N ow that we've covered some of the basic reference material available on AOL, let's take a look at some of the less conventional resources you can find if you look in the right place.

The Straight Dope

If you're from Chicago, you are probably familiar with Cecil Adams, the world's most intelligent human being (according to Cecil Adams). He is a syndicated columnist whose weekly column, The Straight Dope, is carried by over thirty U.S. and Canadian newspapers. Cecil's column is a weekly question and answer piece, dealing with some of life's more unusual questions, such as who invented chewing gum and should you use aluminum foil with the shiny side in or out?

The blending of wit, fact, and irreverence provides some rather humorous and informative reading. To open The Straight Dope window (see Figure 10-21) use the keyword search **straight dope**.

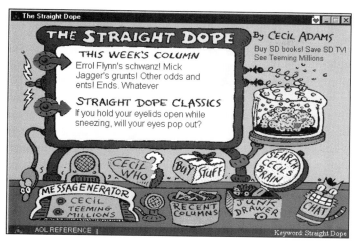

Figure 10-21   Stranger than fiction, The Straight Dope provides answers to readers' questions.

94 Acceptable Two-Letter Scrabble® Words

You know that feeling of frustration. You have only one or two letters left, but no place to put them. Well, the New York Public Library Desk Reference has just what you need — this listing of nearly one hundred legal two-letter words. Before playing, just be sure to take a quick trip to the NYPL 94 Acceptable Two-Letter Scrabble® Words list.

Follow these steps:

1. Click the Keyword button on the Toolbar.
2. Type **nypl** in the Enter Word(s): text box.
3. Press Enter to open the NYPL Desk Reference window.
4. In the Browse Desk Reference display list, double-click the category **Words**.
5. From the Words display list, double-click the category **94 Acceptable Two-Letter Scrabble® Words**.

Big Twin

Even if you've never ridden a motorcycle, I'm willing to bet that at some point in your life, you've dreamed of tossing a couple of tee shirts, some socks, and underwear in your saddlebags, throwing them across your Harley, and driving off into the sunset. Well, it's never too late. If you've got a Harley or you're just dreaming about one, stop by the Big Twin, the All-Harley Magazine online, and find out what's going on in the world of Harley-Davidson. To access the All-Harley Magazine window (see Figure 10-22), use the keyword search **big twin**.

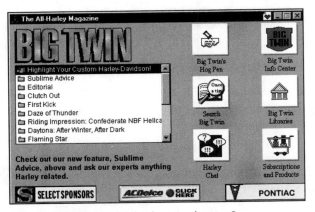

Figure 10-22   Could this be Hog heaven?

Summary

Reference material is not just for kids or students, it is an essential part of everyday life for many people. Maintaining the variety of information resources needed by the different members of your family would require building an addition on the house just to store them. Luckily, with AOL you don't have to do that. The AOL Reference Channel provides access to an abundance of resource material for the whole family.

CHAPTER ELEVEN

ENJOYING THE LIGHTER SIDE

IN THIS CHAPTER YOU LEARN THESE KEY SKILLS

A re you feeling guilty yet about the amount of time you spend online? If not, you just haven't been using AOL long enough — you'll get to that point soon. Are people beginning to use the word "addict" to describe you? Do you find that you lie to people and say you're in the reference section, looking up all the ways to prevent losing the ozone layer?

Don't worry, there are sites on AOL that are educational and fun at the same time. The pleasure you find there is totally guilt-free; it also provides an acceptable reason to be online for hours at a time. Acceptable, that is, to your critical friends who haven't found the joys you've discovered in online life.

This chapter introduces you to some of the interesting cultural areas of AOL, and it provides a brief tour of some highlights.

Hearing the Sounds of Music

H ave you noticed that any discussion of music seems to produce the same intense debating that religion and politics do? Tastes differ, of course, but most of us (myself included) seem to have a desire to convince others that they should like the music we like. I once spent time trying to convince my co-author for this book to like opera. My method was to play "Un bel di vedremo" from the second act of *Madama Butterfly* very loudly. He slammed the door to the room he was in equally loudly. I love Puccini; he likes country-western (which makes me slam doors loudly).

Luckily, the MusicSpace on AOL has plenty for both of us. In fact, there are places we'll run into each other (we both like jazz and rock). To get there, use the keyword **Music** (or click MusicSpace on the Channels window). Arriving in MusicSpace is exciting because there's so much there that you don't know where to start (see Figure 11-1).

Figure 11-1 The expression "kid in a candy store" comes to mind when you look at the offerings in MusicSpace.

Start off by selecting your favorite genre and clicking its icon (see Figure 11-2). After you get inside that space, you'll find even more things to do, choices to make, and areas to explore. It's a never-ending assortment of goodies.

Figure 11-2 This is a great way to keep up with performers, concerts, and new releases.

Each music section has the same format, with icons for featured services, message boards, chat sections, and a list of topics to explore. Many of the items on the list take you to the Internet, where you can gather information and buy music.

Back at the main MusicSpace window, you'll find icons for poking around in MTV, Spin, and Rolling Stone Online (see Figure 11-3).

Figure 11-3 The online version of Rolling Stone keeps you up to date on a daily basis so that you don't have to wait for the printed edition.

The topic list in the MusicScene window presents another wide range of things to read, learn about, and participate in. Check the Member Reviews section to see what AOL users think about concerts, videos, and albums. Even better, add your own comments. There might be something you wasted your money on, and it would be nice of you to warn others before they make the same mistake. Of course, you can also write a good review for a concert you loved or an album you think everyone should own.

New Releases keeps you on top of the latest music news. Pick a topic or a new album release and put yourself one up on everyone else the next time the conversation rolls around to music. Or, be the first one on your block to own the newest albums by buying online (see Figure 11-4).

Figure 11-4 You might want to preview a track from the album before you buy it.

You can download a video or audio clip for most releases, which gives you a chance to decide whether it's worth spending your money on the release.

TIP To view a video clip, you have to have QuickTime software. You can download the software from AOL using the instructions that appear when you choose the video clip.

Don't forget to check out the AOL events (double-click Online Guests) to see what's coming up online.

Touring Show Biz

Everybody connects to the entertainment world, either as a couch potato, a moviegoer, or theater buff. AOL provides everything for people who want to know what's hot, what's not, and where to go to find it all. Start your tour by clicking Entertainment on the Channels window or by using the keyword **Entertainment** (see Figure 11-5).

Figure 11-5 This is more information about show business than anyone could possibly need to know.

Scroll through the Index listings to find the news and gossip you want. There are sites for television networks (including cable), specific TV shows, movies, comic books, and more.

The interest group categories range from kids' shows, to soaps, to those magazines that are displayed at the supermarket checkout counter. Interactive communication is available all over the place, so leave notes, enter contests, and add your thoughts to the conversation.

Keeping an eye on the TV

Does anyone NOT watch television? Of course not, so hit the television beat for a hearty dose of information about shows, listings, and gossip (see Figure 11-6).

Figure 11-6 Click the buttons on the clicker to wander around AOL's television studio.

I'll mention some of my favorites to get your tour of this area started, in case you're overwhelmed. Let's start with the Networks button, where AOL recognizes that there's a lot more to television than the three major network giants. You'll probably find your favorite cable network listed. I headed straight for the Comedy Network, and then clicked Ab Fab (see Figure 11-7).

Figure 11-7 Download pictures, print the air schedule, and buy merchandise from the sites of your favorite shows.

Almost all the sites offer interactive participation so that you can read and write comments. And, there's frequently stuff to buy. Click Tube Talk to join the TV chat room, or click TV & Me and pick your favorite show and climb inside it. You'll find chat rooms, message boards, gossip, plot recaps, and lots more for each show that's listed.

Back at the Main TV Screen, choose News & Reviews to get news, gossip, and opinions. You can read what critics (the ones who are paid to have an opinion) are saying about shows and episodes; you can also read what other AOL users say. Of course, you should add your own cheers and jeers for the shows you watch.

TIP   **If you have children, be sure to check out Parents Soup for reviews and pointers about appropriate programming.**

One of the neat sections in the Television area is the Episode Guide section (click Shows, and then double-click TV Episode Guide). This Web site lists a whole bunch of shows for which you can read summaries of each episode. The air date, writer, director, cast, and a plot summary is included — all the things you have to know to play Trivia or win an argument.

Here are a few other things you should look for:

* The Shows window has an alphabetical listing of popular TV shows. Double-click your favorites to meet the cast, post messages, and catch up on the storyline (see Figure 11-8).

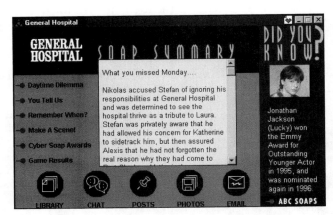

Figure 11-8   If you can't always be there for your stories, you can still keep track of all the plots and subplots.

* If you like to shop, you can buy online, choosing among Star Trek stuff, Friends' greeting cards, Oprah sweatshirts, and lots more.

* The Television section also has a button for Radio. Click it to learn about radio shows and schedules, covering everything from NPR (National Public Radio) to Ham radio.

Investigating the movie scene

Click Movies on the Entertainment window to enter the theater — bring your own popcorn. Information, reviews, and gossip all await you (see Figure 11-9).

Figure 11-9 The movie section is the starting point for lots of cinematic data.

You can read reviews of all the current releases to decide which flick you want to see tonight or to see if your opinion matches Gene Siskel's. There is, of course, a place for you to enter your own review because AOL is always thinking of interactive ways for you to participate.

Scroll through the list to find a topic or feature that interests you. Some of the items you might find interesting include

* Photos of the Stars!, the place to go to download cool pix.

* Movies Store, where you can buy posters, soundtracks, and even screensavers.

* Movie Star Transcripts, where you can read the questions and answers from a star's appearance in an AOL Live event.

* Independent Films, a wealth of information about current and upcoming projects.

* Movie News, a collection of gossip columns, articles, and features.

Click the Home Video icon to visit the largest video store you'll ever find (see Figure 11-10). The stores to visit, reviews to read, and articles to browse are all designed to help you learn about the movies now available on video.

Figure 11-10 Check out the titles, make a decision, go to the video store, order the pizza, and enjoy the evening.

TIP This is another AOL area with plenty of help for parents. If you have children, read the information aimed at helping you decide which home videos are suitable for kids.

Don't forget to stop in the Movies chat room and try to pay a visit to the Message Boards. Reading the messages is amusing, and penning your own notes adds to the fun.

Visiting Cultural Sites

The fine and creative arts are well represented on AOL; if your tastes run in that direction, you'll have a good time at The Arts site (see Figure 11-11). The easiest way to get there is to use the keyword **Arts** (or use the icons for this site in the Entertainment window and the Learning & Culture window).

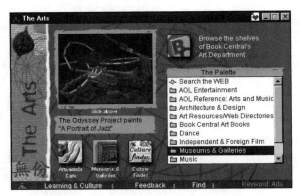

Figure 11-11 The Arts site is a virtual museum, bookstore, theater, and auditorium all at the same time.

When you arrive, the choices are vast. Let's take a quick tour to highlight some of the choices.

Museums and galleries

Open the Museums & Galleries listing to visit most of the great museums of the world. You can pay a virtual visit to the Louvre, the Smithsonian, and lots of other wonderful museums.

When you visit the museums, you can find pictures, stories about the pictures and the artists, and, of course, gift shops so you can buy remembrances of your visit. It's a chance to browse museums you might never get to see, except virtually.

Just to point out some of things that are worth heading for, don't miss the Whitney Museum in New York City, which has an incredible collection of American art. Some of the many shows that have been presented by the Whitney are available for your scrutiny (see Figure 11-12).

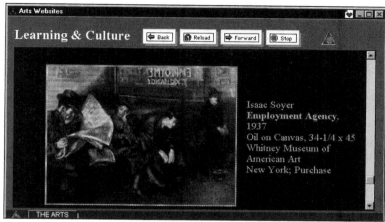
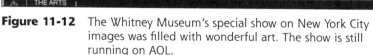

Figure 11-12   The Whitney Museum's special show on New York City images was filled with wonderful art. The show is still running on AOL.

The Smithsonian Museums are a sweeping range of institutions, and the AOL site is replete with information and exhibits about all of them. You can read about (or print or download) the purpose and history of the individual museums, and then take a tour of the exhibits. The National Museum of Natural History (home of the Hope Diamond), the American History Museum, the American Indian Museum, the Arts & Industries Building, the Post Office Museum, the Zoo, and the National Portrait Gallery are just a few of the worthwhile parts of this national treasure you can view on AOL.

All the Smithsonian Museums have sections on upcoming exhibits and special events, so if you're planning a trip to the D.C. area you can coordinate your itinerary. An online search feature lets you download articles and resource guides about an enormous variety of exhibit items. This means the kids have a wonderful resource for homework because the museums cover so many different topics.

Double-click Leonardo da Vinci Museum Online to spend some time being fascinated by art work, scientific drawings, and one of history's most incredible minds (see Figure 11-13).

The da Vinci online site traces this remarkable man's life. You'll see his scientific drawings and notes along with his artistic endeavors.

Figure 11-13 Imagine somebody coming up with the design of a helicopter over 400 years ago.

Music

Double-click Music to enter AOL's cultural auditorium, which offers a treat for people who enjoy the classics and jazz. You'll find links to those areas in the AOL MusicSpace (discussed earlier in this chapter) as well as a number of interesting sites that provide information about the history of music.

Some of your favorite labels are represented, so you can peruse catalogs and buy that CD you want — all online.

TIP If you're a performer, this area has a lot of information you might like to read, such as articles on managing stage fright and on controlling the injuries musicians are apt to experience, such as tendonitis and repetitive motion problems.

Theater

If you're a theater buff, pop in for a visit by double-clicking the Theater listing. Start by opening Playbill On-Line to keep up with the world of thespians. This site has news, interviews, feature articles, chat rooms, and more. Here are some of the offerings on the Playbill site:

* An interesting collection of files available to download, including seating charts for all the New York theaters, photos of scenes from current and past productions, and Playbill covers.

- Casting Call information for upcoming productions on and off Broadway, as well as for road companies. The casting call list includes non-performance jobs that need to be filled.

- Want to know who won awards, which award, and for what? It's right there.

- A trivia section poses questions about shows, dialogue, and performers (the answers are at the bottom of each trivia file).

- Newsletters connected to the theater world are available, including those distributed by SAG (Screen Actors Guild), the Drama League, The Rodgers & Hammerstein Organization, and many others.

You could spend a lot of time and have a great deal of fun on the Playbill site. And, if you get so excited about the ambiance and book some theater tickets and a flight to New York, you might want to consult the online restaurant guide as well.

The New York Times theater section is also represented here. It contains reviews of shows playing on and off Broadway (some of the reviews are better written than the plays they discuss). Listings arranged by show titles or theaters are available, and there are Message Boards for theater, music, dance, and every other fine and creative art.

Keeping Up with Hobbies

Almost everyone has a hobby; it's a common diversion. Have you noticed, however, that some people can't tell the difference between a hobby and a passion? Regardless of your level of enthusiasm, enter the keyword **Hobby** to find other folks who fill their time (and closets) with things they make or collect. You'll find a rich variety of choices at Hobby Central (see Figure 11-14).

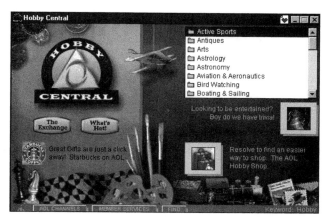

Figure 11-14   Here's the place to find the other person who collects the same unusual thingamajigs that you do.

The first thing to do upon entering Hobby Central is scroll through the list of topics to find the one that matches your own affinity. Because the list is long and varied, you're probably going to find exactly what you're looking for. Some of the sites are just bursting with information and features, and you'll spend many happy moments visiting them.

If you're an antiques buff (or even if you're not), the Antiques site has plenty of interesting features. You'll find magazines, chat rooms, Message Boards, and places to buy and sell old furniture, cars, radios, and other collectibles.

Do-It-Yourself fans have a never-ending supply of hints, tricks, and professional advice to browse through in Hobby Central. Whether you're interested in crafts, woodworking, or a major home improvement project, Hobby Central offers a wealth of useful information (see Figure 11-15).

Figure 11-15   If your hobby is fixing up the house, click an icon to get your project finished without turning your house into a money pit.

If your thumb is green, head to the Garden spot for tips on what to plant, organic gardening, pest control, and when to prune.

Model planes and trains are popular hobbies, so you'll find plenty of other folks to talk with and compare notes. If you like transportation vehicles of the full-sized variety, check out the car section.

BONUS

I f you're not serious about (or obsessed with) some hobby, you may want to check out The Exchange. Just click its icon on the Hobby Central window. When you arrive, you'll find some generic topics that everybody can relate to, not just hobbyists and collectors (see Figure 11-16).

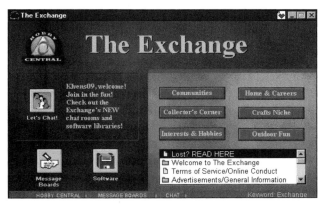

Figure 11-16 There's something for everyone here, even those who aren't beating the bushes for another doohickey to add to a collection.

Click Communities to move to a central clearinghouse for interacting with people who have a heritage or a lifestyle like your own. Most of the ethnic groups are represented, as well as groups organized by profession (this is what we call "networking"). Paramedics, morticians, attorneys, and even professional bodyguards exchange information on these Message Boards.

Click Home & Careers to interact with people who share your interests and to find help on parenting, health, and other family matters.

Check out Support Groups to find people with common problems and backgrounds (see Figure 11-17).

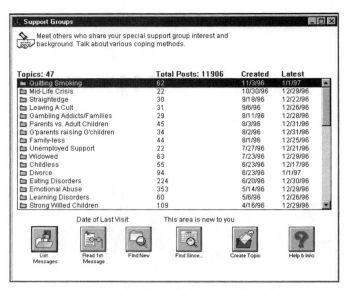

Figure 11-17 Coping with a problem is easier when you can share the experiences of others in the same boat.

Summary

The general interest sections, a few of which are discussed in this chapter, are some of the most worthwhile reasons to use AOL. This is one of the ways to let your whole family enjoy this service.

BECOMING A COMPUTER NERD

IN THIS CHAPTER YOU LEARN THESE KEY SKILLS

12

One of the best things about using AOL is that you don't have to be a propeller-head to figure out how to use it. Of course, to get the best out of it, you have to read this book. But, while you're working in AOL, you don't have to know how a chip is wired, what the kernel of your operating system is doing while you're online, or how a modem really works. You can take all of that for granted.

But for many of us, as we use computers for more and more tasks, curiosity takes over. Why does this work that way? What makes that happen? What's available that's better than the software or hardware I'm using? What utilities and add-ons can I use to make my current software applications work better?

This chapter is a guided tour through the computer information sections of AOL. You'll learn where to find news, advice, tips, software, hardware, and everything else connected to computing. Eventually, by accident, you'll become a computer nerd.

Connecting with the AOL Computer Center

No matter how hard you try to keep up, it seems as if the leading edge of knowledge is miles ahead of you. Things happen so fast in the world of computers that it's mind-boggling. To stay abreast of the current state of the art, you'll have to devote a lot of time to the effort. If that seems a bit much, you can keep up enough to tread water (not much progress, but it's better than drowning) by staying in touch with the information mavens.

There's an enormous range of information about computers and computing on AOL. You find it by clicking the Computers and Software icon on the Channels window or by using the keyword **Computers & Software**. The window that greets you has lots to choose from (see Figure 12-1).

Figure 12-1 This is where the weenies hang out.

Before you head for the freebies and begin downloading (although I know it's tempting), browse. You'll find lot of information that can get you started on the road to becoming a weenie.

Browsing ZDNet

For information and software (the best of two worlds), try ZDNet (see Figure 12-2), an online publication that offers a wealth of information (and yes, they have software that you can download).

Figure 12-2   Articles, software, and tips — so much to learn about!

The **explore** area is a way to browse the online services provided by a host of computer magazines. You don't access the magazines themselves in an online version, but you do tap into special online features that are provided by the publications. In fact, you can usually get a peek at news stories that haven't been printed yet. Luckily, ZDNet provides a search engine so that you can gather only the relevant publications and articles for a specific topic. The search produces any and all articles that contain your search phrase (see Figure 12-3).

Figure 12-3   The search phrase I entered (which was my own name) produced all the articles I was interested in.

Crave is a perfect descriptive title because it tells you everything you want to know about all the things you've been craving for your computer. It's a shopper's guide, which means you can take advantage of lots of information before you decide what to buy. In addition to reading reviews by experts, you can learn what readers have said about the software, hardware, and peripherals they've purchased. A Message Board is available so you can ask everyone who visits it about that CD burner you've had your eye on.

The **mingle** section is ZDNet's headquarters for interactive participation, with Message Boards and chat rooms. Saunter on over to the rotunda, an organized chat room where participants can present questions to a guest expert (and then chat about the answers). This is an interesting way to attend a seminar.

Try the **tweak** section of ZDNet for hints, tips, and tricks for revving up your computer. If you're not ready to gun the motor, there's plenty of basic information available so you can start to understand what tweaking is and whether or not you need it. You'll find articles from a variety of publications, as well as a Message Board (go there to leave a pathetic note when you've pulled your computer apart to add a new peripheral and can't remember what went where — lots of people will be glad to help).

And, of course, make your way to the **download** area for a smorgasbord of software, all arranged by category (see Figure 12-4).

Figure 12-4   Now *this* is like being a kid in a toy store.

Believe it or not, you'll get a great deal of value out of the Advertisers Index. Click its icon to see a list of advertisers in ZD magazines who have Web sites. Head for NetBuyer, where you'll find buying advice, special offers from lots of vendors, and a comparison shopping guide organized into logical categories (see Figure 12-5).

Figure 12-5 This is sure better than taking advice from some salesperson with limited knowledge at a superdiscount store.

Touring the Magazine Rack

The aisles of the computer Magazine Rack are packed with periodicals, reference books, and interactive areas (see Figure 12-6).

Figure 12-6 The Magazine Rack is misnamed because there's a lot more than magazines on its shelves.

If you're too lazy to walk through the aisles, or if you're afraid of new places and need to have your hand held, you can take a guided tour. It's the first item in the listings. You can double-click it to see an overview of the stuff in the racks (see Figure 12-7).

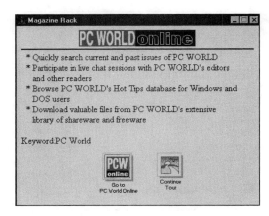

Figure 12-7 One of the tour stops is PC World, which you can visit by clicking the Go to icon.

At every stop on the tour, you can go directly to that area of the Magazine Rack by clicking the Go to icon. When you leave the area, you come back to the tour and pick up where you left off.

The tour doesn't cover every item on the racks, so I'll give you the benefit of my own visits to the Magazine Rack and tell you about some of my personal favorites (some of which do appear on the tour).

BUSINESS WEEK'S ONLINE COMPUTER ROOM

Here is a complete information center. You'll find articles from Business Week's computer coverage (this was the first general magazine to create a specific section dedicated to computers) as well as articles written especially for the Business Week online service. You'll also find Message Boards and software to download. My favorite, however, is the maven, Business Week's expert on computer products (see Figure 12-8).

Figure 12-8 The maven does the homework for me, so comparative shopping is a breeze.

There's even a pricing wizard that lets you put a computer together piece by piece, part by part, peripheral by peripheral, while it keeps a running total of the cost. For each item, you can choose a manufacturer and decide how much you want to spend. It's a pretty nifty exercise.

PC WORLD ONLINE

This is another mind-boggling array of information, software, and interactive activity. Enter PC World by clicking its icon and be greeted by choices that cover pretty much anything you'd want to investigate (see Figure 12-9).

Figure 12-9   PC World is filled with just the information you need to enhance your knowledge and keep up with your propeller-head friends.

Here's some of the neat stuff available in this world:

* Click the picture of PC World magazine to read the current issue.

* Click the shopping bag to visit PC World's shopping mall, where you can buy all sorts of things, including IDG books (of course, you've already bought one, but there are lots more where this came from).

* Click the Software Libraries icon to download software that covers a variety of categories.

* Click the Buyer's Guide icon to get some expert guidance before you purchase anything.

* Click the Q&A icon to ask questions about computing. You'll receive answers from editors, experts, and other users.

* Visit the chat room.

You can spend a long time here without getting the least bit bored.

WIRED MAGAZINE

Welcome to one of the most famous computer publications (see Figure 12-10). You'll see quotes from this publication floating around everywhere in computer-dom — on tee-shirts, in the signatures of e-mail senders, on the lips of geeks. It's funny and irreverent, but full of good information at the same time. This is one of the hot spots for propeller-heads, and if you like what you see (and there's plenty to see) you can subscribe.

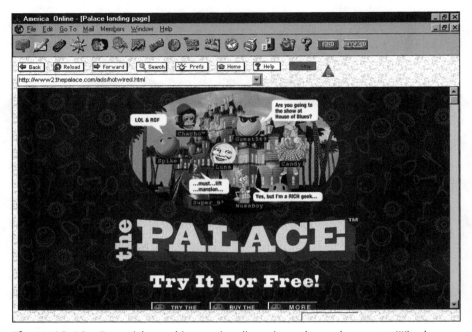

Figure 12-10   For articles and interactive discussions, the geeks meet at Wired.

CNET

This is an online publication filled with news, feature articles, and reviews. The information is relevant and well written, so it's a great source of information for would-be techies (see Figure 12-11).

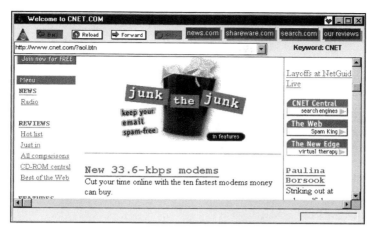

Figure 12-11 Visit CNET to learn about hardware, software, and what's new in the world of computing.

THE COMPUTING DICTIONARY

Here's the place to go when you don't understand a term. Consult it frequently, and eventually you'll be at ease when you find yourself in the company of propeller-heads (see Figure 12-12).

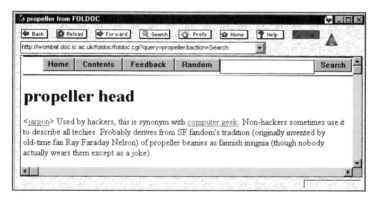

Figure 12-12 I looked it up after I was the target of this epithet.

Besides these favorites of mine, you'll find an enormous selection of periodicals in the Magazine Rack. There's plenty of stuff for Mac users, too.

Homing in on software

Okay, admit it, the freebies and the shareware are two of the main reasons you log on to AOL (the others are e-mail and chat). That just makes you normal. Head straight for the PC Software Center to see what's available. Pick a Category and then—on your mark, get set, go!

Actually, the best place to start is with the Software Help icon, which provides instructions for every level of computer proficiency (see Figure 12-13).

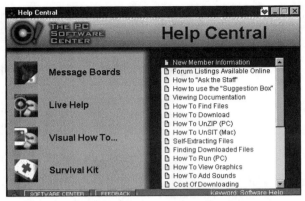

Figure 12-13 Everything you wanted to know about downloading software is in the files in Help Central.

TIP One of the interesting areas in Help Central is the Message Boards center, which is divided by software category. You can read about other users' experiences or ask questions. Any question you ask will have been asked before, and the users who figured out the best answers will respond. You should also take a look at the messages from the Association for Shareware Professions, which will give you the guidelines for using shareware.

After you've garnered all the tips, tricks, and instructions, head for your favorite category. Select subcategories if there are any, and then find the software that looks interesting. Click the listing, and then choose Read Description to learn more about it (see Figure 12-14).

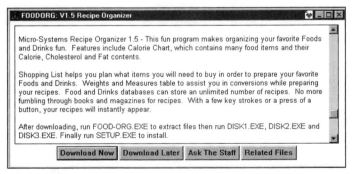

Figure 12-14 Scroll through the description file to learn about the software, the requirements for running it, and instructions on installing it.

If you like it, download it.

Click the File Search icon to search for files that meet your specifications (see Figure 12-15). You can search by choosing one of the date ranges, entering key words, or both.

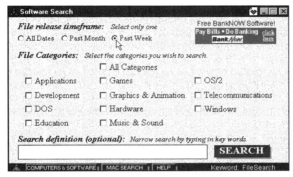

Figure 12-15 If you're a frequent downloader, this is a neat way to see only those files that have been added recently.

After you've entered your specifications, click Search. Then examine the files in the Search Results window and download the stuff you want.

Learning about multimedia

Multimedia is one of the hot technologies for computer aficionados, and the AOL Computers & Software area is right on the leading edge. Choose The Multimedia Zone from the Computers & Software window to join the cognoscenti. This site is really a research site, although there is software you can download. The information is aimed at various levels of computer expertise; you're sure to find something of interest.

You might want to start with the Multimedia Reference Guide, which offers information organized around the questions most people ask (see Figure 12-16).

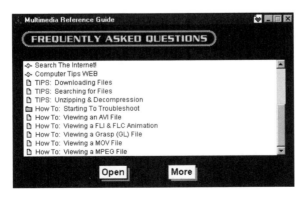

Figure 12-16 Browse the reference guide for basic information about using or writing multimedia applications.

Because video problems account for the most frequent complaints from multimedia users, you can visit the Video Zone to learn more about video setup and to download some helpful software.

Browse the AOL multimedia store at your own risk — it offers a tempting array of products. Digital cameras, video phones, graphics accelerators, and recordable CD-ROM drives are available at the click of a mouse. I could destroy my carefully crafted budget for the next three months with a ten-minute visit to this site.

Playing with electronic toys

My house has a lot of gadgets that beep, light up, or need batteries. And none of them fall into the category of computers. There are all sorts of electronic doo-dads on the market, and the AOL Computers & Software site has set aside an area for them. Select Consumer Electronics from the main Computers & Software window to learn more about these adult toys (see Figure 12-17).

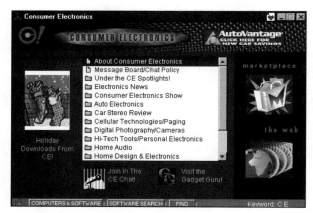

Figure 12-17 If you're interested in thingamajigs and gadgets, come here to learn, chat, and buy.

Audiophiles will love this site, with its sections on stereo equipment for the home and car. Learn what's new, what's hot, what's good, and what's not so good. Of course, there are plenty of places to shop.

The section on Video & Home Theater is perfect for you sports buffs who claim that watching a game on a television set of normal size just doesn't work for you.

For just plain gadgetry, wander over to the Hi-Tech Tools/Personal Electronics section (see Figure 12-18).

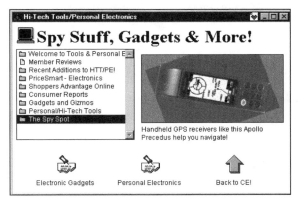

Figure 12-18 For clever items and stuff that's just for fun, browse the stores that specialize in gadgets.

Getting technical support

Installation problems for hardware and software can drive you nuts. You follow the directions, and it doesn't work properly (or at all). You start all over from the beginning, and it still doesn't work.

Of course, even when the installation goes smoothly, there are often problems with hardware performance or software that is supposed to do something but doesn't.

Don't worry; be happy. The AOL Computers & Software area has two sections you can jump into that may make everything okay: the Support Forums area and the Company Connection area. Visiting either (or both) may give you the information you need.

SUPPORT FORUMS

Start with Support Forums, where support information is listed by category (see Figure 12-19).

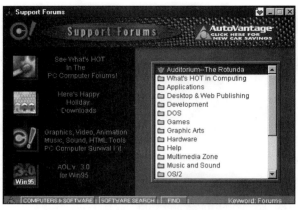

Figure 12-19 Scroll through the categories to find the one your problem falls into, and then double-click to join that forum.

Most of the forums are similar, containing information files, Message Boards, chat areas, and software download sections. Many of the forums also promote conferences or seminars, which are specifically scheduled and have guest experts visiting to answer your questions.

Frequently, a forum has at least one unique section that's specific to its category (see Figure 12-20).

Figure 12-20 The Desktop & Web Publishing Forum provides a great place for learning about or downloading fonts.

Actually, you don't really have to wait for a problem to occur: you should visit the Support Forums area occasionally just to learn. It's another step on the road to computer nerdiness.

COMPANY CONNECTION

Another source of information about using hardware or software is the manufacturer. The Company Connection section of AOL's Computers & Software area is the gateway for getting to manufacturers. When you arrive, you can use the Companies by Category list box to scroll through the categories and double-click the appropriate one, then find the company you need. Or, use the Company Search icon to head right for the company you need to contact (see Figure 12-21). Just enter the company name in the search box.

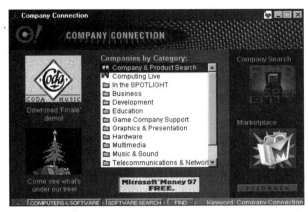

Figure 12-21   Many of the major software and hardware companies are accessible through AOL.

As with the Support Forum, you'll find that most of the sites in Company Connection are similar in content. There are information files on specific topics you can view, save, or print; Message Boards; and software to download (see Figure 12-22).

Figure 12-22   After you've traveled to company headquarters, it's usually easy to find the right location for the information you need.

Some companies have lively graphical pages, and others provide only a list of topics, but there's plenty of opportunity to learn about the company's products and how to use them.

TIP In both the Support Forums and Company Connection, you'll occasionally find links to company Web sites. These are usually worth the extra time because the Web sites tend to be more robust, offering more information or a wider range of information.

Don't wait for a problem to occur before you visit this site. Spending some time browsing here is a good way to learn about what's available that might make your computer more efficient, more fun, or more powerful.

Focusing on the family

Pull up enough chairs for the kids and head for the Family Computing Forum (see Figure 12-23). Traveling here is an easy and quick trip. (The kids don't even have time to ask "Are we there yet?")

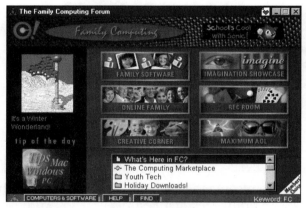

Figure 12-23 There's something for everyone in the Family Computing area.

The Family Software section is, of course, dedicated to software for the family — no surprise there. To avoid all surprises, you might want to postpone your purchase of a particular software title until you see what others have said about it. The Family Software Reviews section has comments by both Family Computing staff members and users who have tried the software (see Figure 12-24). This ought to give you a pretty good idea of what to expect.

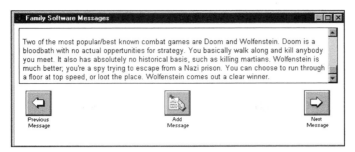

Figure 12-24 Users discuss software in the Reviews Section
Message Boards.

Click Online Family to get an inside view of the Family Computing area. You'll find information about the people who run FC, chat rooms, event calendars, and a place for visitors to exchange greetings (and photos).

The Creative Corner is all about creative arts — mostly creative things you can do with a computer. There's plenty of information about creative software, and you can view some of the output. Try the refrigerator art (named for the way most of us display the artwork our children produce) to see what some kids have been able to do with easy-to-use software.

Try the Imagination Showcase for all sorts of creative fun. The Writer's Nook isn't just for wanna-be authors; everybody will enjoy reading the articles. New Releases is the launchpad for new areas (I found a section on creative ways to keep the family scrapbook). Make sure to visit Retail World to see some amusing cartoons about life in retail stores (from both points of view — customer and retailer).

The Rec Room is a giant online game room. The whole family can participate in the fun (see Figure 12-25).

Figure 12-25 Everybody gets to guess, but the person holding
the mouse gets to pick.

Enter the Maximum AOL section for all kinds of help and advice on interactive computing on AOL. Although it's run by the Family Computing staff, the stuff you learn here will work anywhere on AOL. Read articles, ask questions, and practice downloading and leaving messages on Message Boards). This is a great place for parents to sneak into at night so the kids don't know how far behind them their parents are.

Learning Interactively

One great way to learn is to gather information, see what other people say or ask about the information, and ask your own questions. This scenario is played out frequently on AOL in the form of special chat events, which are almost like seminars. Many of the places you visit in the Computers & Software area sponsor these events. Take note of them as you browse.

Visiting the Rotunda

The majority of interactive learning opportunities for computing information (propeller-head chats) occur in the Rotunda (see Figure 12-26). There are two ways to get there:

* From the Magazine Rack in the Computers & Software area, click Check out Live Events.
* Use the keyword **Rotunda**.

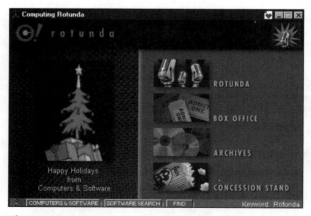

Figure 12-26 The experts come here to chat with you about computing subjects.

The Rotunda is a big building, so let's take a quick tour:

* The Rotunda itself (think of it as an auditorium) is a chat room. When there's no special event, it's empty.

* The Box Office lists the upcoming events and also has a search tool so you can look for specific topics (including past topics).

* The Archives vault holds transcripts of events that took place earlier (see the next section for information about obtaining transcripts).

* The Concession Stand has information files about computer subjects and guest lecturers, schedules of events, newsletters, and places for you to provide feedback about events.

When there's an event scheduled, just head for the Rotunda (get there a bit early to be sure you'll have a seat).

Getting transcripts of events

Reading the transcript of an event enables you to peruse the speaker's comments and the audience's questions at your leisure. Click the Archives icon to enter the stacks (see Figure 12-27).

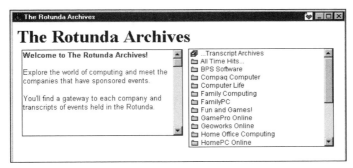

Figure 12-27   Transcripts are indexed by the company that sponsored the event.

Scroll through the list to find the company that sponsored the event of interest, and then double-click its listing.

TIP   If you don't know the name of the company, choose Transcript Archives to see a listing of transcripts arranged by subject.

When you open the company listing, you'll see either a list of topics or a list of years (in which case, you must double-click the year in which the topic you want was presented). Scroll through the listings, double-click the one of interest, and start reading (see Figure 12-28).

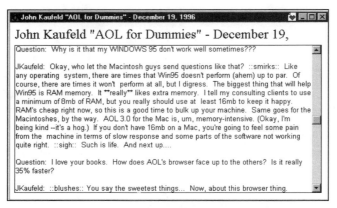

Figure 12-28 There's lots of good information in this event's transcript.

Saving transcripts

Okay, I know, you feel it's a waste of your time on AOL to sit in front of your screen and click the arrow on the scroll bar while you read a transcript. You have a couple of options.

* Click the Print icon on the Toolbar to send the transcript to your printer. This gives you hard copy (computer jargon for a printout of something you're seeing on your screen) that you can refer to whenever you want.

* Save the transcript as a file on your hard drive so that you can load it into a word processor and edit out the bits you have no interest in, saving the good stuff. Then you can print that file or just bring it up whenever you want to get information from it.

To save the transcript, follow these steps:

1. From the AOL Menu Bar, choose File→Save.

2. When the Save File As dialog box appears (see Figure 12-29), enter a name for this file.

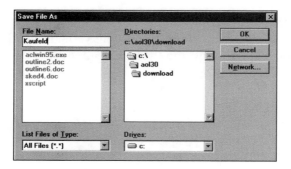

Figure 12-29 You can save any document on your screen for later viewing.

3. Choose the folder (the dialog box calls it a directory) in which you want to save the file.

TIP **By default, AOL saves files in the download folder under your AOL software folder. If you're comfortable with hard drive structures, you can save the file in the same folder where your other word processing files reside instead. That does not change the default download location; the next time you download a file, AOL will return to its own download folder.**

4. When you have chosen the name and location for the file, choose OK.

After the file is on your computer's hard drive, you can view it, edit it, or print it with your word processor or one of the editors that came with your operating system.

BONUS

S ometimes you have to go at this knowledge business sideways. Any site that has some kind of information may have information about computers, and you can take a multi-step approach to get there.

The Reference section (click Reference on the Channels window) has a category list. You can choose Computing & Technology (see Figure 12-30).

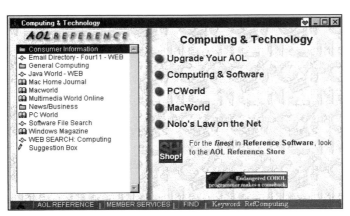

Figure 12-30 Visit any site that seems educational to see if there's a computer section.

The amount of information about computers on the World Wide Web is staggering. It's a safe bet that the manufacturer of every piece of computer equipment you own has a home page on the Web. And there seem to be a zillion places to get information about operating systems and software.

 WEB PATH Click Internet Connection on the Channels window (or use the keyword **Internet**) to get started (see Figure 12-31).

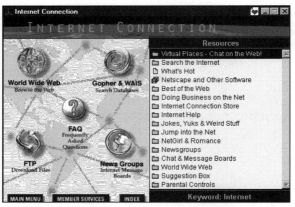

Figure 12-31 Hop on the Internet to find more information about computers and software.

Click World Wide Web to launch the AOL search engine for the Web, or you can pick a resource from the list box.

Summary

People really use computers to get a job done. Sometimes the job is literally a job, and the software you use is your vehicle for getting a paycheck. On other occasions, the computer is used for the very important function of having fun (such as your time on AOL). You don't really have to own all the leading edge hardware and software to make your computer productive; however, the more you learn about computers, the easier it is to make decisions about what you want to add to your machine.

Most important, if you learn a lot about computers, software, operating systems, and other computing categories, you'll work faster, easier, and with far more pleasure when you belly up to the keyboard. The feeling you get when you've learned enough to help others is pretty cool, too.

VISITING DIGITAL CITIES

IN THIS CHAPTER YOU LEARN THESE KEY SKILLS

13

S omebody once said "Getting there is half the fun." That person obviously didn't have small children, a wife who had to pack a pair of shoes to match every outfit, a husband who insisted on taking golf clubs, or a car that burns gas so fast that if you don't turn off the engine during re-fueling, you gain on the pump.

AOL has a service that does make getting there fun. It's a way to visit cities and towns virtually by accessing them via the Digital Cities channel.

This chapter introduces you to Digital Cities and saves you some online time by pointing you to some of the interesting things there. Although it's not possible to figure out what type of city *you* would like to know about, I've chosen a variety of cities and attractions in those cities in the hope that the information will provide some guidance for your own visits to the places in Digital City.

Touring Virtual America

Start the engine, make sure all the kids visited the bathroom, and fasten those seat belts — here you go. You're taking a drive around the country, visiting some of the cities you've always wanted to see. Luckily, you don't have to worry about packing shoes that match your clothing, listen to the kids ask "Are we there yet?," or stop at a gas station to ask directions. (Although, if you're a male you probably would never do that anyway, no matter how lost you were — why is that?)

Get started by clicking Digital City on the Channels window or by using the keyword **Digital City**. The first thing you see is a national map that's divided into sections (see Figure 13-1).

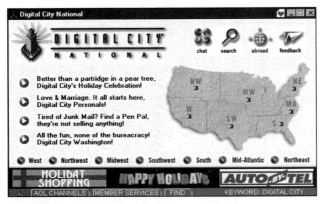

Figure 13-1 Each section of the country has cities you can visit. You can even get to Hawaii without worrying about the car having to float.

Before you settle down somewhere for a while, take a tour of the areas and make a list of the cities you want to return to for a real (as opposed to virtual) visit. If you're not alone in front of the computer, remember that everybody gets a vote.

This section includes stops based on my own experiences because there are a few places I think you should know about.

Touring the Northeast

The northeast section of the country probably contains more big cities than any other area. It's filled with historical sites, recreational areas, and a population that reflects the effects of living in big old towns. (You can interpret that any way you want. Personally, I'm a big-city person, and I get concrete withdrawal if I wander away for more than a couple of days.)

When you see the regional map (see Figure 13-2), the major cities are accessible by a single-click on their names (right on the map). There's a list box to scroll through so you can pick one of the cities included in the area (double-click the listing). Featured cities (which change frequently, so your window may be different) are visited with a single click on their icons.

Today (as I write this) it's Boston and Philadelphia (with the traditional YO! indicated). In case you didn't see any of the Rocky movies, I should point out that most of us who live in Philly say "Yo" all the time. It means "May I have your attention please" when you're initiating a conversation, or "Whaddya want?" when you're responding to somebody calling your name. If you come in the fall, you can attend the YO festival on the banks of the Delaware River and eat soft pretzels, hoagies, and steak sandwiches.

Figure 13-2 Click your way through the cities to find the one that interests you. (Why is Cleveland part of the Northeast instead of the Midwest?)

 WEB PATH Take one of the side roads and visit some of the cities you might not know anything about — or maybe you never even heard of them. You never know what you'll learn, and you may decide to pay a visit there that isn't virtual. For example, one of my favorite places is Cape May, New Jersey, which is filled with wonderful Victorian houses and quaint places to eat and shop. I was surprised to find it on the Digital City list (guess they have an aggressive tourist agency). Double-clicking its entry produced a list of topics about Cape May, and choosing one took me to an information-filled page on the Web (see Figure 13-3).

The larger cities tend to present more than tourist information; you can dive right in and participate in chats, message boards (including personal ads), and other action (see Figure 13-4). Some have a section that permits registration as a digital citizen (you can't vote).

Check out the important things for each city, such as restaurants and theater. (Don't worry about lodging; you can sleep in the car. Finding a good place to eat and good entertainment is much more important.)

Figure 13-3   Like many cities you can visit online, Cape May provides information about lodging, vacation spots, shopping, and community services.

Figure 13-4   It might be nice to have a friend to visit when you travel to a city.

As an example, New York City's online presentation has a fulsome selection of restaurants indexed by neighborhood, price, review ratings, and cuisine. You can read restaurant reviews (as long as they were published in *The New York Times* — I guess the reviewer for *New York Magazine* doesn't rate any cyberspace). There are also Message Boards discussing restaurant experiences.

If it isn't the middle of winter, investigate Buffalo (see Figure 13-5). Of course, if you love the thought of maneuvering your car or your legs through large piles of snow, the middle of winter will suit you fine.

I tend to think of Buffalo as an interesting place to stop on the way to someplace else (no nasty letters, please), but I really believe that the best thing about Buffalo is the incredible combination of Jim Kelly and Marv Levy. Of course, to see them in action, you'll probably have to brave the snow.

Figure 13-5 New York is also the name of the state, and there's plenty to do and see outside of New York City.

Speaking of snow, Maine is another great place for vacations. Portland is represented in Digital City, and it has some interesting spots. Use the Digital City features to find lodging and restaurants there, and when you leave Portland, just keep heading North through Maine; you'll land in wonderful Bar Harbor.

There are several important things to remember about Maine:

✳ Lobster is incredibly cheap.

✳ Lobster is extremely fresh and sweet (you don't even need butter for dipping).

✳ In Northern Maine, summer (the way I define it, at least) lasts from July 4th to July 10th or so. Then it's autumn for a couple of days, and then winter starts. I'm not sure if they have spring or not; I've never been there then.

✳ Lobster is incredibly cheap.

✳ The scenery is incredible — try lying down on the top of Mount Cadillac on a starlit night to watch the Aurora Borealis, which seems close enough to reach out and touch.

✳ Lobster is incredibly cheap.

Let's move on. Okay, it's not in the United States, technically (although some of the residents frequently complain that it's an economic colony of the U.S.), but one Digital City in the Northeast section that's worth peeking at is Toronto (see Figure 13-6).

Actually, there are plenty of U.S. cities (some represented in Digital City) that are a short drive from Canada, and it's quite easy to cross the border (depending on what you've stashed in the trunk of your car).

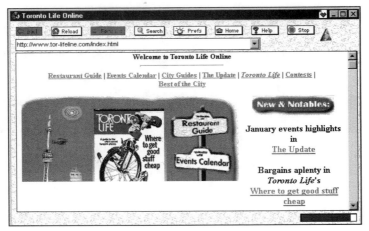

Figure 13-6 Canada is a great place to visit, and the Toronto DigitalCity information is far-reaching and informative.

Exploring the Mid-Atlantic states

It sounds as if it's in the middle of the ocean, but the Mid-Atlantic section of the United States is firmly on land. It's an area rich with history and filled with interesting cities (see Figure 13-7).

Figure 13-7 The Mid-Atlantic region is announcing a new Digital City, something you'll see a lot of as this section of AOL continues to grow.

The heart of the Mid-Atlantic is Washington, D.C., and if you haven't been there yet, shame on you. There are the obvious things to see and do, such as going to the gallery to watch the amusing scenes played out by your elected representatives. (Be aware that it's frequently a very small cast. I've never been there when there were more than a handful of elected officials on the floor of either house — where do you suppose they go during sessions?)

Browse through the D.C. site on Digital City, and you'll be amazed at what's there above and beyond your tax dollars at work. Actually, some of our tax dollars are spent in an extremely worthwhile manner, which you realize when you visit some of the museums. The good ones, like the Smithsonian institutions, are tax-supported so there's no entrance fee (see Figure 13-8).

TIP **One of the neat things on the Washington, D.C., Digital City site is the opportunity to download pictures and information files about some of the important sites in the city. It's a great source for the children's homework.**

Figure 13-8   The Museum of American Art, part of the Smithsonian, is a wonderful place to spend a day.

Halfway between Washington and Philly is Baltimore. (The *Indianapolis* Colts? I'll never get used to it — but then, I'm old enough to remember Johnny Unitas.) This is a city with a great history, going back well before the American Revolution. Head for the Inner Harbor, which has been renovated, rejuvenated, gentrified, and made altogether marvelous. The Baltimore Digital City site provides a map (see Figure 13-9).

Here are some of the great things about Baltimore (some of them are discussed in the Digital City site):

* Hard shell crabs all year round — cooked the proper way.
* There's always some great music in town, for fans of all musical genre.
* Hard shell crabs all year round — served the proper way.
* Great town for sports, and Camden Yards is a beautiful stadium.
* Hard shell crabs all year round.

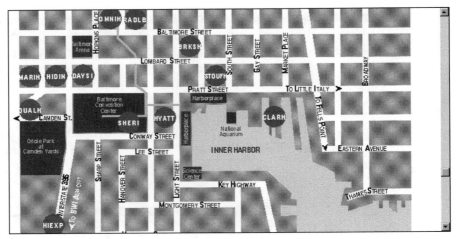

Figure 13-9 You can see how quick and easy it is to walk through the Baltimore Inner Harbor, but you'll be slowed down by yielding to the temptation offered by some marvelous restaurants.

Head to Pittsburgh for another city with plenty to offer. The only large city voted Most Livable (in the *Places Rated Almanac*), it's a cosmopolitan city without the enormous population that makes many cities seem crowded and hypertense. Browse through the Digital City information to see the rich range of activities, events, and resources.

TIP   **Pittsburgh is another virtual site with tons of information that is useful for a child's homework. Its industrial history (which is really the history of industrial America), the heritage of its Native American past that is honored to this day, and the opulence of the historic buildings that were erected by the millionaires who built fortunes from steel and railroads are all mentioned.**

Don't forget that the Steelers sent six players to the Pro Bowl, and the Pirates are always fun to watch (even if they have no taste in caps).

Speaking of history, Virginia is a real find for history buffs. A major influence in the American Revolution through its native sons (George Washington, Patrick Henry, et al), it's also the center of the history of the Civil War.

Richmond provides a wealth of information about its history in a series of articles you can download or print (more great stuff for homework help) in addition to lots of data about vacations, relocating, and entertainment (see Figure 13-10).

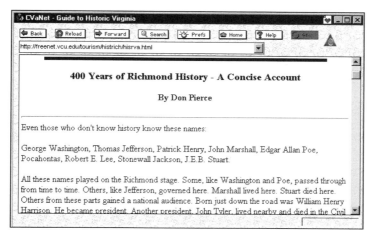

Figure 13-10 From the founding of America through all the significant historical events, Virginia has been in the center of the action.

In central Pennsylvania (double-click Harrisburg, Lebanon, Lancaster) the emphasis is on farming the old-fashioned way. The Pennsylvania Dutch still drive their buggies on the highways and live without electricity or farm machinery. The food and crafts you can purchase online are a sampling of the wonders available when you go there (see Figure 13-11). The best thing in Pennsylvania Dutch country doesn't ship well, however, so you have to visit non-virtually to sample it — funnel cake. It's not really a cake; it's a fried batter with powdered sugar sprinkled atop that starts melting in your mouth instantly. You don't have to work to eat it. You just let it melt while you moan a lot.

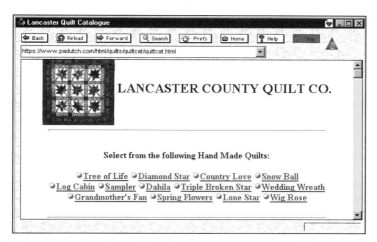

Figure 13-11 The Amish crafts are without peer, and they're still made the way they were hundreds of years ago.

If you're inspired by your virtual trip to central Pennsylvania and decide to go for a real vacation, mosey down the road a couple of miles and go to Hershey, Pennsylvania. Just walk the streets and sniff; it smells wonderful there all the time. The street lamps on Chocolate Avenue and Almond Street are shaped like Hershey kisses. Tour the factories and get samples. And, to continue the process of pointing out things that are useful for children's schoolwork, the town of Hershey is a model of the benevolent approach to business. The entire town — the houses, the schools, and everything else — were built by the original chocolate makers to provide a good lifestyle for the workers.

You might also want to go a little further up the road and visit Happy Valley (the natives' term for Penn State University) and the Nittany Lions, where Joe Paterno still rules after all these years (half the population of Pennsylvania keeps trying to get him to run for governor; the other half is holding out for the presidency).

Heading south

Head south for sunshine, higher speed limits on the highways, cheap cigarettes (the states that grow tobacco don't think much of cigarette taxes), and graceful old mansions in wonderful small towns. There are plenty of big towns, too, and a couple of big cities (see Figure 13-12). It's a mixture of everything, and that's part of the fun.

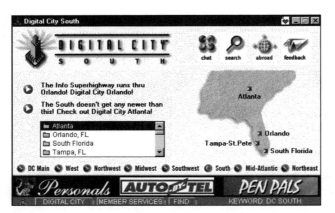

Figure 13-12 Get a virtual taste of southern hospitality in Digital City's South District.

The big city in the South is Atlanta, home of Coca-Cola (I never saw a Pepsi while I was there, but I'm told you can get some) and a gazillion streets and buildings named Peachtree. It's a great urbane city with all the variety of attractions found in any large city. Browse the information about Underground Atlanta; it will make you want to hop a plane and see it. It's what's left of Atlanta after Sherman marched his army through the city during the Civil War — the current city was rebuilt on top of it. This underground small town is filled with great stores. It's an underground mall, and the original old buildings have been joined by newer edifices to house the shops.

In North Carolina, browse the Digital Cities of Raleigh and Durham (yes, they are two separate cities, even though most people say Raleigh-Durham as if it were a single location). There's plenty of history here, with a lot of concentration on the Civil War (see Figure 13-13).

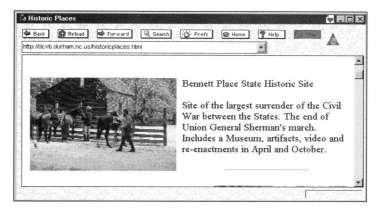

Figure 13-13   Durham has plenty of interesting sites for history buffs.

Shortly after you cross the Florida state line, you come to Jacksonville. This is a large city with all the diversity of any metropolitan area — there's plenty to do. It's even more interesting because it's within spitting distance of some great resort areas (see Figure 13-14).

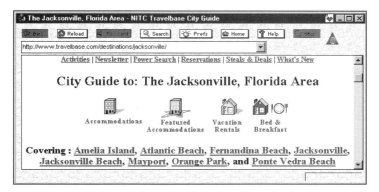

Figure 13-14   The Digital City of Jacksonville, Florida, is a veritable gold mine of information about the area. Point and click your way to the perfect spot to visit.

Florida encompasses quite a bit of land. Every time I drive to Florida, I feel great when I cross into the state, and then I remember there's almost a whole day's drive in front of me to get to Boca Raton. The South Florida area of Digital City is the place to visit to learn about cities and towns in southern Florida (see Figure 13-15).

Figure 13-15 Digital City South Florida is a gold mine of information about the gold coast towns of Florida.

When you click one of the subject buttons (for instance, Entertainment, Sports, and so on), you'll see information for all the locations involved in this enterprising approach to virtual visiting.

TIP **All this togetherness of the South Florida group is limited to the ocean side. Check out Ft. Myers/Naples and Tampa-St. Pete for information on western Florida locations.**

If you're Alabammy bound, there are plenty of cities represented. The same is true for the other southern states.

Moving Southwest

Click SW on the national map to move to the southwest part of the country. When you get there, don't be alarmed; there really is more to the southwest than Texas, regardless of what you see on the map that displays on-screen (see Figure 13-16).

Figure 13-16 Don't worry, your geography teachers were right — the map is just missing a few states and cities.

To see everything, scroll through the listings for the city that interests you. In New Mexico, the Santa Fe/Albuquerque area is noted for its emphasis on art. If you can't find time to visit in person, you can browse the galleries and stores online (see Figure 13-17).

Figure 13-17 Besides great weather, there's great creative art in Santa Fe.

Head for The Big Easy for fun, food (seriously wonderful food), fascinating architecture, and a general party atmosphere (see Figure 13-18).

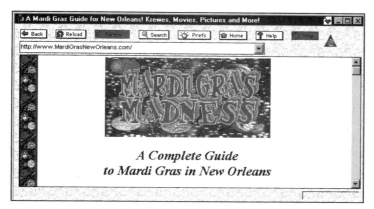

Figure 13-18 Mardi Gras is the big New Orleans event, although there's never a bad time to visit.

El Paso, Texas, is a veritable treasure chest of interesting historical museums. Oklahoma City, Oklahoma, is headquarters for fascinating stuff about Native Americans and the history of the west. Take a peek at the Will Rogers museum, one of the favorite native sons.

Deep in the heart of Texas, the Dallas/Fort Worth Digital City awaits your exploration. There's plenty to see here; it's a big area with plenty of action and interesting sites. After you investigate all the places that offer Tex-Mex food or Barbecued Ribs, you can buy a cowboy hat and boots (everybody in this area seems to wear a cowboy hat). If it's the right time of year, go see the Cowboys play (in Philly, we hate the Cowboys; we love the Iggles).

A few hours of driving (or a click of your mouse, in this case) gets you to Houston and the NASA space center. Talk about interesting things to see! If you get there for real, visit Kids Space Place and watch the kids' faces — this is a magical place.

Touring the Midwest

The middle of the country is a microcosm of the United States. It has large cities, farms, industrial sections, and lots of academic centers (see Figure 13-19).

Figure 13-19   The heart of the nation has lots of Digital Cities to explore.

You'll find a long list of Digital City participants in the Midwest and a wide variety of attractions.

The obvious place to start is Chicago, so blow over there to see one of America's great cities (see Figure 13-20).

Figure 13-20   That toddlin' town has a full range of online features for learning about the city, chatting with residents, and buying items online.

Virtual Chicago has plenty to look at. There are articles about every attraction in the city, lots of information about things to do, people to see, and places to go. Some of the country's best restaurants are here, and there's also a booming nightlife for pub crawlers. The zoo, the beauty of the lake shores, the educational facilities, and lots more keep you clicking away through this online site.

The Twin Cities (Minneapolis/St. Paul, to those who have forgotten their eighth grade geography) are another important area in the Midwest. Mary Tyler Moore does not really live there, and you can reassure your daughter that the Little House on the Prairie family did not live in either of the Twin Cities.

Goin' to Kansas City, Kansas City, USA (imagine that tune playing). When I think about my time in Kansas City, I always remember eating great barbecued meat. Arthur Bryant's Barbecue Restaurant is famous all over the country, and it's a must-go (or a must-read about if you're online). Kansas City is proud of its reputation for good BBQ, but there really is more to this town than grilled food (see Figure 13-21).

Figure 13-21   Something about the attitude of this museum makes me want to visit it.

Actually, the biggest tourist attraction in Kansas City is probably Worlds of Fun, a theme park based on the book *Around the World in Eighty Days*. It's an enormous place, with rides, food, and interesting featured attractions representing all the continents in the world.

Meet Me In Saint Loueeeee, Loueeee (singing again), and explore another great city online. Eero Saarinen's famous arch welcomes real-time visitors (climbing it was more exercise than I was really looking for), but online you can browse through some of the many attractions available here. The Botanical Garden is just incredible (it contains the largest formal Japanese garden in the world), and there are museums, a good zoo, and plenty of other attractions to investigate.

Omaha, Nebraska, is another Digital City you might want to browse. It's the home of Boy's Town (a real place, not just a movie) and played a vital role in the opening and expansion of the west. In fact, it's part of what we call the Wild West.

Exploring the Northwest

Moving into the Northwest (see Figure 13-22), I personally head for the biggest, sweetest oysters I've ever had, followed by the local salmon — which is perfect whether it's poached or grilled. The Seattle-Tacoma site in Digital City points you to more than fishing, however. The climate and clean air attracts a constant stream of visitors and new residents, and there are all the accommodations and attractions you'd expect to find in any cosmopolitan area.

Figure 13-22 This section of Digital America is full of wide-open spaces, so there aren't a lot of Digital Cities listed — but more are added as time goes on.

Portland, Oregon, is an interesting place to visit, virtually or really. I was delighted at the amount of nightlife I found there, and a trip to the Columbia River Gorge is guaranteed to awe you.

Alaska has a Digital City site, too. Apparently nobody pointed out the fact that it's a state, not a city (those little things tend to bother me). Browse the site, however, and you'll be amazed at the amount of information you can gather (see Figure 13-23).

If your only knowledge of Alaska comes from watching Northern Exposure on television, forget it — it wasn't even shot there.

Pointing West

The last stop on our virtual tour of the Digital Cities map is the West (see Figure 13-24).

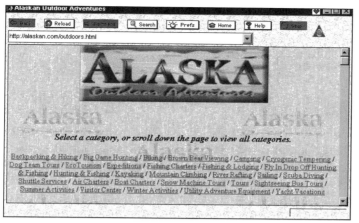

Figure 13-23 Parts of Alaska make you feel like a pioneer, and other parts are just like lots of other cities, which makes Alaska fascinating.

Figure 13-24 There's a long list of Digital Cities to explore in this part of Digital America.

Pardon me while I indulge my own preferences and start in San Francisco. I love this city, and I try to visit several times a year. No matter how long my visit is, it's not nearly long enough to see everything I want to see. There is more fun, more entertainment, more good food, and more interesting exhibits than any other city I've ever been to. Don't tell anyone, but I always visit the Exploratorium in Golden Gate Park — even when I don't have any kids with me (the Exploratorium is a totally hands-on science museum for children that is as much fun for adults as kids). All my favorite places are discussed in the San Francisco online site.

While most cities have museums for art, sculpture, and the like, San Francisco has turned Alcatraz and San Quentin into museums. There's even a museum dedicated to Pez candy dispensers (it's near the airport, in Burlingame).

There are plenty of more traditional museums, and, in fact, I don't think I've ever been anywhere with as many museums.

The North Beach area (right above Chinatown) is pasta heaven. Union Square is shoppers' heaven. Fisherman's Wharf is everybody's heaven.

Clamber around the rocks under the Golden Gate bridge (especially on the Marin side) and see the hidden underground bunkers with little slits for telescopes and guns, built to watch for Japanese ships in the bay during WWII.

As long as you're on the west coast, hop over to Hawaii (something you could only do virtually). The Digital City site for these islands is replete with information about attractions, and it's almost impossible to resist the urge to buy a plane ticket (see Figure 13-25).

Figure 13-25 The Digital City Site for Hawaii is ready to take reservations.

Moving back to the mainland, head for Los Angeles, where the Digital City site is enormous — there are plenty of articles to read. L.A. has something for everybody; it's a large city with attractions and resources that cover the widest spectrum you could imagine.

There's more to L.A. than movie making (it's called The Industry there). There are excellent restaurants and great shopping (if you go, walk along Rodeo Drive where the shops are incredible, the celebrities abound, and the parking meter spots seem reserved for Rolls Royces). It's always beach weather (although as an Easterner, I never get used to the sight of the sun setting into the ocean instead of rising out of it).

Monterey (along with nearby Carmel) is another one of my favorite California spots. The Digital City site is chock-full of information. Don't look for the canneries that Steinbeck wrote about — they're no longer there. Carmel is beautiful and peaceful, full of artists (and stuff to buy) and wonderful places to stay.

Another good site in the west is Colorado Springs (see Figure 13-26). This is a beautiful area of the country with plenty to do. It also has a collection of some of the most interesting residents I've ever encountered.

Also in Colorado, visit Denver's Digital City collection of facts about things to do, see, participate in, and enjoy. There's plenty to choose from.

Check your pocket or pocketbook for loose change and then head for Las Vegas. The Digital City pages tell you all about the city, the activities, and all the places to go to relieve yourself of the weight of those coins. There's also a wedding chapel listing (most of them are also divorce chapels).

Figure 13-26 Read all about Colorado Springs to gain some insights on life in the mountains.

When the warm and sunny climes of Arizona beckon, you should click the Phoenix icon on the map to start browsing for information (see Figure 13-27).

Figure 13-27 Phoenix and the rest of Arizona have put together goo-gobs of information to help you learn more about the area.

You'll find other cities in the west that may interest you — just double-click your way through them.

Making Pen Pals

One of the neat things about being a member of a global community such as AOL is the chance to meet other people as you journey through cyberspace. If you'd like a little more control than you can get in a chat room and you're not comfortable about participating in the personal ads in Digital City, try looking for a Pen Pal. Pen Pals correspond through e-mail.

Pen Pals are part of Digital City, but they're not attached to any particular city; they're global. Click Pen Pals in one site and reach the same place you'd get to from another site.

Getting to the Pen Pal section isn't always a one-step process because different Digital City sites have it at different levels. For example, if the Digital City you're visiting has a People button on its window, click it to move to that level. Then search for a listing named Pen Pals or Digital City Pen Pals. Sometimes that listing comes up along with all the choices for information about a Digital City. Each Digital City has its own way of storing and displaying choices. No matter how you have to delve and meander through the menu system, however, when you find this choice and double-click it, it looks like Figure 13-28.

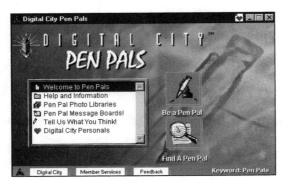

Figure 13-28 Your Pen Pal experience starts here.

TIP A faster way to get to Pen Pals is to use the keyword **Pen Pals**. When the opening Pen Pals window displays on-screen, you can choose between Digital City Pen Pals and International Pen Pals. This section assumes you're interested in Digital City folks (because that's the name of this chapter). When you click that icon, you get to the Digital City Pen Pals window.

There are two ways to approach becoming a Pen Pal.

* You can describe yourself and ask people with similar interests (or personalities or whatever else is important to you) to come forward. This is called Being a Pen Pal.

* You can respond to somebody who has already performed that step. This is called Find a Pen Pal.

Being a pen pal

Click the Be a Pen Pal icon to start your search for correspondents on AOL. The Pen Pals window is a form you have to fill out in order to tell potential Pen Pals about yourself (see Figure 13-29).

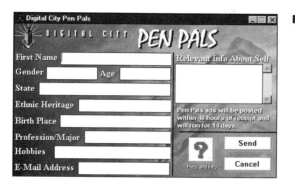

Figure 13-29 Supply the information that will attract the attention of somebody with something in common.

There are some guidelines for filling out this form that you should bear in mind:

✳ The First Name entry can either be your screen name or your real name. Many people start out with their screen name and then decide whether or not to give their real name to the correspondents who reply.

✳ There is no space on the form for a last name, a street address, or a telephone number. Do not supply this information in any field on the form. Unfortunately, there are some loonies out there.

✳ Don't use the Relevant Info space to write your autobiography. One or two descriptive sentences will do. After you begin corresponding, you can tell your Pen Pal your life story.

After you've entered the information, choose Send. The folks in charge of Pen Pals at AOL will get your information into the database within a day or two. Then just keep an eye on your mailbox.

Finding a pen pal

To find someone who has indicated an interest in finding a Pen Pal, choose Find a Pen Pal from the original Digital City Pen Pals window. You are offered two choices for finding somebody to write to (the fine points between the choices are discussed next):

✳ Choose Find a Pen Pal to look at all potential Pen Pals, sorted by age, gender, or both.

✳ Choose Search Pen Pals to enter a word or phrase that is matched on a Pen Pal's form.

If you choose Find a Pen Pal, you're asked to select how you want to proceed. You can select By Age, By Gender, or By Gender and Age.

FINDING A PEN PAL BY AGE

If you choose By Age, you're offered a series of age ranges. They tend to be narrow ranges (for instance, 19 through 21). However, as you move to older folks, the ranges get wider. For instance, there's a choice of 39 through 41, and a choice of 50 through 59. Either there are so few older people on AOL that they're thrown together to look like a crowd, or somebody figures that once you get that old you aren't all that particular. Either way, I take it personally.

Double-click the age range you're interested in to see a list of potential Pen Pals (see Figure 13-30).

Figure 13-30 Salient information from the Pen Pal forms is presented so you can choose someone with interests that match yours.

FINDING A PEN PAL BY GENDER

If you don't care about age and you select By Gender, you get to choose between male and female (well, that's no surprise). The listings aren't much help, but each listing is really a folder, which you have to double-click to open. Inside the folder are the real listings, where information about each person is displayed. The problem is you have to open each folder, close it (use the Close box — it has an X in it — in the upper right corner of the window), open the next folder, and repeat the process over and over.

If you have the personality and patience for this sort of thing, you'll probably find a lot of interesting potential Pen Pals.

FINDING A PEN PAL BY GENDER AND AGE

Clicking By Gender and Age brings up a window with choices sorted to reflect those priorities (see Figure 13-31).

Open the appropriate folder and browse the listings.

TIP If the More button is active (not greyed out), it means there are more listings than are currently displayed. Click it for additional items, and then use the down arrow on the scroll bar to continue your search.

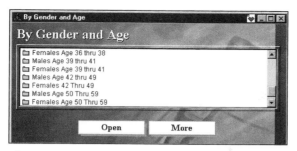

Figure 13-31 Now this makes sense as a sorting pattern.

FINDING A PEN PAL BY SEARCHING FOR WORDS

If you choose Search Pen Pals, instead of being offered the choices about gender or age, you get to decide what you want to look for. The Search window that opens permits words or phrases. Whatever you enter is matched against the forms filled out by potential Pen Pals (see Figure 13-32). When you have entered the words you want to match, choose Find Pen Pals.

Figure 13-32 We all have our priorities.

For instance, if you want to talk about cooking, you can enter **cook**. If you want to find somebody who is male and likes to cook, enter **cook and male** to indicate that both those words must be in the form. If you want to correspond with someone who likes to cook and also likes music, enter **cook and music**. Entering **cook, music** indicates that you'd like to see information on someone who has either word in the form.

TIP   The best way to match words is to use the shortest form of the word. For instance, if you enter **cooking**, you will only be offered those folks who used that word. But, if you enter **cook**, you'll see the forms for people who entered cook, cooking, cookery, and so on.

Contacting a pen pal

When you find someone who looks as if he or she might make an interesting correspondent, click Respond. The Digital City Response Form displays on-screen, which looks like a simple e-mail form with the receiver's e-mail name already filled in (see Figure 13-33).

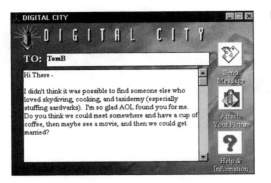

Figure 13-33 Just write a note saying hello and offering a bit of information about yourself, and then see what comes back to your mailbox.

There are plenty of interesting people on AOL, and you all start out with a couple of things in common — you use computers and you use AOL. At least that's a conversation opener.

BONUS

There's a lot more to Digital Cities than we were able to cover in this chapter. And, more cities join every month.

If you live in a city that has a Digital City site, you'll see an icon for it on your Welcome screen when you log on. You can get the latest news, weather, and sports results, and you can join chat sessions or message boards. There's no need to go through the steps for accessing Digital City to get there (although you do have to use the instructions in this chapter to reach other Digital Cities).

Adding your own comments

Almost all the Digital Cities have some form of message board available. You're encouraged to add your own comments about the Digital City site or about the city if you've been there non-virtually (the techie term for "in real life"). It's also okay to ask a question about the city and return to the site later for the answer.

Communicating with people

Many of the sites have chat rooms or personal ads. This is especially true of the larger cities. Now that you can use AOL for a fixed rate each month, using a chat room isn't as financially daunting as it used to be. However, personal ads are fraught with the possibility of danger, and you should approach carefully. Don't reveal real information such as your name, address, or telephone number.

Dealing with technical problems

As you travel through virtual America searching for information on Digital Cities, a great deal of the information is on the World Wide Web. This sometimes causes error messages to appear, but don't worry; it's almost never your fault. Things in Digital City are in a constant state of flux, and Web pages are under construction all the time.

* If the error message says that the Web page you want has moved, it will give you the name of the new page. That's a hot link, and if you click the new Web page URL (Universal Resource Locator — the techie term for the address of a Web page), you'll go there immediately.

* If the error message says the Web page isn't there anymore and offers no additional information, just close the current window to return to where you were in Digital City.

* If the error message seems complicated and deals with browser software, compressed files, or compressed graphics, you may have a compatibility problem. Some of these problems can be solved, some can't, and some are just a matter of whether or not you choose to solve them.

Going abroad

You can also visit Digital Cities on other continents. From any Digital City map, click the Abroad icon. The International Digital Cities window opens (see Figure 13-34). Every continent has a blinking red light to indicate that you can access it.

Use the International Marketplace to order wines from around the world. The Entertainment icon takes you to events like this year's opera season in Paris or news of the royal family's doings in England.

Click a continental red button, and then select a city or country. You can pay the same kind of virtual visit you experienced in Digital City America (see Figure 13-35).

You can access chat rooms and message boards, but most of the time you'll be interacting with other U.S. AOL users, discussing their experiences in foreign countries.

The Global Citizen icon takes you to a window aimed at people who commute abroad (see Figure 13-36).

Figure 13-34 Cross the oceans with a click of your mouse.

Figure 13-35 I thought I'd check to see what's changed since the USSR broke up.

Figure 13-36 When you're ready to go, here's the place to take care of the details.

Hey sports fans, the Sports icon on the International window is the place for hot info and the latest scores on soccer, cricket, fussball, and other games.

Summary

This chapter introduced you to one of the extra benefits of your AOL membership. Learning about other cities and other people is fun. Being able to get detailed information is more fun (and educational). And, planning your vacation and making reservations online is a real time-saver. The best part of Digital City, however, is available to those who are relocating. You can begin your real estate search through Digital City, contact the Chamber of Commerce for information, learn about schools, and so on. Then, when you move, you just continue to sign on to AOL as usual; the only thing you have to change is your access number.

13

CHAPTER FOURTEEN

ENHANCING YOUR FINANCES

IN THIS CHAPTER YOU LEARN THESE KEY SKILLS

"Wealth is not without its advantages and the case to the contrary, although it has often been made, has never proved widely persuasive."

John Kenneth Galbraith, *The Affluent Society,* 1958.

14

Let's face it, the nobility of poverty is appealing to struggling artists and ascetics, but few others. The rest of us realize that although money can't buy happiness, it certainly makes the pursuit a lot less stressful. Unless you've taken a vow of poverty, you're probably interested in improving your financial situation as much as you can. Unfortunately, the number of people who achieve this goal is far smaller than the number who strive for it. The reason is usually due to a lack of solid money management and financial planning. Keeping your personal finances in good shape does not require a special talent. It is a skill that can be honed and improved by using the right tools and techniques.

What better place to pick up those tools and learn those techniques than at the AOL Personal Finance channel? It provides a number of useful resources that enable you to improve your money management skills, plan your financial moves with confidence, and invest your money wisely.

One thing to keep in mind, however, is that any information you find on AOL, like all third-party information, may not be 100% accurate. Just as you would seek a second opinion before undergoing major surgery, try to confirm any information upon which you intend to base an important financial decision with a second or third source. And, **always** remember that any investment, no matter how conservative, is still a gamble.

Getting Started

Taking your money matters into your own hands is easy with all the financial information and resources available on AOL. The place to start is the Personal Finance channel. Here you can find links to the major financial areas on AOL as well as the World Wide Web.

To open the Personal Finance window:

1. Click the Keyword button on the Toolbar.

2. Type **finance** in the Enter Word(s): text box.

3. Press Enter to open the Personal Finance window (see Figure 14-1).

Figure 14-1 Don't gamble with your financial destiny. Shape it with the help of AOL.

Here are some of the resources you can find at the Personal Finance channel:

* **Display List of Resources**. Financial resources, organized by category.

* **Mutual Fund Center**. An area devoted to mutual funds exclusively.

* **Market News Center**. Financial news, stock, bond, fund, tables, and more.

- **Your Business**. Resources for the small entrepreneur who wants to play in the big leagues.
- **Quotes & Portfolios**. Track stocks, bonds, and mutual funds with delayed quotes and your own personalized portfolios.
- **Company Research**. Stop here to get the bottom line on a company before investing in its stock.
- **Online Banking Center**. Information and links to banks that provide online banking and bill paying.

Managing Your Money with AOL

With so many products, both material and financial, to choose from and so many claims being made about each one, it is difficult to spend your money wisely these days. To make intelligent financial decisions, you have to expend a lot of time and effort studying all your options. Actually, you *used to* have to expend a lot of time and effort doing research. Now, because AOL puts a myriad of financial tools at your fingertips, you can sit back, relax, and do the necessary research with a minimal amount of hassle.

Money Whiz

What does it take to be a money whiz? That's easy. An understanding of how to spend your money judiciously, how to keep your debt manageable, and how to make solid plans for your financial future. Where do you go to become a financial ace? The answer is also easy: the MoneyWhiz area of AOL. At the MoneyWhiz Finance Center, you can find advice on credit and debt management, investing, banking, and more.

To access the MoneyWhiz Finance Center, follow these steps:

1. Click the Keyword button on the Toolbar.
2. In the Enter Word(s): text box, type **moneywhiz**.
3. Press Enter to open the MoneyWhiz Welcome window.
4. In the Money Whiz Features display window, double-click The MoneyWhiz Mission.
5. In the bottom right of the MoneyWhiz Mission window, select the MoneyWhiz Finance Center to open the MoneyWhiz: Finance Center window (see Figure 14-2)

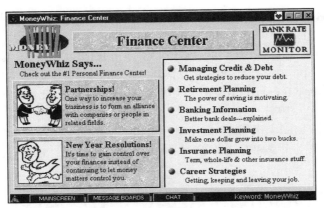

Figure 14-2 With a little training and the right tools, you too can be a master financial mechanic.

The MoneyWhiz Finance Center provides advice and articles on financial topics pertinent to individuals who want to control their own financial destinies. The MoneyWhiz site, which is managed by financial author and journalist Christy Heady, offers Money Management Message Boards and chat room sessions as well as financial information. Some of the categories for which you can find financial resources are:

* **Managing Credit & Debt**. Advice on how to avoid getting in over your head, what to do if you're already in over your head, and how to stay out of debt after you get out.

* **Retirement Planning**. Do you understand 401(k) plans? How do you plan for retirement if you're self-employed? What are some retirement plan options? The answers to these questions and more can be found at the Retirement Planning area.

* **Banking Information**. Find out how to get the best rates, keep your costs down, and take advantage of all your bank has to offer.

* **Investment Planning**. Stop here and take a crash course in investment basics. Stocks, bonds, mutual funds, treasuries, munis, and more are covered. Investing your money is not as daunting a task as it may seem at first glance.

* **Insurance Planning**. What kind and how much insurance do you really need? Find out at the Insurance Planning area.

* **Career Strategies**. Unless you're heir to a multimillion dollar fortune, your financial world probably centers around your ability to earn money in your chosen occupation. Whether you're employed, looking for a job, or thinking about striking out on your own, you can find some useful tips here.

Because there is no direct access to the MoneyWhiz Finance Center, it is a perfect candidate for Favorite Places. Simply drag the red heart that's in the upper right-hand corner of the MoneyWhiz: Finance Center window onto the Favorite Places icon in the Toolbar and drop it. The next time you want to visit the MoneyWhiz Finance Center, open your Favorite Places folder and double-click MoneyWhiz Finance Center.

Consumer Reports

When it comes to product evaluation, there's no better-known or more trusted name than Consumer Reports. For years, they have been providing fair, unbiased testing and reporting on every consumer product from mouthwash to Maseratis. Now they're online with AOL and available to you for quick product research with a few keystrokes. The reports found on AOL are derived from *Consumer Reports Magazine*'s published articles. The policy of No-Commercialization is carried over to the AOL online service, which means no advertisements are allowed in the Consumer Reports area of AOL.

To access the Consumer Reports area:

1. Click the Keyword button on the Toolbar.

2. In the Enter Word(s): text box, type **consumer reports**.

3. Press Enter to open the Consumer Reports window (see Figure 14-3).

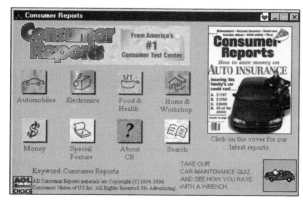

Figure 14-3 Consumer Reports helps you get the most bang for your buck.

Here's some of what you can expect to find in the Consumer Reports area:

* **Automobiles**. In addition to profiles of the major makes and models, you can also find Road Test Reports, reliability reports, and information on a variety of auto accessories.

* **Electronics**. Whatever your consumer electronic needs, you can find valuable information on cameras, computers, fax machines, televisions, and more.

* **Food & Health**. It's Friday night, you just got home late from work, you're beat, and you have no intention of cooking. What do you do? Order pizza, of course. However, which one should you really be ordering? Well, take a look in the Consumer Reports Food & Health to get an evaluation of the major pizza chains as well as supermarket pizzas for taste, nutrition, and cost comparisons.

* **Home & Workshop**. Those tools and appliances that, not too many years ago, were considered luxuries have now become essential elements of almost every household today. Dishwashers, microwaves, and espresso makers are just a few of the items you can find analyzed in this area. Okay, you got me. Espresso makers aren't a necessity in most households, but you can still check them out here.

* **Money**. Need some advice on how to handle the kids' allowances? Or perhaps you're not sure about proper tipping practices. What exactly is a debit card anyway? Check out this area for answers to your money-related questions.

* **Search**. In addition to being able to browse the different categories, you can also perform a keyword search on the entire Consumer Reports area.

Bank Rate Monitor

As we as a nation have become more and more dependent upon credit, it is imperative to stay on top of the latest trends and rates that banks are charging for car loans, mortgages, and credit cards. The Bank Rate Monitor offers an excellent overview of the banking industry nationwide. If you want to find out who's got the best rates on Certificates of Deposit (CDs), this is also the place to stop.

To access the Bank Rate Monitor area:

1. On the Toolbar, click the Keyword button.

2. Type **brm** in the Enter Word(s): text box.

3. Press Enter to open the Bank Rate Monitor window (see Figure 14-4).

Because of easy access to credit, many people find themselves unnecessarily stretched by their debt. One way to avoid this is by keeping an eye on what the prevailing rates are and shopping around for a loan or credit card. In the Bank Rate Monitor area, you can find the following information:

* **Mortgage Rates**. Nationwide highs, lows, and averages for fixed and variable rates, plus state by state information on specific banks, can be found at the Mortgage Rates area (see Figure 14-5).

Figure 14-4   Whether you're borrowing or investing, be sure to get the best rate available.

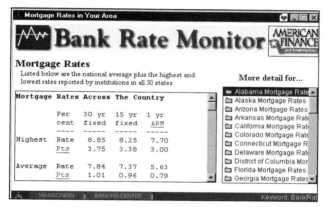

Figure 14-5   A quick stop at the Mortgage Rates area could save you a bundle.

✻ **Highest Yielding CDs**. Bank name, phone number, and rate for the highest Certificate of Deposit rates in the country. Because the best rates are liable to be outside your state, the Bank Rate Monitor also provides tips on how to open out-of-town accounts.

✻ **New Car Loans**. Get the best rate on your new car loan by checking this state by state listing.

✻ **Best Credit Card Deals**. For the best credit card rates around, this is the area to visit.

Planning with AOL

A key element to any campaign, whether in war, politics, or finances is proper planning. Without it, you're on a haphazard course that could lead anywhere. When it comes to your personal finances, you can't afford to wander about aimlessly if you want to secure your financial future. Therefore, planning must be an integral part of your personal finance strategy.

Financial planning

When you mention financial planning, most people think budgets and investments. Although that's part of the financial planning process, budgets and investments are by no means the only elements to a long-term financial plan. The major financial events in your life can, to a great extent, be planned for ahead of time to obtain the most benefit from each one. Housing, automobiles, insurance, and college for the kids consume significant portions of your income and should be planned expenditures — not spur-of-the-moment impulse decisions. Although AOL does not offer a lot in the way of overall financial planning advice, the information is available if you do a little hunting for specific topics.

* **Housing**. Check out the Bank Rate Monitor (keyword: **bankrate**) for the best mortgage rates, and then stop at the MoneyWhiz (keyword: **moneywhiz**) Home and Auto Shopping area for tips on mortgage types, closing costs, and shopping for the best deal. A quick trip to Ric Edelman's Money University (see Figure 14-6) will net you advice on whether it's better to rent or buy, when to refinance, the best way to pay off your mortgage, and more. Use the keyword search **moneyu** to access the Money University, and then select Classroom and double-click Mortgage.

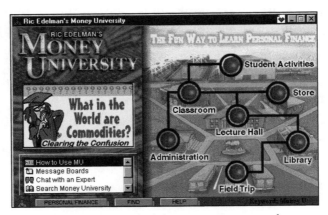

Figure 14-6   You can find the answers to many of your financial questions at Money U.

- **Automobile**. First determine what you need and what you can afford, and then look for the best buys at Consumer Reports (keyword: **consumer reports**). To check for the lowest auto loan rates, head for the Bank Rate Monitor (keyword: **bankrate**) area. The MoneyWhiz (keyword: **moneywhiz**) Home and Auto Center gives you sound advice on buying or leasing as well as car shopping tips.

- **Debt Planning**. It is inevitable that you will find yourself in debt at one time or another. The big question is will you manage your debt, or will it manage you? The answer depends on how well you have planned for your debt. The MoneyWhiz (keyword: **moneywhiz**) Finance Center offers a lot of information on managing debt and credit. Keeping an eye on prevailing interest rates when obtaining loans or credit cards by stopping at the Bank Rate Monitor (keyword: **bankrate**) is always a good idea.

- **Insurance Planning**. All too often an afterthought, or simply left up to the discretion of your local agent, this is an area that should be tackled head on. You can begin by taking advantage of the MoneyWhiz (keyword: **moneywhiz**) Insurance Planning Strategies.

- **Retirement Planning**. You're never too old to plan for retirement. Who knows, if you plan right, you may be able to retire early enough to really enjoy it. A stop at the MoneyWhiz (keyword: **moneywhiz**) Retirement Planning area will give you plenty to think about.

- **College Planning**. The first place to start your college planning is at the Road to College (keyword: **road to college**) found in the AOL reference area. Here you can find tips on selecting, testing for, and applying to colleges, in addition to financial preparation advice. Ric Edelman's Money University (keyword: **money u**) Classroom offers more advice on how to plan for the cost of college.

Tax planning

Although it's true that taxes are inevitable, it is possible to minimize their impact with the proper planning. Planning your financial moves, such as buying or selling a house, stock, or business, can result in a significantly reduced tax burden. The timing and method of major financial transactions can make a big difference in the tax implications. The Tax Planning window of the Personal Finance Channel is AOL's jumping-off point for tax planning.

To open the Tax Planning window, follow these steps:

1. Click the Keyword button on the Toolbar.

2. Type **tax** in the Enter Word(s): text box.

3. Press Enter to open the Tax Planning window (see Figure 14-7).

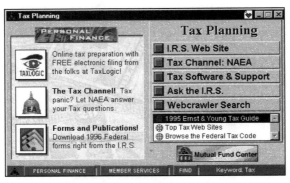

Figure 14-7 Take the pain out of taxes with AOL's Tax Planning.

The following are some of the features you can find at the Tax Planning area:

* **I.R.S. Web Site**. A new World Wide Web site that contains tax law, publications, forms, and more.

* **Tax Channel: NAEA**. A wealth of tax information supplied by members of the National Association of Enrolled Agents who are professional, independent tax advisors licensed by the federal government to provide taxpayer representation before the I.R.S.

* **TaxLogic**. Tax news, advice, and information from TaxLogic's team of tax experts.

* **WebCrawler Search**. A direct link to the WebCrawler search engine and a number of tax-related Web Sites.

THE TAX CHANNEL

The NAEA Tax Channel offers advice and information provided by Enrolled Agents. As independent agents, they are licensed to represent taxpayers going before the I.R.S. They are agents of the taxpayer and not the I.R.S. These individuals must pass rigorous I.R.S. tests or have a minimum of five years working at the I.R.S. in a position that requires the application and interpretation of I.R.S. code and regulations. To open the NAEA Tax Channel (see Figure 14-8), use the keyword **naea**.

Some of the information available on the NAEA Tax Channel includes:

* **Top Tax News**. All the tax news that's fit to print.

* **Tax Tip of the Day**. Tax FAQs (Frequently Asked Questions) as well as current and past tax tips.

* **Tax Web Hotlinks**. In addition to links to federal and state Web taxation sites, you can also find links to a variety of tax products and services.

* **Tax Chat**. Weekly chat sessions hosted by tax professionals.
* **Tax Message Boards**. Members exchange information and experiences on tax matters.

Figure 14-8   Get tax advice from the experts.

TAXLOGIC

The TaxLogic site offers news, advice, and information from the TaxLogic tax experts, many of whom are CPAs. You can also find chat sessions, Message Boards, and links to tax-related Web sites.

To open the TaxLogic window, follow these steps:

1. On the Toolbar, click the Keyword button.

2. In the Enter Word(s): text box, type **taxlogic**.

3. Press Enter to open the TaxLogic window (see Figure 14-9).

Figure 14-9   Tax help is just a mouse click away at TaxLogic.

Investing with AOL

Mastering your financial destiny is a three-step process. First, you must learn to manage the money you have in order to set some aside for investing. Next, you have to establish a plan for the future. Third, you must wisely invest the money from step one to ensure the success of the plan you developed in step two. Whether you're new to investing or an old pro, AOL has something to help you make the right investment decisions.

The Motley Fool

If you haven't heard of the Motley Fool, I can only assume that you've been on retreat in Tibet for the last couple of years. What started as a small circulation, hard copy newsletter in 1993 has grown in the last two years to become cyberspace's most popular alternative investment forum. Giving down-to-earth, money saving, practical advice with a generous dose of humor is the key to their success. It also helps that their portfolio routinely beats the industry averages. To access the Motley Fool (see Figure 14-10), use the keyword **fool**.

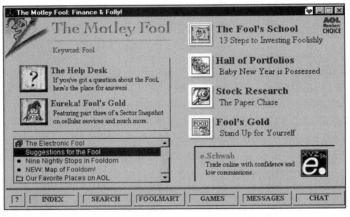

Figure 14-10   Fool's paradise for the maverick investor.

THE FOOL'S SCHOOL

I'll bet you never thought you had to learn what comes naturally to so many of us: acting "foolishly." Fortunately, the Fool's School (see Figure 14-11) teaches you to act as dumb as a fox, using the Motley Fool school of thought. The Fool's School curriculum consists of a thirteen-step investing program that starts from ground zero and walks you through the process of becoming an intelligent and capable investor in your own right.

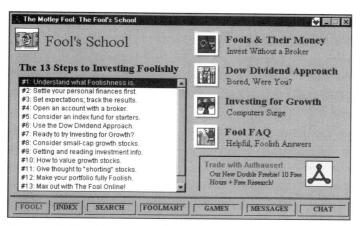

Figure 14-11 Okay — stop fooling around and pay attention;
you may learn something!

The thirteen-step program starts off by advising you to get your financial house in order before jumping into any investments. From there, it offers advice on brokers, market indexes, performing your own research, and the various investment strategies to consider. In addition to the investment lessons, you can also find

* **Fools & Their Money**. This area offers money management tips on such things as saving money, clearing up debt, and even the best strategy for buying a car.

* **Dow Dividend Approach**. A simple investment strategy which, over the last twenty-five years, has consistently outperformed the market by a two-to-one ratio. This area includes an explanation of the Dow Dividend Approach, the statistics behind it, and the Message Boards discussing it.

* **Investing for Growth**. Another investment strategy similar to the Dow Dividend Approach, but containing mid to large cap growth stocks.

* **Fool FAQ**. If you guessed frequently asked questions, you're wrong. What else would it be but Foolishly Answered Questions? No matter what you call them, here you can find answers to common questions about the Motley Fool as well as general investment questions.

HALL OF PORTFOLIOS

Now that you've brushed up on your investment skills, it's time to move on to the real world of investing. The Hall of Portfolios (see Figure 14-12) is precisely that. Here, you can see a comparison of the performance of actual stock portfolios against the S&P 500 and the NASDAQ averages.

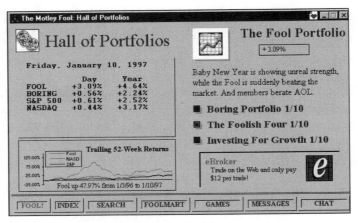

Figure 14-12 Does the Motley Fool investment strategy really work?

✳ **The Fool Portfolio**. Their second day online, the Motley Fool founders David and Thomas Gardner began the Fool Portfolio with six stock purchases. Since its inception, the Fool Portfolio has outperformed the S&P 500.

✳ **Boring Portfolio**. Begun in January of 1996, this portfolio favors the less glamorous stocks that will perform well over the long haul.

✳ **The Foolish Four**. A portfolio, derived using the Dow Approach, that over the last 25 years has compounded at an annual rate of 22.23%. A respectable return in anybody's book.

✳ **Investing for Growth**. The rate of return on the Investing for Growth portfolio from 1980 to 1995 was 26.06%. The portfolio was assembled using the Investing for Growth Strategy discussed elsewhere in this chapter.

STOCK RESEARCH

Unless your investing strategy involves a Ouija board or tea leaves, you should do some amount of research on the stocks, bonds, or other vehicles in which you plan to invest. The Motley Fool crew agree and have provided the Stock Research (see Figure 14-13) area to aid you in your quest for knowledge.

The Stock Research area, in addition to having an abundance of general information on industry sectors, also includes tips on evaluating stocks, weekly earnings reports, and more.

✳ **How to Value Stocks**. Explains how to read a balance and what the different valuation strategies, such as earnings-based, revenues-based, and equity-based mean.

✳ **FoolWire & Specials**. Financial news and editorials

✳ **Weekly Industry Updates**. Weekly reports on the status of various industry sectors, including biotech, healthcare, and real estate — to name a few.

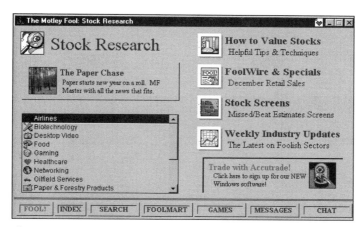

Figure 14-13 A little knowledge can go a long way in making smart investment decisions.

FOOL'S GOLD

Fool's Gold is the Motley Fool's weekly online periodical with news and features to keep you up to date on the latest financial happenings. In addition to previous editions and links to other Motley Fool areas, the Fool's Gold (see Figure 14-14) provides you with more focused information than the other areas.

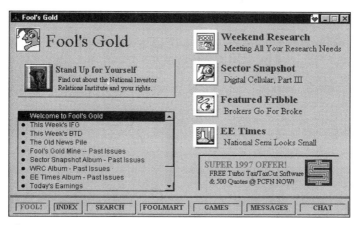

Figure 14-14 When it comes to investing, research is as good as gold.

✳ **Weekend Research**. A listing of the previous week's companies with major announcements. A good starting point for researching potential buys.

* **Sector Snapshot**. A brief analysis of a particular industry sector or group of stocks, plus a look at the individual players in the group.
* **Featured Fribble**. A weekly anecdotal editorial provided by Motley Fool members. Anyone can submit a fribble for consideration. One is chosen each week and is included in Fool's Gold.
* **EE Times**. An online version of the weekly newspaper focusing on the electronics industry.

Quotes & Portfolios

The Quotes & Portfolios area of the Personal Finance channel offers a quick and simple way to get delayed quotes and track the performance of your stocks, bonds, and other investments. To access the Quotes & Portfolios (see Figure 14-15) site, use the keyword **quotes**.

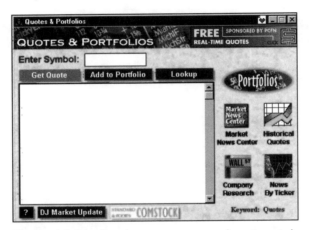

Figure 14-15 Keeping an eye on your investments is key to any investment strategy.

To get a delayed quote, type the stock symbol in the Enter Symbol: text box and then press Enter.

If you don't know the symbol, you can find it by following these steps:

1. Click the Lookup button to open the Search Symbols window (see Figure 14-16).

Figure 14-16 Finding a stock is easy with Search Symbol.

2. Type the first few letters of the company name or symbol (in case you know only part of the symbol) in the text box.

3. If you typed the company name, select Search By Company, otherwise click Search By Symbol.

4. From the display list of stocks that match your criteria, select the one you desire and then press Enter to see the quote (see Figure 14-17). If your stock does not appear, select More to see additional listings that match your search criteria.

TIP Since the stock quotes provided by AOL are delayed quotes, they will not be 100% accurate. The delay is usually at least twenty minutes and sometimes more. Before making any buy or sell decision, it is best to obtain a real-time quote. These are available through your broker.

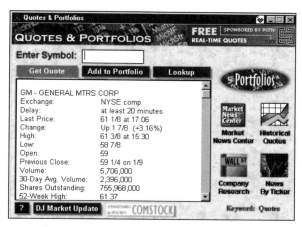

Figure 14-17 You can see at a glance how your stock is performing.

In addition to checking out stock quotes, you can also create portfolios of your investments. Because most of us invest to increase our wealth, it is essential to be able to see at any given moment the value and performance of our investments. Fortunes are won and lost in the blink of an eye on Wall Street. Creating and maintaining a portfolio gives you the ability to closely track your investments and make timely decisions.

To create a portfolio:

1. Click the Portfolios icon on the right side of the Quotes & Portfolios window to open the Portfolio Summary window (see Figure 14-18).

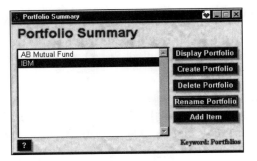

Figure 14-18 Creating a portfolio is as easy as losing money trading options.

2. Select Create Portfolio to open the Add a Portfolio window.

3. Type the name you want to give the new portfolio, click OK, and you're done.

To add items to the portfolio follow these steps:

1. In the Quotes & Portfolios area, click the Portfolio icon to open the Portfolio Summary window.

2. Select Add Item to open the Add Item window (see Figure 14-19).

Figure 14-19 To add an item to your portfolio, you need some basic information.

3. Enter the symbol in the Symbol: field, and then Tab to the next field.

4. Enter the number of shares purchased.

5. Enter the price paid for the shares when they were first purchased, and then select OK to add the item to your portfolio.

TIP If you have purchased the same stock at different times and therefore at different prices, enter each purchase as a separate item to accurately track their progress.

Once you've created a portfolio and have added a few things to it, you can look at it and see how you're doing over-all.

To view your portfolio, follow these steps:

1. In the Quotes & Portfolios area, click the Portfolio icon to open the Portfolio Summary window.

2. Highlight the portfolio you want to see.

3. Select Display Portfolio to open the Portfolio Detail window (see Figure 14-20).

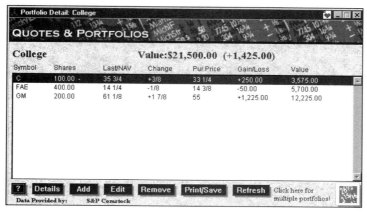

Figure 14-20   The Portfolio Detail view gives you a snapshot of your investments and their value.

In addition to the ability to create portfolios and get stock quotes, the Quotes & Portfolios site offers access to several other AOL areas of interest to investors:

* **Market News Center**. Comprehensive news coverage of all the market sectors.

* **Historical Quotes**. An excellent way to see how a stock has performed in the past, this area allows you to download quotes for a selected period of the stock's life.

* **Company Research**. Detailed information on the financial condition of individual companies.

* **Company News**. Search AOL's news resources for company-specific news using the stock market symbol.

Mutual Fund Center

If you're into mutual funds, this is the place for you. You can find mutual fund advice, information, and news, plus links to many of the major funds online. Check out the Sage area, which includes tips, Message Boards, chat sessions, and a tutorial that all focus on mutual funds. To access the Mutual Fund Center (see Figure 14-21), use the keyword **mutual funds**.

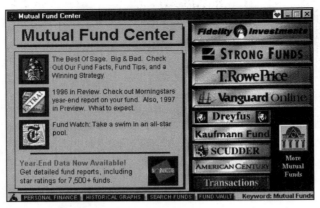

Figure 14-21 If mutual funds are your cup of tea, the Mutual Fund Center is your kind of place.

Stocks and Investing

Another area of interest to investors is the Stocks and Investing area of AOL. Here you can find general information on investing and stock analysis, as well as links to the Motley Fool, Business Week, and more. To access the Stocks and Investing area (see Figure 14-22), use the keyword **pf stocks**.

Figure 14-22 Become a savvy investor by boning up at the Stocks and Investing site.

Some of the features found at the Stocks and Investing area are

* **AAII**. The American Association of Individual Investors, a non-profit organization that's been helping individuals to manage their investments since 1978, is now online at AOL. Stop here for investment basics and expert advice.

* **The Online Investor**. These guys have investment advice to spare.

* **Investor's Network**. A forum for members to exchange investment advice, info, and tips.

- *** Decision Point**. A forum for those investors using technical analysis as a basis for their investment decisions.
- *** Bond Center**. Information on treasury bonds, municipal bonds, interest rates, and more.
- *** Exchange Center**. Find out what makes the major stock exchanges tick at the Exchange Center.

BONUS

We all know how frustrating it is when you need information on your bank account but the bank is closed. Trying to balance your checkbook with a missing check is enough to drive you crazy. You have no idea how much it was for and whether or not you can spend any of the money left in the account. If only you could tap into the bank's system to see if the check has cleared and for what amount! Well, now you can do just that, with online banking.

The opportunity to do your banking online, and pay your bills without writing a check or licking a stamp, is very enticing. For the bank's part, the savings in labor and physical assets such as buildings and furnishings is all too alluring to ignore. We are now in the early stages of a move to electronic banking and bill paying. Although computerized bill-paying services have been around for a number of years, they have not made a great deal of headway — for the simple reason that until recently they have been third-party ventures without widespread support from the banking industry. The tremendous growth in the computer industry is spurring banks to move with the times and provide online banking services. To check out the services offered by the banks at the AOL Banking Center (see Figure 14-23) use the keyword search **bank**.

TIP

Shopping for banking services is no different than shopping for any other product. Be sure to compare services and fees to see that you are getting the best buy for your money. Don't be fooled into paying for services that you don't need. Be sure to inquire about *all* fees that are associated with the account. It won't do you any good to get drawn in with low monthly fees if charges per check, deposit, overdraft, and so on are excessive.

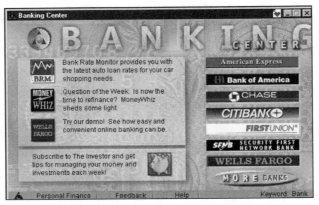

Figure 14-23 Tired of standing in line to transfer money or get a balance? Check out the AOL Banking Center for online banking services.

Summary

Getting your financial house in order takes planning, discipline, and good decision making. By taking advantage of the financial resources available on AOL, you can get your finances under control, plan for the future, and make sound investment decisions.

PART FOUR

USING THE INTERNET

Get ready to enter cyberspace! You're going to the Internet and the World Wide Web. During your trip, you'll learn how to maneuver all the AOL features so your travel is fun and productive.

In an industry where speed is key, mortgage professionals avail themselves of the latest, most comprehensive information to cut their deals. In the past, mortgage lenders would cozy around the fax machine, disseminating their daily rates to mortgage brokers around the country, who could easily number in the thousands, at toll call rates that added up.

MixStar, in its partnership with America Online, has created a brave new world where mortgage lenders can distribute price lists to these thousands of brokers at the click of a button, and where brokers, on the other end, can access key information in a personalized, customized way, without having to plow through vast quantities of irrelevant material.

"We intend to make MixStar the mortgage place in cyberspace," said Kirk Hoiberg, president of the 10-person company in Newport Beach, California, "with the broadest array of content presented in the most user-friendly way. We will add more industry players, more lenders, and we will add value through interactive tools like the trading board."

Beyond the price lists, which constitute the heart of the communication between lenders and brokers, MixStar provides a smorgasbord of related information. One of their menu items hooks subscribers into the Wall Street world with Treasury and mortgage-backed security updates — freshly revised every 15 minutes.

Trading boards allow mortgage professionals to post classified ads relating to the exchange of products and services. For instance, a broker might use the service to locate a lender for a hard-to-fund loan. Subscribers can generate business and literally cut deals online.

In addition to the hard facts, MixStar publishes the *Market Commentary*, which summarizes and articulates economic statistics and market trends, and the *Industry News*, which features news stories and press releases of interest to industry players.

How did MixStar choose AOL for its partner in this exciting venture? "In the beginning, we looked at all the different commercial online services and proprietary networks. AOL was very user-friendly, the simplest to use, and could reach the mass market," said Mr. Hoiberg. Mr. Hoiberg is especially satisfied that the mass-market criterion has been fulfilled.

To give form and substance to the new concept, Mr. Hoiberg said, "We went into intensive design as to content, used focus groups in the industry—people having a mortgage practitioner background, not technical one. We then went to large lenders, and got them to become content partners." As far as Mr. Hoiberg is aware, MixStar is the first business-to-business application on AOL.

USING THE INTERNET

IN THIS CHAPTER YOU LEARN THESE KEY SKILLS

There is no escaping the Internet. Even if you aren't using a computer and modem to connect to the outside world, you are probably totally aware of the Internet. It's an enormous group of computers, located all over the world, all connected by phone lines.

You can connect your computer to any one of those computers if you have the right equipment. Luckily, as an AOL user, you *do* have the right equipment. You have a computer, a modem, and — when you log on to AOL — the software. AOL lets you hop over to the Internet whenever you wish.

In fact, if you've been using AOL for a while and you've been visiting special interest sites, you may have already visited the Internet: many of the sites jump there when you ask to see specific items. Because you didn't specifically choose the AOL Internet Connection, you may not have been aware of it.

This chapter presents an overview of the Internet services you'll find on AOL.

Connecting to the Internet

For a direct connection to the Internet, use the keyword **Internet** (or click Internet Connection on the Channels window). AOL has a collection of Internet Resources, so you can head right to your favorite virtual place or read about the Internet before deciding which part of the Internet you want to join (see Figure 15-1).

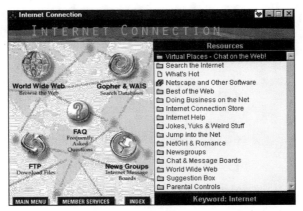

Figure 15-1   AOL has an Internet Connection page that's your launch pad to the virtual world.

Most of the items in the Resources list are informational. It's probably a good idea to browse for the ones that are similar to your own aspirations for using the Net. An even better idea is to click the FAQ (Frequently Asked Questions) icon to get information about all the important Internet topics (see Figure 15-2).

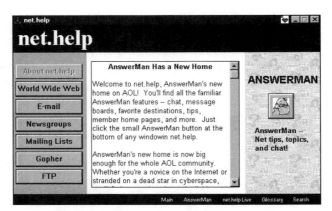

Figure 15-2   All the questions users (along with the answers) have asked are collected for your edification.

The AOL Internet Connection page is just the launch pad for your trip to the Internet, so now let's take off and start traveling.

Browsing the Web

There must be a way to describe the World Wide Web (WWW); there must be some word or phrase — but if there is, I don't know it. This is an awesome place. It's a group of sites all over the world that are linked together by hyperlinks.

Understanding hyperlinks

Let's talk about hyperlinks for a moment because they're very important in understanding how you get information from the Web. So you can better understand the process, I'll create a scenario that's easy to understand.

You're reading a book about the founding of America. A great deal of information about Benjamin Franklin's contribution is in the book, and you become interested in him. You go to the library or book store to get a book about Franklin. As you read the book, you become fascinated with electricity. You go back to the bookshelves for a book about electricity. Isn't the stuff about Tesla interesting? You leave the house again to get a book about Tesla.

Suppose, however, that in the book about the founding of America, you click a mouse pointer on the word Franklin whenever it is mentioned and the book about Franklin just pops into your hands, on top of the book about America. Then, while reading the Franklin book you click the word "electricity" and a book on that subject is magically sitting on top of the Franklin book. It keeps going this way until you've piled up lots of books and are moving from subject to subject as your curiosity is tweaked.

That's how the Web works. Every time you see a word that's in a different color, or an icon that's marked with a subject, you click and fly there. The links are called hypertext links, and they're "webbed together."

Understanding Web sites

A Web site is a place on the World Wide Web that is created and maintained by one entity, such as a corporation, an organization, or a person. On that site, you'll find one or more *Web pages*, which are the smallest element of the Web. Pages usually contain links to other pages on the same site or to other sites.

To find a Web site, you have to know its address, which is called a *URL* (Universal Resource Locator). The URL always starts with *http://* followed by the address. Most of the time the first part of the address is *www*.

Going to the Web

Click the World Wide Web icon on the Internet Connection window to move to AOL's home page on the Web (see Figure 15-3).

Figure 15-3 The AOL Web Browser is ready to travel.

You have plenty of options for traveling the Web from here:

* If you know the URL of the site you want to visit, enter it in the top box (where the AOL URL is) and then press Enter.

* Click AOL Members' Choice to see the Web sites that AOL members think are the best.

* Enter a word or phrase in the Search box and then click Search to begin your hunt for specific information.

* Click one of the topics to go to the Web sites that are related to that topic.

For example, if you wanted to learn more about IDG books (maybe to find another book with detailed information about using the Internet), you could enter the URL (**http://www.idgbooks.com**), or enter **IDGbooks** in the search box. When you get to the site, you'll see lots of links so you can click your way to exactly where you want to be (see Figure 15-4).

TIP **Although using the search box seems easy, it's usually the longest route to any Web site. You can narrow the search by using the tips provided in the search help section, but you'll generally have to move farther and farther through search results to get where you want to go. Using a proper name is generally the fastest way to use the search box.**

There are gazillions of useful things on the Web. Here are some to look for:

* Shareware and freeware, which is great software that you buy on the honor system or get for nothing (make sure you have a virus checker on your computer so you don't bring home any problems).

* Technical support for hardware and software from the manufacturers.
* Groups that offer help and support for software and operating systems.
* Updates for software and operating systems.
* Drivers for printers and other peripherals.
* Beta software you can download, try, and report bugs about to help the company test it. (If you're not comfortable with computers, this can be dangerous.)
* Encyclopedias and other reference books.

There's almost no end to the information on the Internet. It can become totally addictive, so start your first trip at your own risk.

Figure 15-4   Home pages, like this one for IDG, have links to lots of subjects, all of which are just a mouse click away.

Joining Newsgroups

Newsgroups are like Message Boards on AOL. They're a way to read messages from other users and add your own comments. The proper name for this element of the Internet is *Usenet Newsgroups*, but you'll hear the jargon *Usenet* as well as *Newsgroups*.

The groups are established to be focused and single-purposed. For example, there may be 20 different newsgroups for OS/2, with topics ranging from programming to using a specific part of that operating system.

Understanding the newsgroup names

The way to figure out the newsgroup's focus is to read the name of the newsgroup. There are several parts to the name; each part is separated by a period, and each part is a clue to its purpose. The names are hierarchical, and each part of the name narrows the focus of the newsgroup. The first part of the name indicates the newsgroup's category. Most newsgroups fall into one of these categories:

* ✴ **rec**, for recreational topics such as movies, hobbies, sports, and other lifestyle topics.
* ✴ **comp**, for computer information.
* ✴ **soc**, for social issues and also for cultural and ethnic groups.
* ✴ **talk**, for opinions. Any topic is fair game.
* ✴ **sci**, for science, such as chemistry, physics, and so forth.
* ✴ **news**, for discussion about Usenet groups.
* ✴ **alt**, for topics that don't fit into the main categories. These topics are frequently risqué and sometimes deal with topics not suitable for children.

There are other names for categories that crop up from time to time (and disappear from time to time), so this list is probably not complete.

After the first part of a newsgroup name, the following parts of the name hierarchy continue to narrow its focus. For example, comp.os.os2.games represents the following:

* ✴ comp = computers
* ✴ os = operating systems (a subset of computers)
* ✴ os2 = the specific operating system being discussed (a subset of operating systems)
* ✴ games = the particular topic being discussed (a subset of os2)

TIP   The lowercase presentation of terms is not a typographical error. In newsgroups and throughout the Internet, just about everything is solid lowercase (this stems from the UNIX operating system, the origin of the Internet).

Finding and subscribing to newsgroups

To move to the Internet newsgroups, click the NewsGroups icon on the AOL Internet Connection window. The Newsgroups window displays on-screen (see Figure 15-5) and offers a number of choices for your next step.

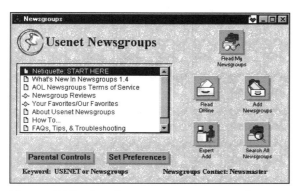

Figure 15-5   Start here to set up your use of newsgroups.

The logical choice for a first step is to find the newsgroups you want to join. (Okay, as a preliminary choice, it's probably a good idea to read one or more of the information files in the list box, so call that step Pre-One and we'll move on to Step One.) You join newsgroups by subscribing to them. You create your own subscription list so that you don't have to wade through every newsgroup on the Internet (there are more than 20,000 of them) when you want to participate.

To begin building your subscription list, follow these steps:

1. Click Add Newsgroups.

2. When the Categories window appears (see Figure 15-6), scroll through the available choices to find one of interest to you.

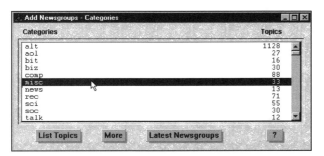

Figure 15-6   I'm in the mood for conversation about
miscellaneous stuff.

3. Double-click the category you want to browse through.

4. The next level of hierarchical names for this category appears in the Topics window. Find the subcategory that looks interesting and double-click.

TIP   Depending on the category and subcategory you've chosen, there may be yet another window in which you have to make a choice as you move through the hierarchy.

5. Finally, you get to the newsgroup you want to put on your subscription list (see Figure 15-7).

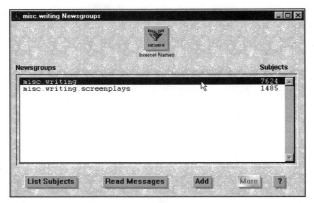

Figure 15-7   I found the newsgroup I want, but I'll never be able to catch up on all those messages!

6. To be sure this is the right group for you, you can click List Subjects to see the subjects of the messages, or you can click Read Messages to begin reading actual messages (you'll start with the first message).

7. If you're already sure (or you already read some messages and have decided you want to subscribe), choose Add.

8. AOL pops up a little message box telling you that this newsgroup is on your subscription list. Click OK to make the box go away.

To subscribe to more newsgroups, follow the same procedures (just back up a few windows by closing the windows).

TIP   If you know the exact name of the newsgroup you want to subscribe to, you don't have to go through these steps. Click the Expert Add icon on the AOL Newsgroups window and enter the name. You must have all the parts of the name spelled correctly and the periods must be in the right place.

Reading newsgroup messages

When your subscriptions are all lined up, you're ready to go. After you log on to AOL, use the keyword **Newsgroups** (or **USENET**) to go to the Newsgroups window.

Then follow these steps:

1. Click Read My Newsgroups to display the Read My Newsgroups window (see Figure 15-8).

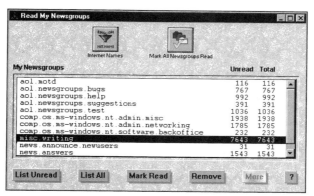

Figure 15-8 The first time you visit your newsgroups, there are an awful lot of messages to catch up on.

 TIP In addition to the newsgroups you chose, AOL adds some to your subscription list. These are newsgroups that have messages about using newsgroups; AOL thinks you might be interested in reading the messages.

2. Click the name of the newsgroup you want to participate in, and then choose List All to see all the subjects being discussed (see Figure 15-9). Subjects are also called *threads* because they're threads of conversations. Messages are also sometimes called *postings* because they've been posted to the Internet site.

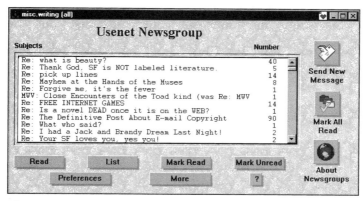

Figure 15-9 You'll find plenty to read here and probably lots of new information to add to your mental data bank.

 TIP The first time you go to a newsgroup, the number of unread messages is equal to the number of messages, so you can click either List Unread or List All (hereafter, you'll want to choose List Unread).

3. When you find a subject or a message you want to read, double-click it. If it's a subject with multiple messages, the first message in that thread displays on-screen (see Figure 15-10).

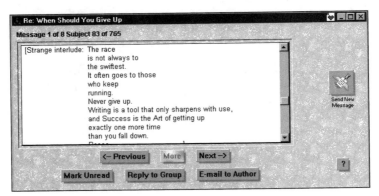

Figure 15-10 I hate coming in in the middle of a conversation, so I always start with the first message of a thread.

TIP If a subject has multiple messages, you can also choose it and then click List. You'll see a display of the names of the people who contributed messages to this subject and the date the message was submitted to the newsgroup. When you find one you want to read, double-click it.

4. When you've read this message (or decided you don't want to bother with it), use one of these actions to move on:

✴ Choose Next to move to the next message in this thread. (If it's the last message in the thread, you go to the next message in the next subject.)

✴ Choose Previous to move to the prior message (which may be the last message in the previous subject).

✴ Choose More (if it is accessible — most of the time it's not) to finish reading a message that is too long to fit into one window. The scroll bar can help you move quickly to the bottom of the window, but the entire message may not be in that window.

✴ Choose Mark Unread if you want the chance to read this message again the next time you go to your newsgroups. (It will show up when you select List Unread.)

✴ Choose Reply to Group if you want to add your own message to this thread in response to the one you're reading.

✴ Choose E-mail to Author to send a private e-mail note to the person who wrote this message.

✳ Click the Send New Message icon to enter a message that is not a direct reply to the one you're reading but that is connected to the subject matter being discussed.

 5. When you have finished reading, select another subject and continue this process.

Unless you have absolutely no life at all outside of AOL, you probably won't even want to attempt to read all the messages that have piled up in your selected newsgroup. However, they'll keep showing up as unread and continue to get in your way. There's a solution to this dilemma: lie. Tell AOL you read the messages even if you didn't.

To do this, take these simple steps:

 1. Close windows until you arrive back at the Read My Newsgroups window, where the newsgroup name is highlighted.

 2. Choose Mark Read to tell AOL you read all the messages.

 3. When AOL pops up a message telling you it has marked all the messages in this newsgroup as having been read, click OK.

The next time you go into this newsgroup, you'll see only those messages that are new since your last visit. That should be a much shorter list.

Canceling a subscription

If you decide you're no longer interested in a newsgroup, you can remove it from your subscription list. This is really a simple procedure; in fact, it's a no-brainer. Just highlight the newsgroup in the Read My Newsgroups window and choose Remove.

Incidentally, many people *browse* the newsgroups that AOL provided, and after they've gotten the help they need, they remove them.

If you change your mind later, you can always add the newsgroup by choosing it as described previously.

Contributing your thoughts

Of course you're going to want to add your own messages to newsgroups. There are two ways to do this, and each method has a slightly different result.

If you choose Reply to Group while you're reading a message, the Post Response window opens so you can enter your contribution (see Figure 15-11). Click inside the Reply box and begin typing.

Here are some things you should know about replying to an existing message:

 ✳ Don't change the text in the subject box, in order to make sure your message continues the thread.

* Keep your message short and to the point. Long, rambling discourses are not a good idea in newsgroups.

* Although you can't see it while you're entering your contribution, a reference to the message you're responding to as well as its text will be in the message you send.

* You can choose to contact the author of the original message via e-mail if you want him/her to see it immediately instead of waiting until the next time the author visits this newsgroup.

* You can add a *signature* to your name. A signature is a sentence or two that is appended automatically to the end of any message you enter (see the section that follows on signatures).

If you instead click the Send New Message icon, the Post New Message window opens. It looks very much like the Post Response window except for two things: you have to fill in the subject text and there's no option to send anyone a simultaneous e-mail message.

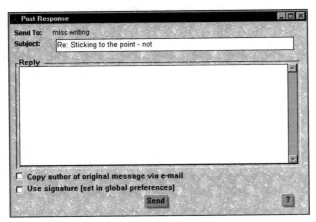

Figure 15-11   When you respond to a message, the subject is filled out for you.

Setting preferences

You can configure your Newsgroups windows to display contents in a way that makes it easier for you to browse the message, although most of the time you'll find that the established settings work just fine. And, while you're setting up your own configuration, you can also add a signature that will appear whenever you post a message in a newsgroup.

To set preferences, follow these steps:

1. Use the keyword **Newsgroups** to go to the AOL Newsgroups window.

2. Click Set Preferences to display the Preferences window (see Figure 15-12).

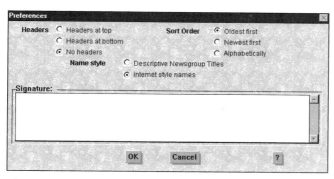

Figure 15-12 Set your own Configuration Preferences for newsgroups, including a signature to enhance your messages.

3. If you want to see any headers for messages (the route they traveled as they navigated the Internet), choose whether you want Headers at top or Headers at bottom. (Headers crowd your screen. The default of No headers is the best choice.)

4. If you want to change the way messages are presented in a window, you can change Sort Order. Instead of seeing the oldest messages first, you can have the latest messages at the top of the window. Or, you can choose to have the messages sorted alphabetically by subject.

5. The Name style choice is for changing the name of the titles of the newsgroups to descriptive names instead of the Internet names that were explained earlier in this chapter. It's not a particularly good idea to do this because when you're on the Internet you should get used to the way it works. Besides, it isn't that hard to figure out what a newsgroup is about from its Internet name.

After you've made any preference changes, you're ready to consider whether or not you want to add a signature to every message you leave. This is a sentence or short paragraph that is automatically appended to the end of the text you type. People use signatures for many reasons: to describe themselves, to send a message, or to voice an opinion. As you browse messages, look at the signatures people use, and then decide whether you want to use one — and what type of message you want to send if you do use one. When you're ready to write your signature, return to the Preferences window.

Using Gopher

Gopher is a cute, buck-toothed tyke (all gophers are buck-toothed; I'm not making fun of the Internet's Gopher) who scurries hither and yon all over the Internet looking for information for you.

Before we get into the technical stuff about Gopher, I'll bet you're asking why in the world anything as high-tech as an Internet search engine could be called something as silly as Gopher. Well, there are two reasons. The first reason is that you send this hairy little creature all over the world to retrieve information from databases, which makes him a go-fer. The second is that the Internet started as a cooperative venture between a large group of universities and the federal government. Gopher was invented by Mark McCahill, who was part of the Internet link at the University of Minnesota. The mascot for U of M is the Golden Gopher.

To get to Gopher, go to the AOL Internet Connection window and click Gopher's icon. The Gopher window displays (see Figure 15-13).

Figure 15-13 Gopher's ready to tunnel through the Internet and bring back whatever you need.

 TIP **The Gopher icon has the title Gopher & WAIS. The WAIS part of that name is merely a technology that works with Gopher and isn't anything you have to worry about. You never have to configure it or think about it (in fact, you won't ever see a reference to it while you're using Gopher).**

Here are the most important things to remember about using Gopher:

* Menus lead to menus, which lead to menus, but eventually you get to exactly the file you want (usually an article about a subject or an entry in a database).

✳ To back up to a previous Gopher window, use the Back button on the top of the window. Don't close the window; if you do, you'll have to start all over again.

There are special Gopher computers all over the Internet — thousands of them — and we call this Gopherspace. Most of the information in Gopherspace is in the form of files (information about a specific subject) or a database record (the e-mail address of somebody on the faculty at a certain university). There are, however, some graphics, sound files, and other miscellaneous file types.

When you get to the information you want, click it. It's downloaded to your computer and displayed on your screen. You can read it and move on, or you can save it.

The easiest way to understand Gopher is to start using it. You have a couple of choices, which are covered next.

Using the Gopher Directory

Click the Gopher Directory icon and look at the choices. These change from time to time, so I won't bother to list them or show you a picture of them. However, two of the choices are All Gopher Sites in the World and Gopher Jewels. The latter is a collection of Gopher categories, presented in simple English, without all the mumbo-jumbo of Internet techno-babble, and it's the most logical place to start. To get there, double-click Gopher Jewels (see Figure 15-14).

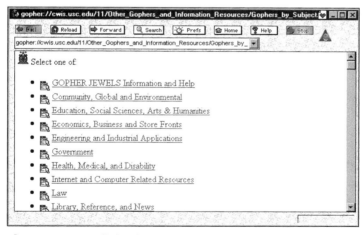

Figure 15-14 All the databases and locations are compiled by category to make it easy to use Gopher.

Select a category by placing your pointer over the category name. When the pointer turns into a hand, click once. Keep selecting text until you get to a specific file, which is usually a text file replete with information about its subject (Gopherspace is often very academic).

If you enjoy being overwhelmed, choose All Gopher Sites in the World, where the processes work the same but the choices are much larger.

Using the Gopher Treasures

Another way to start off is to click the Gopher Treasures icon in the middle of the Gopher window. When the window opens, it displays lots of choices. Use the scroll bar to see all of them (see Figure 15-15).

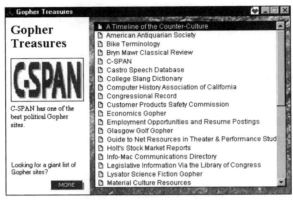

Figure 15-15 Gopher's collection of treasures has everything from the Congressional Record to Monty Python movie scripts.

The process is much the same; as you click subjects, you are either brought directly to a Gopher site or to another set of menus that help narrow your choice as you make your way to the site.

Using FTP

FTP means *File Transfer Protocol*. It is more complicated and less user-friendly than any of the other processes we discuss in this chapter. Therefore, I'm going to give you a very brief overview of what it is and how it works because the odds are you won't need to use it often — if at all.

When you use FTP, you make a direct connection between your computer and a computer that's on the Internet. You can exchange files directly; there is no software between you and the other computer, no friendly lists, and no help. It's a simple file copy. You have to know the file name and where it is in order to use FTP properly. You can, if you want, search through FTP sites because you think one of them might have a file you need or want, but you'll get no assistance as you browse the computers.

To make this all a bit less scary, AOL has provided some FTP sites so you don't have to know the exact Internet address of the site in order to get there. If you want something that isn't part of the AOL group, however, you have to determine the exact name of the site, and then you have to know how to find the file when you get to the computer.

To access FTP, click its icon on the AOL Internet Connection window. When the FTP window opens (see Figure 15-16), you see several choices.

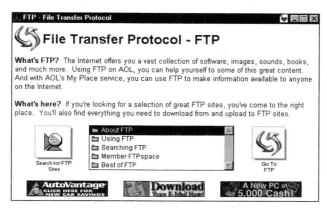

Figure 15-16   Take advantage of the explanations in the AOL files before venturing further.

* Choose a file from the list box to read more about FTP on AOL.
* Click the Search for FTP Sites icon to go off on your own. Enter a word or phrase that describes what you're looking for and see if the FTP search engine can match that with its database.
* Click Go to FTP to see the AOL selection of sites (see Figure 15-17).

Figure 15-17   AOL has a collection of FTP sites, but there's not a lot of information available by reading these listings.

The AOL selection consists of FTP addresses, each of which represents a computer on the Internet that has made files available to users. Note that the window says *Anonymous FTP*, which indicates that the sites don't require any special access codes or passwords in order to access the files. The majority of FTP sites work that way, but there are some that require you to make arrangements ahead of time. Those arrangements include a user name and password for that site.

As an example, Figure 15-18 shows the Microsoft FTP site (which is on the AOL list). This is as user-friendly as it gets — which isn't very user-friendly. The listings with folders indicate directories, where you can expect to find additional directories as you search for files you can transfer to your computer.

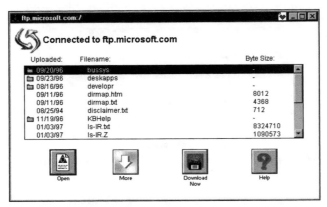

Figure 15-18   Microsoft has a lot of files. It isn't terribly difficult to find them. (Hint: bussys means business systems.)

If you know what you want and where it is, you can select Other Site from the Anonymous FTP window (the one shown in Figure 15-17), and enter the FTP address (don't forget to indicate a request for login name and password if you aren't going to an anonymous site).

If you do have an address of an FTP site and want to head there directly, be aware that you might not see cute folder icons indicating categories. For many FTP sites, you have to be very comfortable with DOS or UNIX directory structures to navigate the computer at that site.

There are some other things to be aware of when you use FTP:

✳ Never use a file you've taken from an FTP site without running a virus check on it first.

✳ Keep an eye on the extension to the filename. If it is .zip, you probably have the right software to unpack it; if it isn't, you may not be able to get to the file. Some extensions are for Mac, some for UNIX or XENIX, and some will work in DOS or Windows if you have the right software.

If the concept of directory structures makes you twitch, don't even bother with FTP. Many of the files (especially from software companies) are available on the Web.

BONUS

One of the advantages of the AOL connection to the Internet is yours without even going to the AOL Internet Connection window. It's the ability to send and receive e-mail with folks who have Internet accounts but who aren't on AOL.

If you know a person's e-mail address, you can send him a message. AOL sends it through all kinds of circuitous routes, if necessary, to get it to your recipient. The same thing happens when someone with an Internet e-mail address sends mail to you. It travels hither and yon around the Internet to get to your AOL mailbox.

> **TIP** If you're interested in seeing the route that mail has traveled, read the header that comes with your mail. Usually found at the bottom of the message (outside AOL, the header is usually at the top of the message), it traces all the stops along the Internet as the note was sent from point A to point B.

There are two ways to give your e-mail address to somebody:

* Get the person's e-mail address and send a note. Your e-mail address is on the note when it's received, and the recipient can add it to his/her Address Book.

* Write it down and give it to the person. Your e-mail address is *screenname*@aol.com. Don't forget to substitute the screen name you log in with for the word *screenname*.

There are many places besides AOL that are used for Internet access and e-mail. The recipient you want to correspond with can be at any of them. For instance, there are many companies that provide Internet access with no other services beyond that gateway. These are called ISPs (Internet Service Providers). People who use an ISP have an e-mail address that follows the format *username*@*isp*.com or *username*@*isp*.net (where *username* is the person's username and *isp* is his/her ISP). Other people use services similar to AOL, such as CompuServe. On AOL, their addresses are *xxxx.xxxx*@compuserve.com, where *x* indicates the CompuServe number (people on CompuServe have numbers, not names). There may be more or fewer *x*s in any particular user's name.

> **TIP** If a CompuServe user gives you his or her address in person by writing it down, you're likely to be looking at something like 12345,67. You have to replace the comma with a period, and then add @compuserve.com to the end of it to translate the CompuServe address into an Internet address.

15

There is one thing to be aware of, however: you probably won't be able to attach files to a user whose e-mail mailbox isn't on AOL. Each software package that is used for Internet access has its own way of converting files so they can be read by the recipient.

TIP **If the file you want to send to another user is a word processing file, open the program in which you created it and use Copy and Paste to move the text to your message.**

There are a few other caveats about sending and receiving e-mail when the other person is not on AOL:

* You cannot check the status of mail to see if it has been read.
* Messages you receive are formatted the way they were sent (AOL does not reformat messages), so the way sentences wrap may look a little strange if the recipient has different margin settings.
* Received mail that is larger than 1MB will probably be split into multiple messages. AOL will number the messages so you can read them in the correct order.
* AOL won't send a message that is larger than 32K (which is about 7 pages of text). If you're sending a long message, split up the message. AOL does not automatically split and number outgoing mail.

None of these restrictions could be classified as onerous, so now that you're on AOL, you can correspond with anybody who has an e-mail address. It's going to save you a fortune in long-distance phone calls.

X-REF **For more information about e-mail, see Chapter 4.**

Summary

The Internet is your world-wide connection to information, e-mail, files, and fun. AOL makes it easy to travel into the virtual world of the Internet. However, remember that none of the Internet is as protected as AOL. There are no guides and no rules, and absolutely nobody is in charge. This is particularly important for parents to remember. Mostly, though, the virtual world that awaits you on the Internet is fun, interesting, and totally addictive.

DISCOVERY CENTER

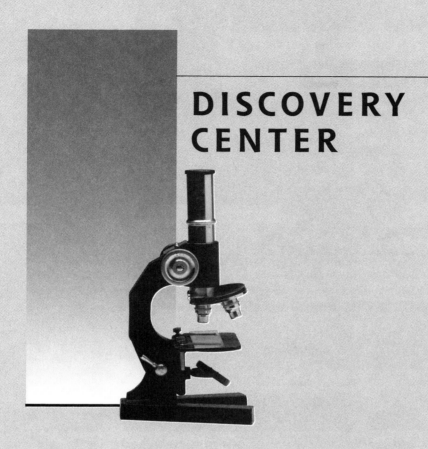

I n this section, you'll discover many of the important steps for how to accomplish tasks in America Online. The Discovery Center serves as a handy reference to the most important tasks in the chapters. These quick summaries include page references, referring you back to the chapters if you need more information.

CHAPTER 1

To start AOL (page 13)

* In Windows 95, double-click the desktop icon or double-click the AOL file in Explorer.
* In Windows 3.*x*, open the America Online program group, and then double-click the America Online icon.
* For Macintosh, double-click the America Online folder, and then double-click the America Online icon.

To sign on to AOL (page 22)

After opening the AOL software, use the choices on the Welcome window.

Your screen name
(only displayed after
you've been through setup)

Enter your password.

Choose Sign On to dial AOL.

Choose Help to get assistance
on this window.

Choose setup to edit your
setup, usually to add new
access phone numbers.

To find more local access numbers (page 26)

1. Sign on to AOL.
2. Use the keyword **Access** to go to the Accessing America Online window.
3. Choose Search Access Numbers.

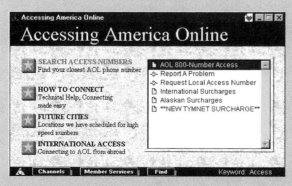

CHAPTER 2

To visit AOL's main areas from the Welcome window (page 38)

Channels are the main gateways to AOL's most popular sites.

Find out what's new, exciting, and hot on AOL.

Send and receive e-mail.

Enter the world of live chat.

Your window to the World Wide Web and other Internet features

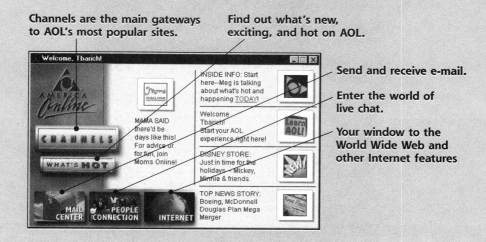

To get the inside scoop on what's really hot (page 39)

Tips and advice on how to get the most out of AOL

Currently the most popular sites

A listing of features unique to AOL

New features and refurbished sites

Online sales and special offers

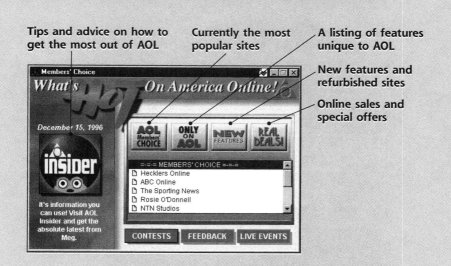

1. Click the Keyword button on the Toolbar.

2. Enter the keyword to search on.

3. Click Go to search.

Enter the keyword(s) to search on.

Click to search for a specific AOL area.

Click to search for any area containing the keyword(s).

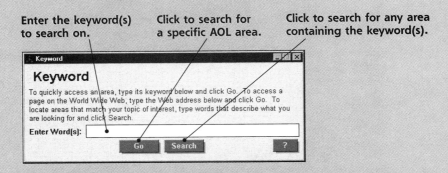

Enter the keyword(s) to search on.

Click the appropriate tab to search for related information.

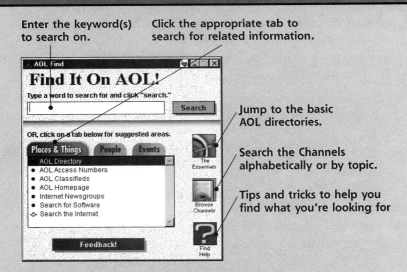

Jump to the basic AOL directories.

Search the Channels alphabetically or by topic.

Tips and tricks to help you find what you're looking for

To save a site as a Favorite Place (page 37)

Click the heart to add this
site to your Favorite Places.

CHAPTER 3

To create a screen name (page 60)

Type a name (three to ten
characters, beginning with a letter).

Click to create a
new screen name.

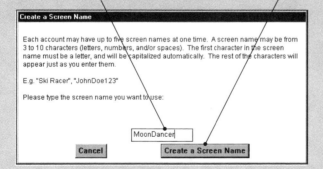

To implement parental controls on a screen name (page 61)

Select this option for unlimited access to all AOL and Internet features.

Select this option for unlimited AOL access but limited Internet access.

Select this option for AOL access limited to Kids channel and approved Web sites.

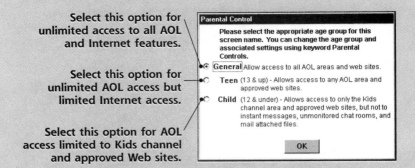

Parental Control

Please select the appropriate age group for this screen name. You can change the age group and associated settings using keyword Parental Controls.

General Allow access to all AOL areas and web sites.

Teen (13 & up) - Allows access to any AOL area and approved web sites.

Child (12 & under) - Allows access to only the Kids channel area and approved web sites, but not to instant messages, unmonitored chat rooms, and mail attached files.

OK

To change your password (page 61)

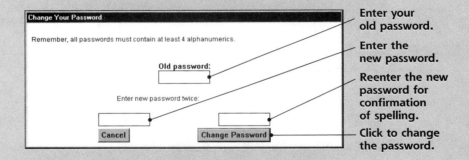

Change Your Password

Remember, all passwords must contain at least 4 alphanumerics.

Old password:

Enter new password twice:

Cancel   Change Password

Enter your old password.

Enter the new password.

Reenter the new password for confirmation of spelling.

Click to change the password.

Click to delete your
Online Profile.

Select to go to the
My AOL area.

Enter your
personal
information
(it's not
advisable to
post street
addresses
or phone
numbers).

Click here to
update and
save your
Online Profile.

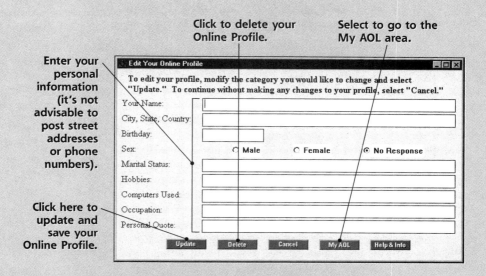

To manage Buddy Lists (page 63)

Existing
Buddy Lists

Click to create a
new Buddy List.

Click to edit the
highlighted Buddy List.

Click to access the
Member Directory.

Select to delete the
highlighted Buddy List.

Select to open the
Preferences window.

Click to open the
BuddyView window.

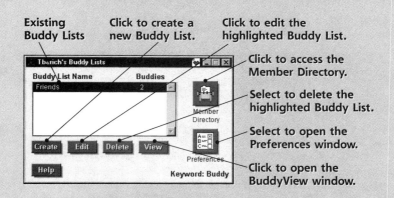

To create Buddy Lists (page 64)

Enter the name for the new Buddy List.

Enter a screen name to add to the Buddy List.

Click to add the newly entered name to the Buddy List.

List of members included on the new Buddy List

Click to save the new list.

Highlight a name on the list and click here to remove from the list.

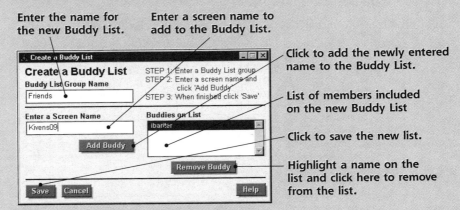

CHAPTER 4

To get new e-mail (page 88)

1. Click the Mailbox icon to open the New Mail window.
2. Highlight the e-mail message to read.
3. Click Read to open the message.

When the flag is up and the door is open, you have new mail.

The New Mail window

Unread messages

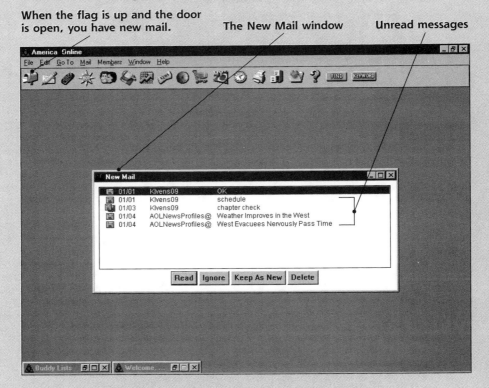

To add e-mail addresses to your Address Book (page 97)

1. From the Menu Bar select, Mail → Edit Address Book .
2. In the Address Book, click Create to open the Address Group form.
3. Enter the individual's real name in the Group Name text box.
4. Enter the e-mail address of the person in the Screen Names text box.
5. Click OK to add the new address to the Address Book.

Enter the person's real name here. **Enter the e-mail address here.**

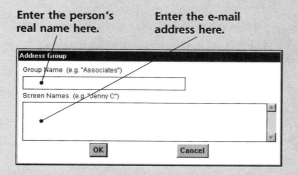

To create an e-mail message (page 98)

1. From the Toolbar, select the Compose Mail (pencil and envelope) icon.
2. In the Compose Mail window, click the Address Book to select an address to enter in the To: field.
3. Enter a brief description of the message in the Subject: field.
4. Type your message in the text window below the Subject: field.
5. Click Send to transmit the message.

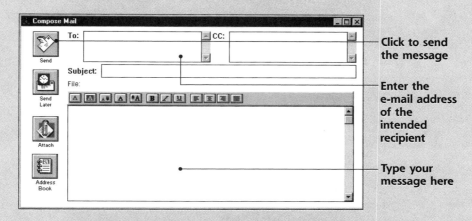

Click to send the message

Enter the e-mail address of the intended recipient

Type your message here

CHAPTER 5

To visit a chat room, use one of these methods (page 112)

* Click the People Connection icon on the AOL Toolbar.
* Click the People Connection icon in the Welcome window.
* Click People Connection in the Channels window.
* Use the keyword **People Connection**.

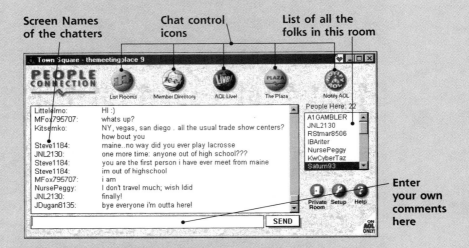

Screen Names of the chatters

Chat control icons

List of all the folks in this room

Enter your own comments here

To move to a different chat room (page 113)

Click List Rooms, and then pick a category and a room.

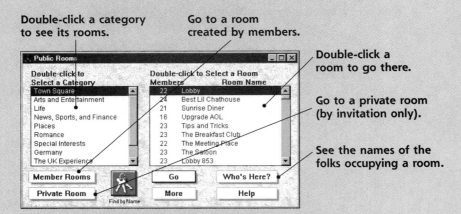

Double-click a category to see its rooms.

Go to a room created by members.

Double-click a room to go there.

Go to a private room (by invitation only).

See the names of the folks occupying a room.

To use Instant Messages (page 124)

1. Press Ctrl+I to open the Instant Message window.
2. Enter the recipient's name and the message text.
3. When a response arrives, continue the conversation back and forth.

The conversation thus far

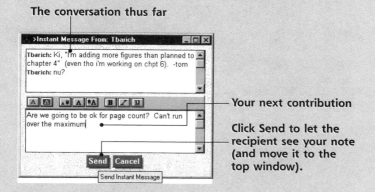

Your next contribution

Click Send to let the recipient see your note (and move it to the top window).

CHAPTER 6

To access the Travel Channel (page 134)

1. If the Channels window is open, select Travel.
2. If the Channels window is not open, click the Keyword button on the Toolbar.
3. Enter **travel** in the text box, and then click Go.

Check this area to get ideas for your dream vacation.

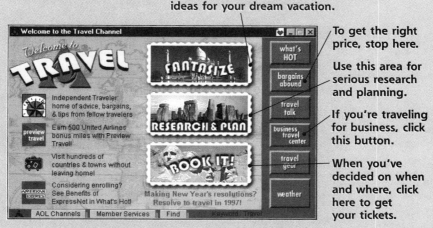

To get the right price, stop here.

Use this area for serious research and planning.

If you're traveling for business, click this button.

When you've decided on when and where, click here to get your tickets.

Look for vacation ideas that match your hobbies and interests.

See what other AOL members are raving about.

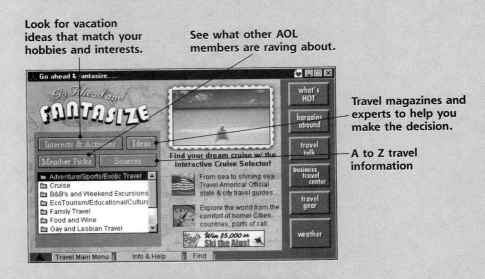

Travel magazines and experts to help you make the decision.

A to Z travel information

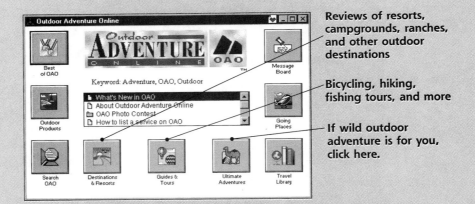

Reviews of resorts, campgrounds, ranches, and other outdoor destinations

Bicycling, hiking, fishing tours, and more

If wild outdoor adventure is for you, click here.

For member input on Domestic travel, click here.

For hobby- and activity-related message boards, click here.

Click this button for member feedback on International travel.

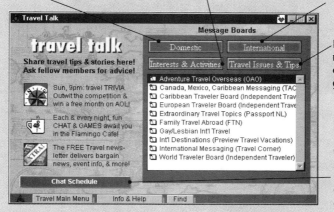

Find out what AOL members have to offer in the way of general travel tips.

Click to get a schedule of upcoming travel chat sessions and events.

General travel information for the business traveler

Stay informed with News & Reference.

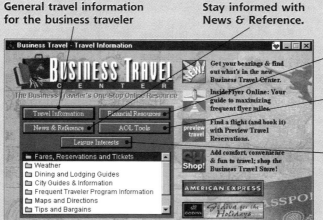

Keep track of the financial world.

Let AOL help you make the most of your business trip.

Get away for a little R&R.

CHAPTER 7

To get to Today's News (page 146)

You can take any one of these routes to get to AOL News:

* ✳ Choose Today's News from the Channels window.
* ✳ Click the Today's News icon on the toolbar.
* ✳ Use the keyword **News**.

To read a summary of the latest news stories (page 147)

1. Go to Today's News.
2. Choose Highlights in the US & World News mini-window.
3. Read the summary stories in the top box.
4. In the bottom box, double-click the listing of any full story you want to read.

To keep up with celebrity gossip (page 154)

1. Go to Today's News.
2. Choose Highlights in the Entertainment mini-window.
3. Scroll through the items in the Entertainment Features box and choose any one of the columns (try Extra's Daily Spotlight News).
4. Double-click each story you want to read.

To find a magazine or newspaper to read (page 156)

Choose Newsstand from the Channels window to find a host of publications and special features.

Special feature icons give you one-click access to selected publications.

Scroll through the list of publications and double-click your favorites.

CHAPTER 8

To get to the AOL Marketplace (page 172)

Choose one of these options:

* Choose Marketplace from the Channels window.
* Click the shopping cart icon on the AOL toolbar.
* Use the keyword **Marketplace**.

Marketplace major categories

Currently featured stores

Special events

Click Search to get to the Marketplace Directory of stores.

Marketplace services

To buy an item from a Marketplace store (page 176)

1. Go to the item's window and read the information.
2. Choose Click Here to Order.
3. Answer the questions, choosing Continue to advance through the purchase process.
4. Choose checkout to complete your transaction.

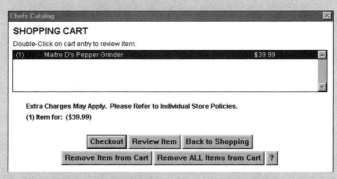

To buy or sell items through the Classified Ads (page 178)

Enter the keyword **Classifieds**.

Pick a classified section or an information message.

Choose a subject to match the item you're looking for.

Choose a geographical area to search.

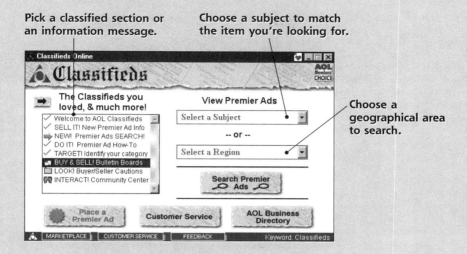

CHAPTER 9

To visit the AOL Kids Only Area (page 188)

1. Use the keyword **Kids Only** or click the Kids Only button on the Channels window.

2. Click the icon for the area you want to visit.

Today's special feature

Search engines for What's Hot and finding specific items

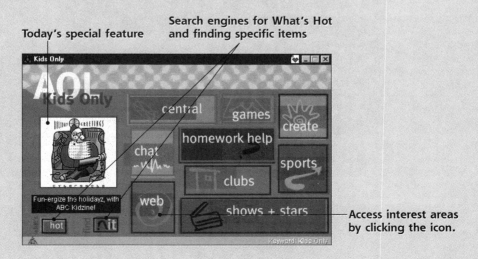

Access interest areas by clicking the icon.

To get help for homework assignments (page 197)

From the Kids Only window, click Homework Help.

Leave a note for a teacher. The answer will arrive by e-mail.

Learn about interesting things, even if it's not part of your homework.

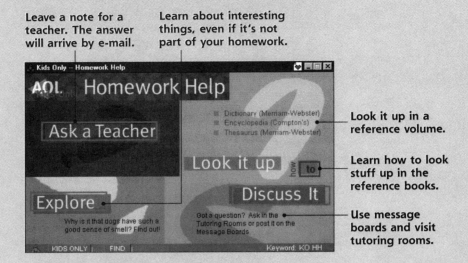

Look it up in a reference volume.

Learn how to look stuff up in the reference books.

Use message boards and visit tutoring rooms.

To head for the games (page 202)

Choose Games from the Channels window or use the keyword **Games**.

Pick a game type or enter a contest.

CHAPTER 10

To access the Reference Channel (page 212)

1. Click the Keyword button on the Toolbar.
2. Type **reference** in the Enter Word(s): text box.
3. Press Enter.

Ask the Experts.   Reference resource categories   General reference materials

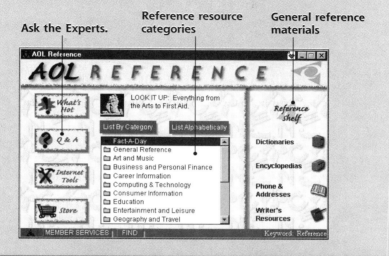

To access the New York Public Library Desk Reference (page 218)

1. From the Toolbar, click the Keyword button.
2. In the Enter Word(s): text box, type **nypl**.
3. Press Enter.

Reference resource categories   Click here to search for specific information.

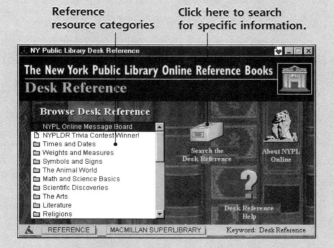

To access the Consumer Reports area (page 223)

1. Click the Keyword button on the Toolbar.

2. Type **consumer reports** in the Enter Word(s): text box.

3. Press Enter to open the Consumer Reports window.

Product categories

Click here for
the latest reports.

To search for a specific
word or topic, click
this icon.

CHAPTER 11

To learn about the latest releases in music (page 229)

1. Use the keyword **Music**.

2. Click the New Releases icon.

3. Scroll through the list of new releases to find the one of interest, and then double-click.

To keep an eye on the world of entertainment (page 230)

Use the keyword **Entertainment**. Then choose a topic and click your way through all the levels of information.

Click the name of a topic to enter its special area on AOL.

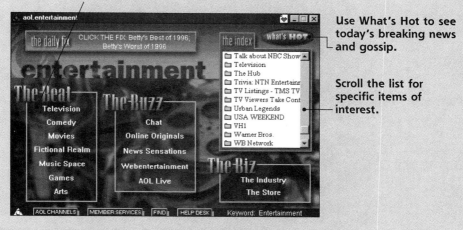

Use What's Hot to see today's breaking news and gossip.

Scroll the list for specific items of interest.

To dive into your favorite hobby (page 237)

1. Use the keyword **Hobby**.

2. Double-click the category you're interested in using to eat up time or money.

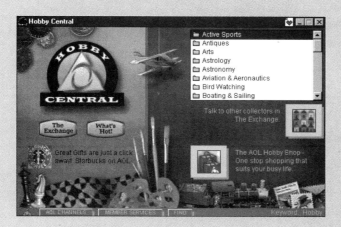

CHAPTER 12

To get to AOL's area about computers (page 242)

1. Click Computers & Software on the Channels window (or use the keyword **Computers & Software**).

2. Choose a topic by clicking its icon.

To get expert help designing and pricing a system (page 246)

1. Go to Computers & Software.
2. Choose Magazine Rack.
3. Choose Business Week's Computer Room.
4. Choose the Maven, BW's Computer Buying Guide.
5. From the Maven Web site, click the word PRICEWIZARD.
6. Follow the easy directions for designing a computer system.

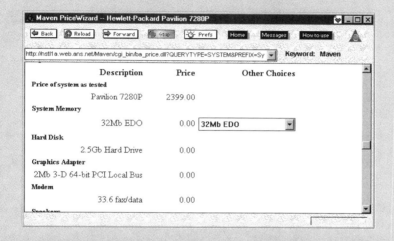

To get support for a hardware or software problem (page 253)

Choose Support Forums from the Computers & Software window, and then pick the appropriate category.

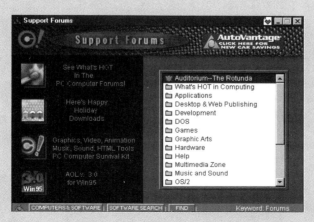

CHAPTER 13

To get to AOL's Digital City feature (page 264)

Choose Digital City on the Channels window or use the keyword **Digital City**.

To locate a specific city (page 265)

Click the section of the country in which it's located.

Scroll through the list of cities to
find the one you want to explore.

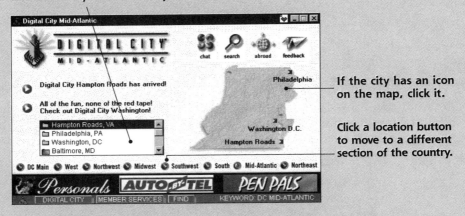

If the city has an icon
on the map, click it.

Click a location button
to move to a different
section of the country.

To correspond with a Pen Pal in another city (page 283)

Use the keyword **Pen Pals**, and then fill in information about yourself that
might interest other AOL visitors to Digital City.

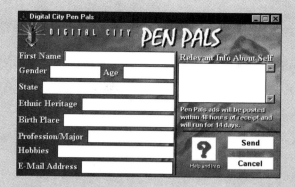

CHAPTER 14

To access the Personal Finance channel (page 292)

1. Click the Keyword button on the Toolbar.
2. Type **personal finance** in the Enter Word(s): text box.
3. Press Enter.

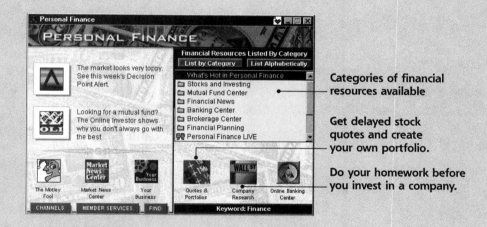

Categories of financial resources available

Get delayed stock quotes and create your own portfolio.

Do your homework before you invest in a company.

To go to the Motley Fool site (page 302)

1. Click the Keyword button on the Toolbar.
2. Type **motley fool** in the Enter Word(s): text box.
3. Press Enter.

Answers to all your questions about the Motley Fool

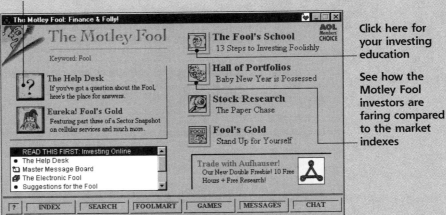

Click here for your investing education

See how the Motley Fool investors are faring compared to the market indexes

CHAPTER 15

To go to AOL's Internet Connection (page 315)

Use the keyword **Internet** (or choose Internet Connection from the Channels window).

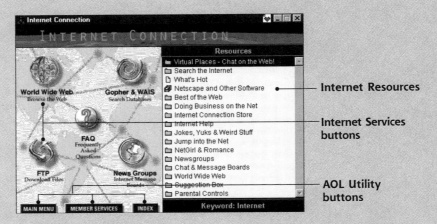

Internet Resources

Internet Services buttons

AOL Utility buttons

Go back to previous Web page

Reload the current page

Go forward (to where you were before choosing Back)

Open a search program

Configure Web preferences

Go to the AOL home page

Web address of current page (URL)

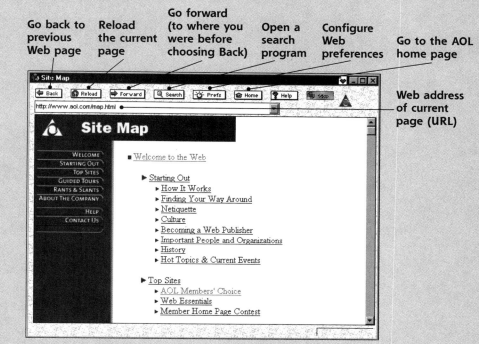

1. Use the keyword **Internet** to get to the AOL Internet Connection window.

2. Click the Newsgroups icon.

3. Choose Add Newsgroups.

4. Double-click a Category (and subcategory if there are any).

5. Find the specific newsgroup that suits your mood or purpose, highlight it, and then choose Add.

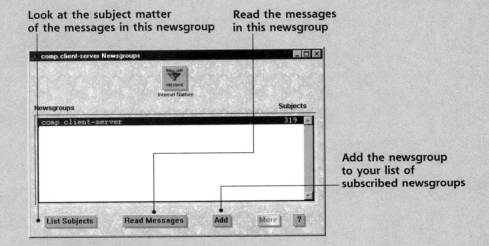

Look at the subject matter of the messages in this newsgroup

Read the messages in this newsgroup

Add the newsgroup to your list of subscribed newsgroups

VISUAL INDEX

Finding What You Need

If you don't know the name of the AOL area you want to visit, use Find to search for it with a word or phrase that is connected to it.

Click the Find button on the Toolbar, and then enter the word or phrase in the Find box. [Ch 2]

When the results of the search appear, double-click the entries to go to the indicated area. [Ch 2]

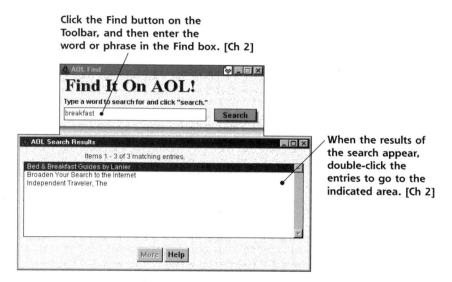

Creating a Buddy List

Put your friends on your buddy list so you know if they're online at the same time you are.

Name the list. [Ch 3]

List of screen names you've added are displayed here. [Ch 3]

Enter the screen name of a buddy, and then choose Add Buddy. [Ch 3]

Delete a buddy you don't want to track online anymore. [Ch 3]

Save your buddy list. [Ch 3]

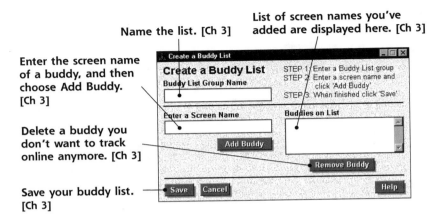

Creating Your Profile

Users on AOL can check you out, so be careful what you say about yourself. Every field is optional (you can even choose not to have a profile).

Screen names can be obscure, so you may want to indicate your gender. [Ch 3]

Enter your name (last names may not be a good idea). [Ch 3]

Let people know where you're from. [Ch 3]

Your birth date doesn't necessarily have to include the year. [Ch 3]

Your hobbies may make another user want to get to know you. [Ch 3]

A lot of people like to know what kind of computers other people use. [Ch 3]

Have a quote that sums up your philosophy of life? [Ch 3]

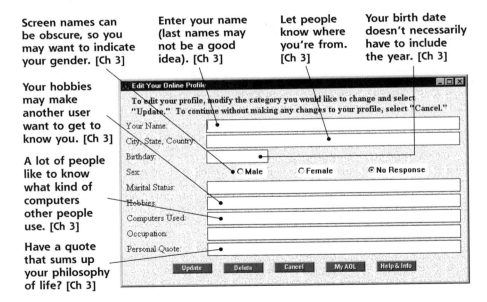

Composing E-mail

Writing a note and sending it electronically is a lot faster than using the post office.

The recipient's screen name (or e-mail address if he or she isn't on AOL) [Ch 4]

The subject of your note [Ch 4]

The e-mail address of anybody you want to send a carbon copy [Ch 4]

The message [Ch 4]

Send now [Ch 4]

Send when you're ready to sign off [Ch 4]

Attach a file (to AOL users only) [Ch 4]

Keep a list of e-mail addresses [Ch 4]

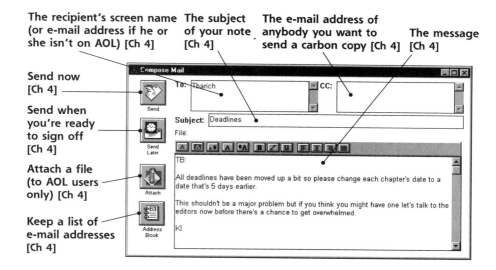

TROUBLESHOOTING GUIDE

AOL software is quite easy to use, and once you're signed on, AOL is easy to navigate. But we're talking about computers, computer software, and computer-operated systems, so there's bound to be an occasional problem. Most of the time, the problem isn't serious and the solution is simple. This section helps you with common problems and is organized alphabetically by topic.

Billing

I'd like to know how much time I've used. You can always check your AOL bill by using the keyword **Billing**. Your current month's bill displays on-screen, and you can ask to see a more details or see the previous month's bill by clicking Request Detail Billing Info.

Where's the button for canceling my account? Don't be silly; they're not going to make it that easy. Canceling your account isn't difficult, it's just not accomplished online. Call 1-800-827-6364, and the AOL service representative will cancel your account. You should receive a letter confirming the cancellation within ten days of that call.

I ordered something online and now I've changed my mind. You can cancel an AOL Store order by calling 1-800-884-3372. You should also use that number if you have a question about an online purchase. If you'd rather not call (sometimes it's busy and it takes a while to get a service representative), you can contact the Customer Service department while you're online by using these steps:

1. Use the keyword **AOL Store**.

2. Choose Customer Service.

3. Click the Ask Customer Service icon.

4. Enter your question.

5. Choose Send.

Your question or complaint is sent directly to the order department of the AOL Store.

Connection

I was in one of the AOL areas and the system suddenly said good-bye and shut down my software. This is really rude, and I'm sure AOL feels badly, but it happens. It's usually impossible to figure out why, although a call waiting beep will frequently cause this (make sure to turn off call waiting during your sign on), as will excessive static on the telephone lines. But sometimes, it's just one of those things. Sign on again and pick up where you left off. Incidentally, if this happens a lot, say once a week, have the telephone company come to check the lines (they often find that squirrels have chewed away the insulation and created noise problems on the line).

Sometimes when I click on a Channels choice, I see an hourglass for a long time, and then I get a message about response. The message means that AOL has noticed that your request to go to a specific area has been ignored for a long time and you probably can't get there from here right now. This is because a lot of people are using AOL at the same time you are, and the system just can't keep up with everyone's requests. There's nothing you can do about it except to try to sign on during less busy times@mdremember that the evenings are the busiest. You can try again later. In the meantime, mow the lawn or do another household chore.

When I download a large file it doesn't finish, usually my whole system freezes up. First, try downloading during less busy times on AOL. If that doesn't help, and the problem is constant (or frequent), there are a few things to check before you do anything drastic about this:

* If you have call waiting, make sure you disabled it in the AOL Setup configuration (click Setup in the first Welcome window).
* If you use a screen saver, it will kick in during a download because there isn't any keyboard or mouse activity, so disable the screen saver.

If neither of those is the culprit, the solution could be a bit more complicated. It could be your modem. All modems are not created equal. Just because you have a modem that's rated for 28,800 bps, that doesn't mean it's going to work as well as my similarly rated modem. That's because different modems have different features built in. And, in fact, you can usually tell by the price you paid. You do get what you pay for, and if you found an incredible bargain when you bought your modem, you may have one without the features you need to perform all the tasks you want to. Many inexpensive modems use a technology called RPI, and it's not necessary to go into long techy explanations of what that means, but it is necessary for you to understand that these modems are less efficient when it comes to downloading files.

AOL has some solutions for RPI modems that may work for you (and then, again, they may not). To try, follow these steps:

1. In the first Welcome screen, choose Setup.

2. Choose Setup Modem in the Network & Modem Setup window.

3. Look at the current settings and write them down because if the solutions I'm offering don't work, you'll want to go back to the original setting so you can at least sign on properly.

4. Scroll through the modem list and look for the WinRPI Modem (you're look for this exact listing at this point, not the listing that has a plus sign after it). Click the listing, and then click OK twice to get back to the first AOL window.

5. Try to download again. If it works, great. If not, sign off and repeat these steps, but use the WinRPI+ Modem.

6. If downloading still doesn't work, buy a better modem or just use your modem for all the other features in AOL.

If you don't have an RPI modem (check the box or the documentation), then there's probably no sense in going through these steps.

E-mail

I got an e-mail message last week that I wanted to read again, but it disappeared. After you read your e-mail, it remains in your mailbox for three to five days, but after that it's gone to e-mail heaven. The easiest way to have a permanent copy of e-mail is to print it when you read it. To print an e-mail message, click the Print button on the Toolbar while the message is open.

Incidentally, if you don't open your e-mail and read it, it won't wait around forever either. Unread mail is deleted approximately 27 days after it's received.

I sent a nasty note, and now I want to unsend it but AOL won't let me. Either you sent the e-mail to a recipient who is reached through the Internet and is not on AO, or the recipient has already seen your note. There is no way to unsend a message unless it was sent to an AOL user and has not yet been read. Next time, it might be wiser to think before you send. You probably ought to make a quick phone call and apologize.

I absolutely have to know if my brother read the e-mail I sent, but AOL won't tell me. Your brother probably has an Internet e-mail address. If your brother isn't on AOL, you cannot tell if the message is sent. Only e-mail sent to other AOL users can be checked for its status.

INSTALLING AOL FOR WINDOWS

Relax and rejoice; the installation process for AOL is one of the easiest, least complicated installations you can find. These instructions cover both Windows 95 and Windows 3.x, and the steps you have to follow are pretty much the same for both operating systems.

If you are using the CD that accompanies this book, put it in your CD-ROM drive. For the purpose of clarity (and to make it easier for myself), I'm going to refer to that drive as drive D. If your CD-ROM has been assigned a different drive letter, substitute that letter for D.

If you are using a disk that came in the mail — put that in a floppy drive (which will probably be drive A but might be drive B).

Okay, let's get started. Make sure your modem is connected to a port and turned on. (If you have an internal modem, it takes care of itself and you don't have to check anything.)

If your computer is running Windows 95, follow these steps:

1. Click Start on the taskbar.

2. Choose Run to open the Run dialog box.

If your computer uses Windows 3.x, you only have one step:

1. From the Program Manager menu bar, choose **File** → **Run** .

At this point, the procedure is the same for both operating systems, and there's not very much to do. Just follow these simple instructions:

1. In the Run dialog box, enter the path to your AOL software, followed by **setup**, as follows:

   * If you're using the CD, enter **d:\setup**.

   * If you're using a disk in the floppy drive, enter **a:\setup** or **b:\setup**.

2. Press Enter or click OK.

TIP It doesn't matter whether you use all caps, lowercase, or a combination of both when typing in these paths.

The America Online software launches its Setup program, and you can sit back, relax, and let AOL do all the work for a while.

AOL checks out your equipment (it flashes a message telling you about it) and then finally decides to install the software (see Figure A-1).

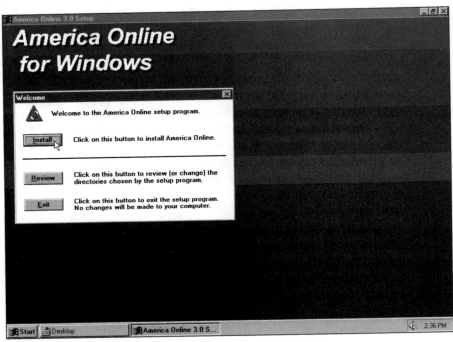

Figure A-1   Okay, now we're really going to start the installation.

Click Install to begin the process of installing all the AOL files onto your computer. If you're curious to see the path AOL has chosen to use for the software, you can click Review. In fact, you could change the path, but there's really no reason to do that because AOL isn't interfering with any other software by placing its own software in a folder (directory) that's already being used by another application.

There's some disk churning and flashing lights on disk drives as the AOL Setup program begins transferring files (see Figure A-2).

After all the software files have been transferred to your hard drive, the AOL Setup program proudly announces that it has completed its job (see Figure A-3).

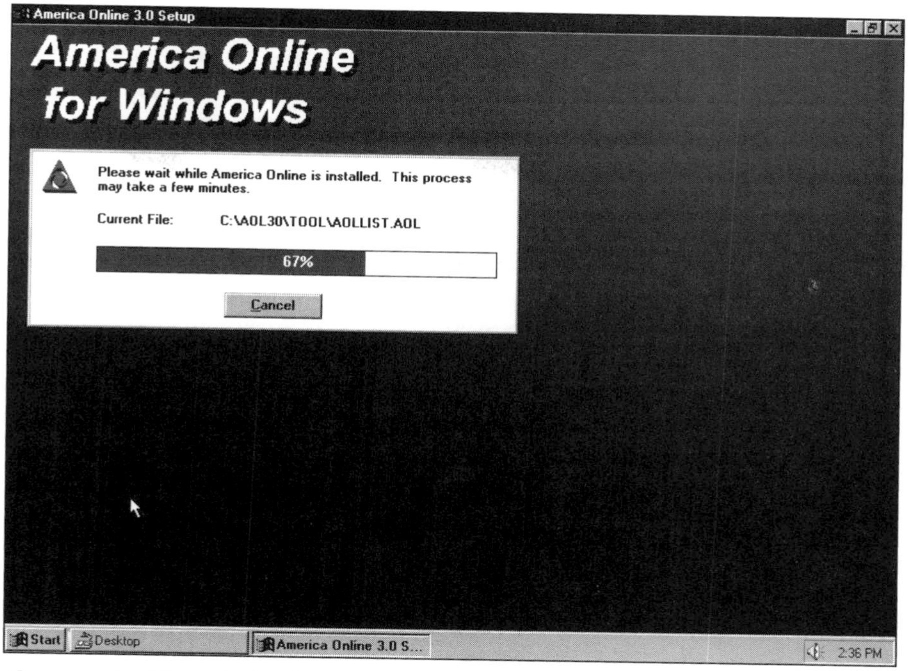

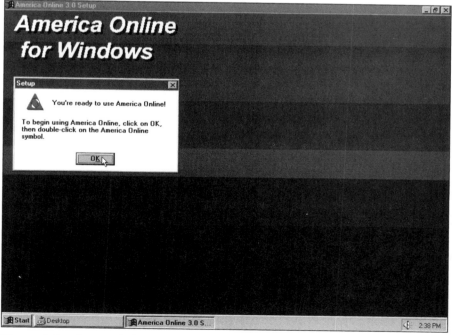

Figure A-2 When the horizontal bar turns solid blue and the percentage figure is 100%, you know that all the files have been installed.

Figure A-3 Congratulations to you and to AOL for a successful installation.

Click OK to make the announcement go away.

If you're using Windows 3.*x*. you return to the Program Manager. You'll see that AOL has placed a program group on your desktop, and it has an AOL icon in it. Go to Chapter 1 of this book to learn how to start and configure AOL and sign on for the first time.

If you're using Windows 95, you are returned to the desktop and there is supposed to be an AOL icon there. However, there may not be one, because this part of the installation process doesn't always work the way it should. Don't worry, we'll tell you how to correct this in Chapter 1. Go to Chapter 1 now and learn how to start and configure AOL and sign on for the first time.

NOTE **When you start the AOL software as a new user, you will be prompted for the registration number and password (as discussed in Chapter 1). If you've installed AOL from the CD-ROM that accompanies this book, the registration number is 3A-5661-3405 and the password is DUSTY-CRANNY.**

APPENDIX C

INSTALLING AOL ON A MACINTOSH

Version 3 for Macintosh is the latest AOL software. If your Mac has a CD-ROM drive, you're set because we've provided it for you on the CD-ROM that comes with this book. If you have a disk version of the Macintosh software, make sure the label on the disk says it is version 3. If it doesn't say that, call AOL and tell them to rush you a disk immediately. After it arrives, come right back here and start reading.

NOTE **You could possibly have hardware considerations that require version 2.7 for Macintosh. The CD-ROM that is provided with this book includes version 2.7, although the default installation is 3.0. I do recommend using the latest software to take full advantage of AOL's features. Call AOL at 1-800-827-6364 if you have any questions or require the installation software on disk.**

The instructions for installing AOL are very simple — your computer and the AOL software do all the work, and you just have to nod approvingly at each step. Well, nodding isn't quite enough. You'll also have to click Continue on a couple of dialog boxes to let the software know you're paying attention and have complete confidence that everything that's happening is OK with you. Here are the steps:

1. Place the disk in its drive (either CD or floppy) and wait a second or two.

2. When the AOL icon appears, choose Continue to say you want to continue the installation process.

3. Click Continue again when AOL tells you that it's going to install files to your hard drive.

4. Click OK when you're told that the installation is complete.

That's it, wasn't it easy? Now go to Chapter 1 to learn how to start AOL so you can configure the software and sign onto AOL for the first time.

NOTE **When you start the AOL software as a new user, you will be prompted for the registration number and password (as discussed in Chapter 1). If you've installed AOL from the CD-ROM that accompanies this book, the registration number is 3A-5661-3405 and the password is DUSTY-CRANNY.**

CD-ROM INSTALLATION INSTRUCTIONS

To install America Online from the CD-ROM that came with this book, follow these basic instructions (for more information, see Appendix B if your computer is a Windows machine and Appendix C if your computer is a Macintosh):

1. Insert the CD-ROM into your computer's CD-ROM drive.

2. Double-click on the Install America Online icon.

3. Follow the on-screen instructions. When prompted, enter your registration number and a password.

INDEX

(continued)

BRB = Be Right Back (chat room
    shorthand), 122
Browse Channels icon, 35, 36
Browse Folders icon, 44
BTW = By The Way (chat room
    shorthand), 122
Buddy List Preferences window, 64
Buddy Lists, 63–67, 125
BuddyView, 66
bulletin boards for classified ads, 178,
    179–180
Business Week Online Computer
    Room, 246–247
business-related information and sites
    Business Directory window, 185
    Business News window, 153
    Business Travel Center, 143–144
    Company News area, 220–221
    Hoover's Business Resources,
        219–220
    IPO Central, 220
    Plunkett's Almanacs, 220
    Your Business area, 221–222
busy signal avoidance, 18, 26–27
BUY & SELL! Bulletin Boards
    (Classified Online window
    option), 178, 179–180

C

California, virtual tour of, 278–280
call waiting, turning off, 10–11
Cape May (New Jersey), virtual tour
    of, 265–266
capitalization

ignored in keyword searches, 34
ignored in news searches, 167
ignored in screen names, 19
usually absent on Internet, 320
car shopping, 186–186, 295, 299
    loan information, 297, 299
careers information
    on Learning list, 201, 202
    on MoneyWhiz Finance Center, 294
    sharing on Home & Careers area of
        The Exchange, 239
cartoons
    from Howdy window, 57
    on Kids Only channel, 198–199
    in Politics forum, 152
case sensitivity. *See* capitalization
CCs (carbon copies) of e-mail, 2, 99
CDS (certificates of deposit), 297
centering text in e-mail, 99
Champion catalog, 175
Change Your Password window, 61
Channel Find feature, 36
channels
    browsing, 36, 38–39
    Computers & Software. *See*
        Computers & Software channel
    Digital City. *See* Digital City
        channel
    displaying at sign-on, 72
    Entertainment, 230–234
    Games, 202–203
    Internet Connection, 315, *See also*
        Internet
    keyword searches, 8, 33–34

(continued)

deletions, specifying confirmation prior to, 77

demoware, 51

Denver, virtual tour of, 281

dialing "9" to get outside line, 10, 15, 16

dictionaries
  of computer terminology, 249
  for kids's use, 197
  on Reference Shelf, 212, 213

Digital City channel
  advantages of touring, 264
  International, 287–289
  Mid-Atlantic states, 268–272
  Midwest, 276–278
  Northeast, 264–268
  Northwest, 278–281
  Pen Pals, 104–105, 282–286
  South, 272–274
  Southwest, 274–276
  West, 278–281

digital telephone lines, 11

direct payment from checking accounts, 19

Disney Adventures Magazine, 159

Door Bell/Slam Sound Installer, 65

Dow Dividend Approach area (Fool's School), 303

Download Manager dialog box, 94

Download Preferences window, 73–74

downloading files
  Across Lite utility, 151
  antivirus protection, 318, 332
  attached to e-mail, 93–94

automatically during FlashSessions, 82

confirming additions to list of, 74

Door Bell/Slam Sound Installer, 65

file–compression utilities, 101

games, 190–191

with Gopher, 329

how to, 49–51

New York Times crossword puzzle, 151

Personal Publisher, 81–82

retaining information about, 74

setting options for display of graphics, 70, 73

setting preferences, 73–74

Web browsers, 183–184

from ZDNet, 244

drivers, on Internet/Web, 319

Durham, North Carolina, virtual tour of, 273

E

EcoTourism, 136

Eddie Bauer catalog, 175

Edelman's Money University, 298

Edit Your Online Profile window, 63

Education Connection window, 216–217

education/research resources. *See* references

800 numbers, preceding with "1," 16

El Paso, Texas, virtual tour of, 275

housing mortgage rates, 296, 298

Houston, Texas, virtual tour of, 276

Howdy window, 57

http:// as Web URL prefix, 317

hyperlinks to Web pages, 317

I

I Need Help! window, 128

icons

getting descriptions from ToolTips, 33

on Toolbar, 33

putting on desktop as AOL shortcut, 14

See also channels

IDG Books, Web page address for, 318

Ignore button, 3

images. *See* graphics

IMHO = In My Humble Opinion (chat room shorthand), 122

IMO = In My Opinion (chat room shorthand), 122

IMs (Instant Messages)

Buddy Lists, 63–67, 125

described, 66, 124

replying to, 125–126

reporting scams, 127–128

sending, 125

shutting off, 128–129

In Depth button (Today's News window), 147

Industry News, 314

Industry News window, 153

Instant Messages. *See* IMs (Instant Messages)

insurance planning, 294, 299

interactive discussions

in chat rooms or message boards, 165–166

for help from AOL representatives, 54, 258

on ZD Net (computer-related information), 244

See also chat rooms

interactive learning, on Computing Rotunda, 258–261

interests. *See* hobbies and interests

Internal Revenue Service Web page, 300

international activity

access, 26

map references, 86

Other Countries chat rooms, 117

pen pals, 104–105, 282–286

virtual touring, 287–289

Internet

access through AOL, 12–13

access through providers, 12

browsing, 317–319

caution on children's use of, 204

connecting to, 315–316

described, 48

FTP (File Transfer Protocol), 330–332

Gopher, 328–330

hyperlinks, 317

newsgroups, 319–327

popularity of, 315

See also Web (World Wide Web)

Internet button, 41

Internet Connection channel, 315

Internet Tools, on Reference channel, 215

investment planning, 294, 302–311

Investor's Network, 310

IPO Central, 220

ISDN telephone service, 11

ISPs (Internet Service Providers), 333

italics for text in e-mail, 99

J

J.C. Penney catalog, 175

Jacksonville, Florida, virtual tour of, 273

JPEG graphics, 71

justifying text in e-mail, 99

K

Kansas, virtual tour of, 277

Karate International Magazine, 161

Keep As New button, 3, 96

keyboard shortcuts. *See* hot keys

Keyword button, 34

keyword searches, 8, 33–34

Kids Only channel, 187–188

    ages appropriate to, 187

    club meetings, 195–197

    creative activities, 191–193

    discussion rooms, 197–198

    games, 188–191

    homework help, 197–198

    pen pals, 196–197

    show business stars, cartoon characters, etc., 198–199

    sports, 194

    teacher pager, 198

    See also children's features; parental controls

KidSoft SuperStore, 175

L

La Vigne, Diana, 132

Las Vegas, virtual tour of, 281

Learn To Use America Online window, 42, 49

Learning & Culture channel, 201–202, 234–237

L'eggs catalog, 175

libraries online

    New York Public Library desk reference, 200–201, 218–218

    See also references]

Life chat rooms, 115

line breaks, saving text with, 72

List Message icon, 45

List Rooms icon, 47, 113

locations, multiple, adding AOL access telephone numbers for, 28

LOL = Laughing Out Loud (chat room shorthand), 122

Los Angeles, virtual tour of, 279–280

Louvre museum, 234

LTNS = Long Time No See (chat room shorthand), 122

lurking in chat rooms, 118

M

McCahill, Mark, 328

Macintoshes, starting AOL from, 13–14

Mad Magazine, 159

magazines
  from Magazine Rack (Computers & Software channel), 245–249
  at Newsstand, 157–161

mail and mailbox. *See* e-mail

Mail Center button, 39–40

Mail Center window, 40, 89

Mail Controls, 105–107

Mail menu, 90–91
  Edit Address Book command, 97–98

Mail Preferences window, 74–75, 94–95

Mailbox icon, 33, 88

Mailing List Directory window, 103–104

mailing lists (e-mail), 103–104

Maine, virtual tour of, 267

Market Commentary, 314

marketing, setting preferences, 77–79

Marketplace
  accessing, 172
  Bargains category, 175–176
  Big Stores and Outlets, 175–176
  classified ads, 178–183
  Clothing and Accessories category, 175
  Food category, 175
  House goods category, 174
  Lillian Vernon, 175–176
  purchasing from, 176–178
  viewing directory, 173

Marvel Comics, 160

Member chat rooms, 40, 112, 120

Member Directory icon, 47

Member Help Interactive window, 54–55

member profiles
  caution on believability of, 47
  caution on revelations in, 62–63
  setting preferences, 62–63

Member Rooms, 40, 112, 120–121
  creating, 121

Member Services, 51–53
  Quick Answers, 52, 53

Members' Choice window, 40

Members menu
  Buddy Lists command, 63–65
  Preferences command, 56, 69

Menu Bar, 32–33

menus
  Help, 53, 54
  Mail, 90–91, 97–98
  opening, 32
  Sign Off, 25
  See also File menu; Go To menu; Members menu

Message Boards
  in chat rooms, 130
  described, 43–46
  on Travel Channel, 142

messages. *See* e-mail; IMs (Instant Messages); newsgroups

Mid-Atlantic states travel tips (Digital City channel), 268–272

(continued)

Portland, Oregon, virtual tour of, 278
ports for modems, 12, 15
Ports of Call travel options, 138
Preferences window, 56, 69, 77–78
    Chat, 69–70
    Download, 73–74
    General, 72–73
    Graphics, 70–72
    Mail, 74–75
    Marketing, 77–79
    Multimedia, 79–80
    Personal Filing Cabinet, 76–77
    WWW (Web), 75–76
Premier Ads window, 180–183
PriceSmart, 176
Print window, 96
Printer icon, 95
printers, specifying, 96
Private chat rooms, 40, 112, 121
Pro Football window, 162
Public chat rooms, 40, 112
public–domain software, 51
Public Rooms window, 114
publications
    computer-related, 157–158, 243, 245–249
    for kids, 158–160
    on hobbies and interests, 160–161
pulse telephone dialing, 10

Q

Q&A (Reference channel), 214–215
Quick Answers in Member Services, 52, 53

Quick Start tutorial, 23–24, 42
quotations in e-mail in AOL style, 75, 92–93
Quotes & Portfolios area (Personal Finance channel), 306–309

R

Raleigh, North Carolina, virtual tour of, 273
Read 1st Message icon, 45
Read button, 3
Read My Newsgroups window, 323
real time interaction
    in chat rooms, 111
    See also interactive discussions; paging
.rec (recreational) newsgroup category name, 320
recreation. *See* hobbies and interests
Reebok Store, 175
Reference channel
    Computing & Technology, 261–262
    described, 8, 212
    Internet Tools, 215
    Q&A, 214–215
    Reference Shelf, 212–214
    Store, 215–216
    What's Hot, 214
references
    advantages of AOL for, 211, 216
    dictionaries, 212, 213
    in Education Connection window, 216–217
    first aid information, 222–223

.soc (social/cultural/ethnic issues) newsgroup category name, 320

software
beta versions on Internet/Web, 319
copyrights for, 51
downloading from Internet, 50–51
from PC Software Center, 249–251

Software Search window, 50

sound cards, 2, 23

sounds
AOL sound installer requirement, 65
in chat rooms, 70, 72, 122–123
setting preferences for, 72
upon sign-on/off of Buddies, 65
See also voice messages

Sounds Library icon, 65

South and Southwest travel tips (Digital City channel), 272–276

Special Interests chat rooms, 116–117

speed considerations, of
downloading files attached to e-mail, 94
graphics files, 70–71
modems, 12, 13, 17
multimedia graphics, 79–80

spelling, checking when seeking help, 197

sports
games and polls for kids, 194
going interactive with chat rooms or message boards, 165–166
on AOL Sports Newsstand, 160–161
on AOL Sports Stars Online, 164
on Kids Only channel, 194

on Sports (category of Today's News Channel), 146, 155–156
scores, 162–163
Sports Calendar, 164–165
in Sports, News, and Finance chat rooms, 115
TV listings, 165

Sports Superstore, 176

Starbucks Coffee, 175

starting, AOL, 13–15

Stock Research area (Fool's School), 304–305

Stocks and Investing area (Personal Finance channel), 310–311

Store (Reference channel), 215–216

The Straight Dope (Cecil Adams), 224–225

Study Break window, 200

subscribing or unsubscribing to newsgroups, 320–322, 325

Support Forums (Computers & Software channel), 253–254

support groups, 239–240

T

Tab key for next box in window, 18, 99

.talk (opinions) newsgroup category name, 320

Tax Channel: NAEA, 300–301

Tax Planning area, 299–301

TaxLogic, 300, 301

IDG BOOKS WORLDWIDE, INC.
END-USER LICENSE AGREEMENT

<u>**Read This**</u>. **You should carefully read these terms and conditions before opening the software packet(s) included with this book ("Book"). This is a license agreement ("Agreement") between you and IDG Books Worldwide, Inc. ("IDGB"). By opening the accompanying software packet(s), you acknowledge that you have read and accept the following terms and conditions. If you do not agree and do not want to be bound by such terms and conditions, promptly return the Book and the unopened software packet(s) to the place you obtained them for a full refund.**

1. <u>**License Grant**</u>. IDGB grants to you (either an individual or entity) a nonexclusive license to use one copy of the enclosed software program(s) (collectively, the "Software") solely for your own personal or business purposes on a single computer (whether a standard computer or a workstation component of a multiuser network). The Software is in use on a computer when it is loaded into temporary memory (i.e., RAM) or installed into permanent memory (e.g., hard disk, CD-ROM, or other storage device). IDGB reserves all rights not expressly granted herein.

2. <u>**Ownership**</u>. IDGB is the owner of all right, title, and interest, including copyright, in and to the compilation of the Software recorded on the disk(s)/CD-ROM. Copyright to the individual programs on the disk(s)/CD-ROM is owned by the author or other authorized copyright owner of each program. Ownership of the Software and all proprietary rights relating thereto remain with IDGB and its licensors.

3. <u>**Restrictions On Use and Transfer**</u>.

   (a) You may only (i) make one copy of the Software for backup or archival purposes, or (ii) transfer the Software to a single hard disk, provided that you keep the original for backup or archival purposes. You may not (i) rent or lease the Software, (ii) copy or reproduce the Software through a LAN or other network system or through any computer subscriber system or bulletin-board system, or (iii) modify, adapt, or create derivative works based on the Software.

   (b) You may not reverse engineer, decompile, or disassemble the Software. You may transfer the Software and user documentation on a permanent basis, provided that the transferee agrees to accept the terms and conditions of this Agreement and you retain no copies. If the Software is an update or has been updated, any transfer must include the most recent update and all prior versions.

4. <u>**Restrictions on Use of Individual Programs**</u>. You must follow the individual requirements and restrictions detailed for each individual program in Appendixes A and B of this Book. These limitations are contained in the individual license agreements recorded on the disk(s)/CD-ROM. These restrictions may include a requirement that after using the program for the period of time specified in its text, the user must pay a registration fee or discontinue use. By opening the Software packet(s), you will be agreeing to abide by the licenses and restrictions for these individual programs. None of the material on this CD-ROM or listed in this Book may ever be distributed, in original or modified form, for commercial purposes.